A JUDEO-CHRISTIAN APPRAISAL OF MAJOR THEORIES OF TRUTH

A Judeo-Christian Appraisal
of Major Theories *of* Truth

JOSEPH B. ONYANGO OKELLO

WIPF & STOCK · Eugene, Oregon

A JUDEO-CHRISTIAN APPRAISAL OF MAJOR THEORIES OF TRUTH

Copyright © 2025 Joseph B. Onyango Okello. All rights reserved. Except for brief quotations in critical publications or reviews, no part of this book may be reproduced in any manner without prior written permission from the publisher. Write: Permissions, Wipf and Stock Publishers, 199 W. 8th Ave., Suite 3, Eugene, OR 97401.

Wipf & Stock
An Imprint of Wipf and Stock Publishers
199 W. 8th Ave., Suite 3
Eugene, OR 97401

www.wipfandstock.com

PAPERBACK ISBN: 979-8-3852-1363-4
HARDCOVER ISBN: 979-8-3852-1364-1
EBOOK ISBN: 979-8-3852-1365-8

05/21/25

To Sophia Munyao-Okello and Sean Amani Okello—
my biggest cheerleaders in the academic world

Contents

Acknowledgments | ix

1. Introduction | 1
2. Relativism as a Theory of Truth | 16
3. Pragmatism as a Theory of Truth: Peirce and James | 40
4. Pragmatism as a Theory of Truth: Rorty and Putnam | 58
5. Postmodernism as a Theory of Truth: Lyotard, Foucault, and Derrida | 77
6. The Correspondence Conception of Truth | 104
7. The Coherence Theory of Truth | 133
8. The Bible and Truth | 155

Bibliography | 183

Index | 189

Acknowledgments

ALTHOUGH WRITING A BOOK of this sort entails the work of a single author, many more individuals helped to put everything in place in the process of completing this manuscript. I wish to begin by thanking Asbury Theological Seminary for making it possible for me to spend my sabbatical preparing this manuscript. The first three chapters were completed in my first sabbatical, which I spent in Kenya. I had hoped that being in Kenya would keep me from unnecessary distractions. I was wrong. I found myself in the midst of additional projects, which, though important, slowed me down in the process of writing the book. However, I did manage to fulfill my sabbatical goals for that period.

The remaining chapters were completed in my second sabbatical. Having learned a lesson from my previous Sabbatical, I decided not to travel outside the United States in preparing the remaining chapters. Still, more distractions came my way and, once again, I found myself doing much more than I had intended during that sabbatical. At any rate, I did complete the project and was ready to submit the material for publication. For one reason or another, I kept postponing the submission process. I finally decided it was time to submit the material for publication, the result of which is the book you now hold in your hands. But I say all this to express my gratitude to Asbury Theological Seminary for their patience with me.

In addition, I am specifically grateful to my students at the Orlando campus of Asbury Seminary who continued to challenge my views in ways that allowed me to give my arguments in this book a much sharper focus. I believe I have been able to address their concerns as I shared some of my findings with them during my in-class and out-of-class conversations about the topic and the nature of truth. My hope is to give this topic additional treatment in the coming days in a way I hope will shed more light and stimulate further discussions.

ACKNOWLEDGMENTS

I wish to express my gratitude to Judy Seitz for reading the entire manuscript and offering suggestions for improvement. Her keen mind and undivided attention to detail rescued me from making embarrassing mistakes in my sentence structures and grammatical expressions. Whereas I give her credit for the masterful corrections she made, I take full responsibility for any errors in the possible philosophical argumentations one could find in this work.

I am also grateful to my wife and my son for their patience with me as I spent countless hours away from them trying to complete this project. My son has always wondered what I write about when I begin to think philosophically around him. In a Wittgensteinian way, he thinks philosophy is almost a fuss about nothing! Just the same, he thinks it has some merit, though he is not exactly sure how it would look like. For that reason alone, he has been supportive at every stage. My wife, though, remains undyingly supportive in all ways. She has lived through intense moments of physical suffering. But I appreciate her commitment to the cause of what she believes is my calling in the area of philosophical truth.

Finally, I am a philosopher who is also committed to belief in the existence of the Judeo-Christian God. I write from this perspective because I believe, as Descartes did, that only from such a vantage point is one's knowledge complete. You might believe otherwise, but that, of course, is a matter of debate. Still, I write this work in the hope that my musings will shed further light on the nature of God and stimulate the kind of glory he alone deserves.

1

Introduction

IN RECENT TIMES, DEBATES on the nature of truth have gained considerable attention in academic circles. The public square has not been spared either. The nature of truth remains at the center of the discussion, ranging from whether or not two contradictory statements could both be true simultaneously to a denial of the existence or the possibility of truth itself. The question needing an answer, then, seems to be of the sort that demands an explanation of the nature of truth. Is truth an entity, and, if so, is it external to us? Is truth some kind of an unfolding or an obtaining of states of affairs in our world, or should truth be limited to specific propositions internally coherent or corresponding to the external world around us? Not surprisingly, these questions and their possible answers continue to dominate public discourses in different areas of life, including the philosophical world.

What, then, is truth? In the biblical world, Pontius Pilate asked Jesus this question but walked away without waiting for an answer. Jesus claimed to be the truth, identifying himself fundamentally with it. As I will show in various chapters of this work, some theories of truth confine it only to propositions in ways that leave it deficient of metaphysical reality. The implication of confining truth only to propositions in this way is that the absence of propositions renders truth nonexistent. The biblical view of truth seems to regard truth as having a genuine metaphysical reality. It seems to give truth the quality of personhood, specifically in the person of Jesus Christ. More importantly, it suggests that truth is alive in the same sense that you and I are alive. The question to be asked is "which view is more correct?"

If truth is, indeed, confined only to propositions, then truth may not be alive in the sense that both you and I are alive. More importantly, since propositions seem to have their origins in sentient beings such as ourselves, truth had no being prior to our existence, and truth ceases to exist the moment we, the originators of those propositions, cease to exist. This view would imply that truth is dependent on the existence of the human mind, for without the human mind, propositions would not exist along with the truths they try to express. Indeed, Peter Gibson arrives at this very conclusion by drawing attention to a specific standard view of truth, namely: if minds were nonexistent, lots of facts would still exist, but truth would not exist. He notes, here, how thinkers routinely view truth as a relationship between mind and facts, and that this relationship is what he calls the *getting it right* relationship.[1] If Gibson is right (and I think he is), then a naturalistic conception of truth faces the problem I have already alluded to, namely, the existence of truth prior to the arrival of the human mind through natural selection.

However, if truth is a person, then truth really possesses a certain quality of being. If truth has its being in the nature of a person with infinite, eternal qualities such as omniscience, then the being of truth has remained an obtaining state of affairs from eternity past and will remain in that state of affairs into the eternal future. This view may present its own problems. One is the objection that if truth is a specific person *P*, then persons not identical to *P* are non-truths. Such an implication seems quite bizarre.

However, things need not plummet to this level, as I will show in the following consideration. The belief that truth is a person is fundamental to Christian theology. Truth is the nature or the attribute of a person called Jesus Christ from whom other subcategories of truths emanate, including descriptions of the persons he, as deity, created. In this sense, then, persons not identical to *P* are not non-truths but the logical outworking of *P*'s creative actions. According to Richard John Neuhaus, Jesus implied, by that claim, that an honest and sincere search for truth will lead the seeker to Jesus.[2] In addition, Dallas Willard notes correctly, I think, that if a substantial reality and nature to truth itself does not exist, then we lack any substantive reasons for having a conversation concerning the evidence and significance

---

1. Gibson, *Philosophy*, 29.
2. Neuhaus, "Is There Life," 25.

of different claims to truth.³ Additionally, Laura Smit postulates, as we will see later in this section, that human access to truth is courtesy of God's gracious revelation made possible by the illuminating work of Jesus—the truth.⁴ Notice Smit's ascription to Jesus as the truth, thereby making him identical to it.

Neuhaus notes how contemporary conversations about truth seem unwelcome to most people, especially those in academic settings. This fact, he argues, becomes clearer when such conversations turn to religion and ethics.⁵ To this very point, Os Guinness observes how a believer in the existence of objective truth gets regarded as Neanderthal, arrogant, and wrongheaded,⁶ and, as Timothy Keller argues, the exclusivity of truth serves as one of the reasons people have trouble believing orthodox religions and Christianity in particular.⁷

Thus, the question of truth itself, along with its various facets, remains decisively extirpated in many areas of culture-forming influence. Neuhaus blames this influence on anti-foundationalism and deconstructivism of postmodern thinking.⁸ Guinness seems to agree with Neuhaus when he shows how deniers of objective truth hold that truth, at best, is relative in the sense that it is contingent upon a person's interpretation and perspective. At worst, truth must be seen as a social construct, as a testament to the community that makes it stick by saying it.⁹

Subscribers to the Judeo-Christian tradition hold to the view, or should hold to the view, that truth exists and that all truths, which I call subsets of truth, ultimately serve one truth. For Neuhaus, one truth exists because only one God exists revealed in Jesus Christ. Believing such a postulate and articulating it is the responsibility of those subscribing to the dictates of the Judeo-Christian tradition.¹⁰ Similarly, Guinness finds truth central to faith for the Christian believer specifically because the personal infinite God himself is the true one. Therefore, he will speak and act truly in a way that allows his actions and words to be checked out in history. In

---

3. Willard, "Introduction," 19.
4. Smit, "In Your Light," 177.
5. Neuhaus, "Is There Life," 26.
6. Guinness, "Time," 40.
7. Keller, "Reasons," 59.
8. Neuhaus, "Is There Life," 26–27.
9. Guinness, "Time," 40.
10. Neuhaus, "Is There Life," 28–29.

an apparent reference to the Gospel of John, Guinness makes the claim that ultimate truth is, in the end, a matter of who God is.[11]

Keller would add to this thought by stating that the person claiming to know God and to know what God is like makes an important claim to truth. The person is saying he or she knows the truth and knows what spiritual reality is like. The person claims to possess the truth. Moreover, the person, by implication, claims that the unbeliever in the Judeo-Christian God does not possess the truth,[12] identified as the person of Christ, though such a person may possess subcategories of that truth, such as the truth that the person in question exists.

According to Neuhaus, when Aristotle urges his readers to deliberate, as rational, reasonable beings, on the question of how humans should order their lives together, Aristotle presupposes the existence of a truth to be deliberated upon. More specifically, Aristotle presupposes the existence of many right answers to specific questions and, by implication, many wrong answers. However, the deliberation would not be futile in light of this presupposition. Still, when people give up talking about truth, we find no way of discussing how they ought to order their lives.[13] Hence, for Neuhaus, as for Guinness, truth is a precious, simple, and fundamental human gift whose absence makes it impossible to negotiate reality and handle life.[14]

The absence of truth has serious consequences. Neuhaus illustrates how one such consequence played out in real life. For example, at the end of the twentieth century, humans had witnessed the bloodiest century in all of human history. Significantly, this event happened simultaneously with the period that produced ideologies that denied the Christian and classic Aristotelian view of truth. Our responsibility to engage each other in our search for that truth more fully was largely dropped.[15] Guinness affirms this observation when he notes how the present crisis of truth has gone in tandem with a crisis of character and ethics.[16]

In his seminal work, *Trinity and Truth*, Bruce D. Marshall postulates a theory of truth similar to the views presented by Keller, Guinness, and Neuhaus—a view I also endorse. According to Marshall, the New Testament

---

11. Guinness, "Time," 46–47.
12. Keller, "Reasons," 55.
13. Neuhaus, "Is There Life," 29–30.
14. Guinness, "Time," 40–41.
15. Neuhaus, "Is There Life," 30.
16. Guinness, "Time," 41.

INTRODUCTION

presents truth as a genuine attribute of the second and third persons of the Trinity. In John 14:6, for example, truth is a predicate, an attribute of Jesus Christ. In 1 John 5:6, it is also a predicate, indeed, an attribute, of the Holy Spirit. Marshall shows how sentences and beliefs function chiefly as truth-bearers. However, the person of Jesus is a truth-bearer if, in fact, Jesus is the truth. If the New Testament is correct, Marshall argues, then ultimately truth is a person.[17]

In a later chapter, I will explore Tarski's notion of truth. For now, however, I draw minimal attention to Marshall's observation about Tarski's notion and, specifically, Marshall's view that Tarski's notion of truth could face annihilation if it proves incompatible with the assertion that truth is a person in the sense I have already stated. Tarski famously pointed to a version of the correspondence theory of truth using the following example: *Snow is white* is true if and only if snow is white. According to Marshall, if we take Tarski's approach and apply it to Christian theology, no serious orthodox Christian will deny the truth of the following claim: *Jesus is risen* is true if and only if Jesus is risen. According to Marshall, a Christian believes that the person who holds *Jesus is risen* true has a true belief and the person who finds it false has a false belief. Marshall finds this outcome theologically acceptable. Informatively and less misleadingly, it seems to capture a part of what traditional theological appeals to truth as correspondence were aiming at. For this reason, theological discipline seems to find Tarski's account of truth quite untouched and intact.[18]

Marshall, however, thinks Tarski's view and John's Gospel seem, quite possibly, to speak about different things when they speak of truth. Bear in mind that the claim "*Jesus is risen* is true if and only if Jesus is risen" does not make Jesus himself true. Neither does it make Jesus the truth with respect to the sentence Jesus is risen. It makes the person Jesus a truth-bearer for *Jesus is risen* in exactly the same sense as grass is a truth-bearer for *grass is green*. Suppose, Marshall argues, having this location on the right branch of a Tarski sentence makes Jesus *the truth*. It will equally well make grass *the truth*. Clearly, John's Gospel does not imply this conclusion when it predicates *is truth* of the person of Jesus.[19]

Tarski, in Marshall's view, is speaking about truth as borne by sentences and beliefs, and Jesus is speaking of truth as borne by the person of

---

17. Marshall, *Trinity*, 242.
18. Marshall, *Trinity*, 242–3.
19. Marshall, *Trinity*, 243.

Jesus. Still, Marshall thinks a link between the two uses of truth remains implicit in the common view of recent exegesis. Thus, in John 14:6 Jesus is *the Truth* in the sense that he is the unique revelation of the Father, being the one uniquely and adequately making the Father known. He brings about the knowledge of the Father on account of his particular relation to him. Stated differently, as the Father's word became human flesh, this flesh expresses the total being of the Father.[20]

Marshall then draws the following inference from his aforementioned supposition: if Jesus is the truth, he imparts knowledge of the Father to us. If he imparts knowledge of the Father to us, we have some true beliefs, and we hold true some true sentences. Hence, if Jesus is the truth, we have some true beliefs, and we hold true some true sentences. These findings by Marshall lead him to conclude that *truth*, as applied to sentences and beliefs, is logically necessary for *the truth* in which the person Jesus Christ is.[21]

According to Marshall, this finding implies that Tarski's approach by itself remains inadequate for a theological account of what truth is. It gives us no clue about how to connect truth to a person as its bearer. In addition, Marshall maintains that the concept of truth as applied to sentences and beliefs cannot be utterly disparate from the concept of truth that applies to the person of Jesus.[22]

Laura A. Smit advances a similar motif by proposing what she calls a Christocentric epistemology. Getting her cue from Bonaventure, the thirteenth-century Franciscan thinker, Smit shows how Christ, together with the other two persons of the Trinity, remain at the center of the act of a person's knowing whenever that person knows anything true. In her view, the person of Christ remains key both to self-knowledge and to knowledge of the external sensible world.[23]

Smit draws our attention to Bonaventure's assumption that a person P may call some given knowledge K true only if K is essential. According to Bonaventure, and presumably to Smit as well, only essential things are lasting. One cannot ascribe truth to changing and ephemeral things. The very nature of truth must be lasting and essential. For Smit, Bonaventure's assumption is fundamentally scriptural for at least one major reason: Jesus identifies himself as the truth, and no one gains access to God the Father

---

20. Marshall, *Trinity*, 243–4.
21. Marshall, *Trinity*, 244.
22. Marshall, *Trinity*, 245.
23. Smit, "In Your Light," 167.

INTRODUCTION

except through Jesus. For Smit, this claim is quite literally true. The incarnation is a point of contact between God and human beings.[24]

Hence, when Jesus says he is the truth, he is saying more than the claim that he is a truthful person. Jesus is saying he is truth in a preeminent sense, in much the same way that he is the preeminent source of life and point of access to God the Father. According to Smit, the terms in John 14 are properly and primarily applied to God and only analogically applied to creatures. John's Gospel, Smit argues, positions this claim of Jesus to be the truth in the context of an understanding of Jesus as the Word of God who reveals God and sustains life.[25]

Smit draws our attention to this link between Christ as truth and Christ as *logos* by appealing to the insights gained from the work of David Crump.[26] Crump shows how the supreme disclosure of God who revealed himself to Moses really presented himself as the incarnation of God in the *logos*. Hence, Jesus shows us God as he really is. In this assertion, Jesus sets the stage for John's use of the truth. Reminiscent of Marshall, Crump contends that truth is personal, not merely intellectual. One acquires truth through the revelation of God rather than through mental application. Crump categorically affirms that God is truth. His eternal reality is ultimate reality. No external standards or benchmarks exist to evaluate his reality. Knowledge of Jesus entails knowledge of God the Father. In this way, Jesus can say that he, too, is the truth. Hence, Crump's claim that God is truth is commensurate with the claim in John's prologue that the *Logos* is God.[27]

These considerations help to set the stage for the overall goal of this work, namely, an elucidation of an adequate account of truth, which, as I see it, finds its origin in something beyond propositions alone, in the origin of a divine mind. For this mind to be an adequate candidate of truth, it must first be in possession of the infinite set of all true statements or, for that matter, propositions. In addition, it must be in possession of maximum knowledge. In short, such a mind must be omniscient, as I will attempt to show in what follows.

An inquiry into the nature of truth seems to provide evidence for the existence of God as long as the inquirer expresses commitments to specific assumptions about the occurrence of truth. This work is an attempt

24. Smit, "In Your Light," 168–9.
25. Smit, "In Your Light," 169.
26. Smit, "In Your Light," 169.
27. Crump, "Truth," 861.

to demonstrate how one could formulate such an inquiry. I call this argument the alethic ontological argument. I use the term *alethic* from the Greek word for truth. It is ontological in the sense that it argues for the being of God as the epistemic possessor of all true propositions. I begin with the widely accepted assumption among epistemologists about truth viewed as a property of statements or propositions. Roughly, I use the term *propositions* interchangeably with *statements*. In the various definitions of truth on the epistemological market, epistemologists routinely cast truth in the following way: a statement S or a proposition P is true if and only if x. In this formula, x takes the place of the definition to which the epistemologist remains committed. The first part of the biconditional gives us the impression that truth is a property or an attribute of a given proposition or statement.

Statements (i.e., propositions) seem contingent on their utterers, namely, statement-makers and/or proposition-makers. In this reading, statements or propositions do not occur on their own owing to the facticity of their intentionality. By intentionality, I refer to the goal of conveying specific information both encoded and implicit in the statement or proposition in question. Thus, statements are dependent upon statement-makers; they are contingent *things*. They do not occur on their own. Some sentient rational beings, such as ourselves, must utter them. This vantage point, admittedly, runs contrary to the view that such propositions or statements exist independently in the way, for example, Platonic forms exist. However, the assumption that statements or propositions are contingent, mind-dependent descriptions of states of affairs implies that without the existence of statement-making rational beings or agents, such as ourselves, the statements or propositions would not exist. Rational beings must utter them into existence. A curious and possible scientific fact seems to emerge from this observation. The history of natural selection suggests that humans are relative latecomers into the universe. For billions of years, the universe existed without human beings. Moreover, so far as we can tell, human beings seem to be the only rational creatures we know about existing in our geophysical world, assuming epistemological naturalism is correct in its suppositions. The curious scientific fact can then be located as follows: prior to the arrival of human beings into the universe, statement-makers remained nonexistent specifically because no human beings existed to utter those statements. Even more curious is the conclusion that owing to the nonexistence of statements prior to the arrival of humans, truth did not

INTRODUCTION

exist either specifically because truth is a property of statements. Hence, just as human beings are relative latecomers into the universe, statements, propositions, and truth are also relative latecomers, and a time exists in which truth did not exist either.

A certain kind of truth, however, does exist and seems to have been in existence before rational creatures, such as ourselves, came onto the scene. This truth, I claim, is the property of an infinitely long true statement. A finite human being cannot be the utterer of an infinitely long and true statement. An infinitely long, true statement would not only exist for an infinitely long period of time, but it would also be contingent upon an infinitely old rational being to produce it. The task we have, then, is to show how an infinitely long and true statement is even possible. If we can locate the possibility of such a statement, then it points to the existence of an infinitely old statement-maker, for the simple reason that an infinitely long statement requires an infinite old statement-maker as its utterer.

How, then, can one locate the possibility of an infinitely long statement? Consider the following infinite set of rational numbers: $N = \{1, 2, 3, \ldots\}$. Roughly speaking, we can represent set N verbally: $N = \{\text{one, two, three,} \ldots\}$. Moreover, interpreting this set as follows is entirely in order: $N = \{\text{the number one exists, the number two exists, the number 3 exists,} \ldots\}$. This set is infinite, and each statement forming the members of the set is true. If we form a conjunction of all its members, it will yield an infinitely long set of true statements. Either humans uttered these statements into existence, or an infinite being uttered these statements into existence following the observation that meaningful statements conveying or expressing specific ideas do not exist independently. Such statements remain fundamentally dependent on statement-makers such as ourselves.

However, a finite human being cannot be a statement-maker of an infinitely long and, therefore, an infinitely old set of true statements. The task of producing an infinitely long true statement requires an infinite amount of time to accomplish, which no finite human being can accomplish. An infinite being remains the best and only possible candidate as the maker of an infinitely long set of true sentences. Since we know an infinitely old set of true sentences actually exists and no statement, infinite or finite, can be made or uttered without a sentence-maker, it follows that an infinitely old, omniscient statement-maker exists who remains the originator of all true statements.

We can formulate this argument formally as follows:

1. Truth is a property of statements.
2. Statements need statement makers to exist.
3. At least one infinite set of true statements exists.
4. A conjunction of true statements in the infinite set of true statements forms an infinitely long true statement.
5. Thus, an infinitely long true statement exists.
6. If an infinitely long true statement exists, it must be contingent, for its existence, upon an infinitely old statement-maker and must have, therefore, been made, or uttered by an infinitely old statement-maker.
7. Finite rational animals such as ourselves are not statement-makers of the infinitely long conjunction of true statements.
8. An infinitely long, true statement, therefore, must have been made by an infinitely old statement-maker.
9. An infinitely old statement-maker is identical to an infinite being.
10. This infinite being is omniscient.
11. Hence, an omniscient and infinite being exists.
12. These attributes of omniscience and infinitude are identical to those we find in the Judeo-Christian description of God.

The naturalist could object to this argument by arguing for the possibility of the existence of mind-independent propositions. One could say, for example, that such propositions do exist independently of beings, such as ourselves, thinking them. Plato, as already insinuated, did make a case for the existence of something similar. Perhaps the nontheistic naturalist could appeal to Platonic forms as a way of raising this objection. However, appealing to a Platonic theist would seem to undercut the naturalist's pushback because, I would imagine, the naturalist would be factoring in the Platonic demiurge into his or her objections, the very entity whose existence he or she takes pains to reject.

I would see how a Platonic idealist could raise this objection. I could even entertain such an objection from a nominalist theist. I doubt, however, that a nontheist scientific naturalist, or a nontheist methodological naturalist, could succeed in raising this objection without abandoning some of the fundamental assumptions of methodological naturalism, namely, that only the objects studied by science are real. We have no scientific way of proving the being (or the existence) of numbers or propositions. We only have representations of numbers and proposition, such as *ii* + *ii* = *iv* for the expression *two plus two equals four*. Both sentences express the same thing, but they look radically different or, more accurately, we write them radically differently. What science cannot do is locate and verify the being of the proposition expressed by these two statements. But the scientist would want to believe the proposition exists, that it has being, a belief beyond the reach or scope of science. The scientific naturalist only assumes their existence (that is, of numbers and propositions) and, based on that assumption, proceeds to carry out his or her scientific experiment. My postulation, therefore, that truth and omniscience seem inextricably linked seems quite promising on philosophical grounds but is firmly established on biblical grounds.

One could use the powerset objection, a more formidable one than those hitherto adumbrated, as a way of undercutting the alethic argument presented. For example, without being committed to the conclusions of the objection, William Wainwright shows how the notion of a powerset reveals an oddity that not even an omniscient being could escape. God's omniscience, the objector would argue, is a sufficient condition for the existence of things T that only God can know. No other being would have cognitive access to T. Hence, suppose we have a powerset P of the set of all true propositions. Since the powerset P of any set S is greater in size than S, more true propositions exist in P than there are members of S. However, such a state of affairs seems impossible since S is the set of all true propositions. This observation seems to warrant the following conclusion: no set S of all true propositions exists. Thus, the objector would conclude that not even God can be omniscient.[28] Wainwright is not committed to this conclusion. To be sure, he defends God's omniscience by stating, quite clearly, that God does know all truths in spite of the possibility that we may not coherently state those very truths propositionally.[29]

This objection does not seem to have much force. Specifically by virtue of the logical rule of redundancy,[30] we can reduce any multiplicity of identical propositions to one. The rule of redundancy says the statement "either P or P" can be reduced merely to P. It also allows a reduction of the statement "both P and P" to P. To illustrate, consider a given finite set S

---

28. Wainwright, "Omnipotence," 50.
29. Wainwright, "Omnipotence," 51.
30. This rule is also called *idempontence*. See Bergmann et al., *Logic Book*, 222.

with members A, B, and C. We capture this idea as follows: $S = \{A, B, C\}$. Since the powerset P of S is the set of all subsets of S, the powerset P of S would have the following members: [{A}, {B}, {C}, {A, B}, {A, C}, {B, C,} {A, B, C}]. It is true that the powerset P of S would therefore be greater than S. However, the redundancy rule in logic allows us to reduce all occurrences of A, no matter how many, to a single letter A. We can do the same with B and C so that, in the final analysis, we end up with the original three letters A, B, and C.

This rule could be applied with equal force to the powerset P of the set S of all true propositions. Each member has an infinite number of identical propositions, thus assuming an infinite set, give it the letter name I, of all true propositions exists and some of them are represented by the letters of the alphabet: $I = \{A, B, C, \ldots\}$. Presumably, the powerset of I, call it I^p, would consist at least of the following subset of I's members: $I^p = [\{A \ldots\}, \{B \ldots\}, \{C \ldots\}, \ldots]$. Notice that the powerset would be infinite as well. Presumably, the number of identical propositions represented by the letter A would also be infinite. Just the same, by applying the redundancy rule of logic, we can reduce all the infinite numbers of identical propositions represented by A to one letter, namely A. We would also do the same with B, C, and with all the infinite number of members of set I, thereby mapping the number of the members of the powerset I^p of I on a one-on-one correspondence with I itself. Thus, the powerset I^p of I would not surpass I in greatness by this logical maneuver. Similarly, we would also not need to worry about the powerset of our earlier set P of infinitely true propositions surpassing S as far as the number of its members are concerned. Hence, whereas the notion of a powerset surpassing the original set in the number of its members seems convincing at first, the redundancy rule in logic renders it innocuous.

Having shown how truth and omniscience are linked, an overview of this work is in order. My goal is to show how this overview measures up, or fails to measure up, to the biblical understanding of truth. In the second chapter, I focus on relativism as a theory of truth, beginning with a basic definition of the relativistic understanding of truth as presented by a select group of scholars and ancient thinkers such as Protagoras and proceeding to later thinkers such as Emrys Westacott. The chapter then offers a more detailed definition of the relativistic view of truth and a detailed analysis of how relativism arrives at this conclusion, drawing from the writings of Rueben Abel, Timothy Mosteller, and Stephen Luper. The detailed analysis of epistemological relativism distinguishes between subjective relativism and pluralistic relativism in which the former denies the existence of a correct or authoritative epistemic standard of judgment while the latter insists on the existence of more than one such correct or authoritative fundamental epistemic standard. The chapter also explores Gordon Kaufman's relativism—the view that values and even truth are relative to the historical context or to the individual personality. At the end of the chapter, I offer an evaluation of relativism so construed, exposing what I believe to be its strength and what I take to be its weaknesses.

In the third and fourth chapters, I focus on pragmatism as a possible theory of truth. Roughly speaking, it is the view that the workability of a given notion or statement confirms the truth of that notion or statement. I explicate variants of this understanding by highlighting the thoughts of Charles S. Peirce, William James, Richard Rorty, and Hilary Putnam. I begin with Peirce because many philosophers consider him the initial formulator of pragmatism. I move on to James because, according to H. S. Thayer, James revived pragmatism by reformulating it as a theory of truth. I then present my critique of James and Pierce at the end of the third chapter.

In chapter 4, I explicate the thought of Rorty, who sought to replace the correspondence theory of truth with the view that one should understand truth as solidarity in the sense of tolerance, respect for divergent views, and a willingness to listen to those views. Some thinkers believe Rorty's views properly belong to the postmodern camp. His explication for the text I have chosen, though, seems to be more pragmatic than postmodern. Still, both views are considered poststructuralist in approach. I then close my survey of pragmatism by highlighting the thought of Putnam, who adopted a conceptual relativist position with regard to truth, one he called pragmatic realism. I draw attention to William Alston's critique of Putnam and then close the section with my personal critique of both Rorty and Putnam.

The fifth chapter is an exploration of the postmodernist account of truth, beginning with Jean François Lyotard's definition of postmodernism as some kind of incredulity toward metanarratives. I give an extended treatment of his rejection of modernism's tendency to legitimize itself—a move it makes, in his view, with frequent reference to a meta-discourse. From Lyotard I examine the work of Michel Foucault. I focus on what he terms the general politics of truth, which he thinks involves the types of discourse society accepts and makes—a discourse, he believes, functions as true. I then conclude the section with the work of Jacques Derrida, drawing attention to his rejection of the possibility of objective truth. At the end of the chapter, I offer what I take to be some strengths of their views. I then conclude the section with the areas I find problematic with the postmodernist account of truth.

The sixth chapter is a survey of the correspondence theory of truth. Beginning with Aristotle's and Bertrand Russell's definition of this theory of truth, I compare it with Ludwig Wittgenstein's, H. B. Acton's, and Patricia Marino's definitions. I then present an explication of Alfred Tarski's defense of the theory based on his illustration demonstrating the truth of the statement "*Snow is white* is true if and only if snow is white." He bases this illustration on his contention that the truth of a statement consists in its correspondence to reality. I also explore Marino's concurrence with this view following her contention that true statements, sentences, or beliefs correspond to the way things are in the world while false ones do not. Marino presents her view as a Modest Correspondence Theory of Truth, and highlights five features of this version. Though I find the theory quite intuitive, I note several problems with it: one presented by David Lewis and one I find in its explications. I observe that some truths seem invisible to the correspondence theory. I suggest at the end that the correspondence theory may need the coherence theory if it has to be exhaustive in its explication of truth.

In the seventh chapter, I offer an explication of the coherence theory of truth, which holds that a statement is true if and only if it coheres with a system or set of other statements and false if it does not. In expounding his position, I outline Harold Joachim's strong coherence theory of truth, which holds that the conceivablity of something is a sufficient condition for its truth and understood as a systematic coherence. I also outline L. Jonathan Cohen's defense of the strong version of this theory. I then move to the weak coherence theory of truth—a version James O. Young espouses, highlighting Young's argument for believing the view's neutrality about idealism as a reason for its weak stance. I highlight the non-factuality problem as one among several of the concerns afflicting the strong version and the nonobjectivity problem as one afflicting the subjective features of the weak version.

I position the eighth chapter as a critique of all the theories of truth hitherto examined by showing how the biblical version of truth possesses all the features of the correspondence and coherence theories while also possessing a foundational feature lacking in all the theories presented. I show how the examined features limit their conception of truth to propositions while the theocentric account offers a personalistic feature of truth, thereby giving truth a transcendental understanding. I begin by exploring the etymology of truth in both Hebrew and Greek settings following the writings of Bible scholars. I also explore the writings of the church fathers who link truth to logos. This exercise highlights the works of Theophilus of Antioch, Athenagoras, Clement of Alexandria, Hippolytus, Novatian, Athanasius, Gregory of Nyssa, Jerome, Nazianzen, Bonaventure, and Aquinas. In addition, the section examines the work of contemporary writers such as Greg Welty and Laura Smit, all of whom independently accept the personalistic feature of truth. Let me now embark on an extended overview of relativism as a theory of truth.

2

Relativism as a Theory of Truth

HAVING GIVEN A PRELIMINARY ACCOUNT of what the Judeo-Christian view of truth looks like, let me explore the nature of relativism and its contribution to the debate on truth. Gordon D. Kaufman, a defender of relativism, notes in *Relativism, Knowledge and Faith* how many contemporary writers take for granted the view that the relative nature of truth and value is a demonstrated fact.[1] Also, in his book *The Closing of the American Mind*, professor Allan Bloom makes an observation widely regarded by a variety of scholars as descriptive of how relativism continues to gain currency in American institutions of higher learning. According to Bloom, one thing a professor can be absolutely sure of is the fact that almost every student entering the university believes or claims to believe that truth is relative.[2] Francis Beckwith and Gregory Koukl remark that this observation by Professor Bloom is not merely a trend. It is a revolution started, as most revolutions do, with an idea whispered in many different environments and diverse situations. It started in the halls of learning, the academia, and eventually engulfed the common person.[3]

The results of two national surveys conducted in 2000 by Barna Research—one among adults and the other among teenagers—underscore this fact. The participants were asked whether, in their opinion, unchanging moral absolutes existed or moral truths were binding only to the person subscribing to a specific value system (i.e., whether moral truths

1. Kaufman, *Relativism*, 3.
2. Bloom, *Closing*, 25.
3. Beckwith and Koukl, *Relativism*, 3.

are relative). By a three-to-one margin, adults held the belief that truth is always relative to the person and to his or her situation. The research found the perspective even more lopsided among teenagers than among adults. Eighty-three percent of the teenagers believed moral truths depend on circumstances. Only six percent of them found moral truths absolute and unchanging.[4]

These facts suggest a strong influence of relativism over a significant portion of the American population. In order to understand its appeal, an appropriate starting point would include an exploration of the nature of relativism as presented by its adherents as well as by those who attempt to describe it without, necessarily, demonstrating a commitment to its tenets. In this section, I give a basic outline of the relativistic theory of truth, beginning with a working definition of relativism derived from a select group of scholars in that field of thought. Epistemological relativism, which is a more focused definition, follows this treatment. I focus more on epistemological relativism as opposed to other forms of relativism, such as ontological relativism and ethical relativism, because epistemology, by definition, belongs to the branch of philosophy dealing with theories of knowledge. This enterprise, therefore, places epistemology at the heart of our discussion on truth.

More importantly, my goal in this section is to show how relativism remains vulnerable to the charge alluded to in chapter 1, namely, that on a naturalistic reading of the universe's origin, truth could not have existed prior to the arrival of humans into the world if truth is, indeed, only and strictly a property of propositions. Because truth, as presented by a certain variety of theories of truth, remains a property of propositions, then prior to the arrival of proposition-makers such as ourselves, propositions could not have existed. According to relativism, truth remains heavily dependent on a person's perception of states of affairs; hence, the absence of the perceiver implies the absence of the perceived truth.

Before attempting to define relativism, I concur with James K. A. Smith's contention concerning the haziness afflicting any attempts to locate the tenets of relativism, let alone defining it. According to Smith, relativism remains a very vague viewpoint such that a school of relativistic thought seems extremely difficult to explain.[5] Also, according to Stephen Luper, the definition of relativism is unclear and, for this reason, we cannot always tell

---

4. George Barna Group, "Americans," para. 2.
5. Smith, *Relativism*, 17.

where relativism leaves off and where other views, such as skepticism or subjectivism, begin. Moreover, the grounds for relativism remain unclear. This reality makes a critique of relativism extremely difficult.[6]

In spite of these realities, Emrys Westacott notes how all varieties of relativism possess at least two features despite the fact that many different kinds exist. First, all varieties assert that one thing is relative to some particular framework or standpoint and this one thing could range from moral values, beauty, knowledge to taste or even meaning. The standpoint could range from an individual subject, a conceptual scheme, to a culture, language, or era. Second, they all deny that any standpoint remains uniquely privileged over all others as the sole custodian of objective truth.[7] This denial, as I will show here, needs the very assumption it rejects in order to advance its postulation and, hence, is self-defeating. In other words, it assumes that no standpoint remains uniquely privileged over all others as the sole custodian of objective truth. One would imagine that the relativist believes this assumption is objectively true. Otherwise, it would be a false assumption, which the relativist would not want to admit. Nevertheless, if the assumption is objectively true, it undercuts the very claim it makes. In that sense, it is self-defeating. These initial considerations help pave the way for a general definition of relativism. The procedure will then formulate a framework for a definition of epistemological relativism. A survey of how this relativistic view has been defended will follow. Thereafter, I will close the chapter by highlighting the various criticisms brought against this view of truth.

A DEFINITION OF RELATIVISM

Protagoras, a pre-Socratic philosopher, remains widely regarded by epistemologists as the key progenitor of relativism. In Plato's *Theaetetus*, Socrates quotes Protagoras's definition of truth: human beings are the measure of all things, including those that do not exist.[8] Protagoras held the view that things are as they appear to you or me at any moment.[9] Timothy Mosteller called this definition *Protagorean Relativism*. Beckwith and Koukl echo this version of relativism in their attempts to define relativistic truth: *true in*

---

6. Luper, "Epistemic Relativism," 271.
7. Westacott, "Relativism," para. 3.
8. Plato, *Theaetetus*, 152a.
9. Plato, *Theaetetus*, 152a.

relativism means *true for me* and nothing more.[10] Neither Beckwith nor Koukl accept this view of truth.

As noted earlier, this version of relativism remains surprisingly persistent, earning the approval of a variety of philosophers and non-philosophers alike. For example, in his book, *Man Is the Measure*, Reuben Abel postulates this version of relativism with apparent approval when he notes how the central claim of his work stems from a view boldly stated long ago by Protagoras but quite possibly never fully grasped nor properly applied.[11]

A definition more helpful than the one offered by Protagorean relativism can be located in Mosteller's writings. According to him, the nature and existence of items of knowledge qualities, values, or logical entities nontrivially obtain their natures and/or existence from certain aspects of human activity, including but not limited to beliefs, cultures, and languages.[12] This definition is helpful because I find it more specific and informative than the affirmations of Protagorean relativism.

So far, we have only considered what relativism affirms in our attempt to define it. In order to foster a deeper understanding than what we have considered, a look at what relativism denies might be helpful. For example, according to Luper, relativism can be ideally defined in contrast to absolutism. More accurately, it should be defined as the denial of absolutism, whether epistemological, which holds that a single objectively true characterization of reality exists, or ontological, which states only one correct or authoritative fundamental standard for assessing epistemic merit exists.[13]

Similarly, James K. A. Smith sees in relativism the very antithesis of absolute truth of the sort proclaimed in Judeo-Christian teachings.[14] Still, Smith's explication of relativism seems rather conciliatory to the extent of attempting to draw some lessons from relativism for the Christian community. At any rate, his contention that relativism remains a view antithetical to the existence of absolute truth remains. This denial of the existence of absolute truth reflects the second feature alluded to by Westacott, namely, the denial that any standpoint is uniquely privileged over all others. The implication here, of course, is that all points of view are equally valid.[15]

---

10. Beckwith and Koukl, *Relativism*, 20.
11. Abel, *Man Is*, xxi.
12. Mosteller, *Relativism*, 3.
13. Luper, "Epistemic Relativism," 271–72.
14. Smith, *Relativism*, 16.
15. Westacott, "Relativism," para. 1.

This short overview of relativism in general presupposes some form of subjectivism on the part of the relativist. In order to understand how subjectivism plays itself out, Beckwith and Koukl make a helpful distinction between subjectivism and objectivism in the following way: they consider the fact that something can be subjectively true or objectively true. For example, consider scenario *A*. Under this scenario, suppose I say, "Haagen-Dazs butter pecan ice cream is absolutely delicious." I have made a true claim specifically because the claim reflects, accurately, my personal taste. What I have said is not really about ice cream. I have not made a claim about an object external to me. Rather, the claim is about the subject—me. My statement about the ice cream is a subjective truth. The statement is true for me, the subject, but not for the object, the ice cream itself. The ice cream does not perform the act of tasting; I do. The experience of flavor pertains to me as a subject and not to the ice cream as the object. Tastes are personal and private. Seemingly, you should not be faulted for having different subjective tastes about desserts than someone else.[16]

Additionally, Beckwith and Koukl ask us to consider a different scenario, which I call scenario *B*. Suppose, they hypothesize, my claim was about numbers rather than about the flavor of ice cream. If I say that the sum of two plus two is four, I would be making a different sort of claim than stating my taste about the ice cream. I would be conveying my belief, as a subject, concerning an external objective truth. Suppose you disagreed with me and said two plus two equals five. I could claim you were wrong and would not be accused of impropriety. In themselves, mathematical equations are either true or false, having one right answer. They do not have a variety of right answers that vary according to one's individual tastes. Thus, any disagreements about the sum would be adjudicated with the goal of determining the right answer rather than that of sharing personal feelings.[17]

The reason for this observation rests on the conviction that truth is objective or "out there" rather than subjective. Subjective truths rest on internal preferences and change according to our whims. Objective truths, in contrast, are realities in the external world. External facts are what they are regardless of what we feel about them.[18] Relativism, however, denies the existence of this kind of truth. Relativism insists on the first scenario presented by Beckwith and Koukl. To be sure, relativism seems to hold that

---

16. Beckwith and Koukl, *Relativism*, 26.
17. Beckwith and Koukl, *Relativism*, 26.
18. Beckwith and Koukl, *Relativism*, 26.

all matters of truth and falsehoods seem determined by one's individual subjective preferences.

We are now in a fairer position to give a general but formal definition of relativism. Seemingly, a formal definition for relativism would run as follows: a given statement S remains true for an individual P if and only if S seems subjectively true for P. Stated differently, S's apparent truth for P is a necessary and sufficient condition for S being actually true for P.

Does this definition count as an accurate characterization of relativism? It remains consistent with the first of Westacott's double features of relativism alluded to at the beginning of this chapter. What remains unclear, though, is whether it satisfies the second part of Westacott's double feature of relativism, namely, the denial that any standpoint is uniquely privileged over all others as the sole custodian of truth. Our definition of relativism needs to include this aspect. This definition might run as follows: for any statement S and for any person P, S is true for P if and only if S expresses a viewpoint subscribed to by persons other than P. This definition seems to meet the requirement expressed by the second feature. Both definitions, once coupled, provide an overview of relativism. Thus, both definitions could be coupled as follows: for any statement S and for any person P, S is true for P if and only if S seems subjectively true for P and S expresses a viewpoint subscribed to by persons other than P. Does this expression meet the requirements of the definition?

Consider the second part of the definition, namely, S seems subjectively true for P and S expresses a viewpoint subscribed to by persons other than P. Should this definition be stated as a disjunction or as a conjunction? If stated as a conjunction, it would seem to entail that both conjuncts obtain in order for the definition to remain an accurate representation of relativism. This way of characterizing relativism would imply that a full-fledged relativist must be both a pluralist and a subjectivist, which may not necessarily be the case, as has been argued by Stephen Luper.[19] To be charitable to both of them, the definition of relativism seems best served by stating this part as an inclusive disjunction: for any statement S and for any person P, S is true for P if and only if S seems either subjectively true for P or S expresses a viewpoint subscribed to by persons other than P or both.

This definition seems charitable enough to meet Luper's explication of relativism and Westcott's as well. Whether or not this overview remains

---

19. See Luper, "Epistemic Relativism," 273.

consistent with itself will be determined later in this chapter. For now, I turn to a more focused version of relativism, namely, epistemological relativism.

A DEFINITION OF EPISTEMOLOGICAL RELATIVISM

In his explication of relativism, Mosteller recollects from Harvey Siegel what he calls a "standard conjunct" and a "neutrality conjunct" in epistemological relativism. According to Mosteller, the standard conjunct says that for any knowledge-claim p, p can be established only according to another set of background principles and standards of evaluation $S_1 \ldots S_n$. The neutrality conjunct says, given a different set of background principles and standards $S_1 \ldots S_n$, no neutral way exists of choosing between the two or more alternative sets in evaluating p with respect to truth or rational justification. The truth of p and its rational justifiability remain relative to the standards used in evaluating p.[20]

Notice the use of "background principles" in Mosteller's definition. What principles does he have in mind? Possible examples include the denial of objective standards and a preference for subjective ones spoken about by Luper. Seemingly, Kaufman gives us a clue. An extended explication of these subjective background principles will receive a considerable treatment later in this section when we turn to Gordon Kaufman's argument for relativism.

Meanwhile, let us examine Stephen Luper's definition of epistemological relativism. Luper sets parameters for defining epistemological relativism by noting how epistemic relativism rejects the idea that claims can be assessed from a universally applicable objective standpoint. This version of relativism suggests that the real basis of our views is something fleeting, such as, following Thomas Kuhn, the techniques of mass persuasion or, following Richard Rorty, the determination of intellectuals to achieve solidarity.[21]

Moreover, Luper notes the subjective and pluralist nature of certain varieties of epistemic relativism: subjective relativism denies the existence of a correct or authoritative epistemic standard. Rather, epistemic merit always gets assessed relative to standards that are entirely subjective. Pluralistic relativism insists on the existence of more than one correct or authoritative fundamental epistemic standard. In this view, the assessment of

20. Mosteller, *Relativism*, 8.
21. Luper, "Epistemic Relativism," 271.

epistemic merit is relative to a range of competing standards, each applied in exclusion of the others as a way of avoiding "incoherent hodgepodge." However, each remains objectively correct in some sense, which the pluralist must eventually supply.[22]

According to Luper, subjective relativism remains closely related to standard subjectivism, which denies the objective correctness of any epistemic standard. Subjectivism, in this context, expresses the notion that an epistemic standard's claim to acceptability remains wholly contingent upon the features of an individual subject. Subjective relativism maintains that accepted subjectivist standards vary from person to person or group to group. Luper notes, however, that subjectivism remains incompatible with pluralist relativism.[23]

This observation of incompatibility by Luper need not be the case if and only if we consider a state of affairs where a multiplicity of individuals (hence pluralistic) could have identical intersubjective affirmations concerning a given viewpoint. Luper, however, could counter this view by noting how the identical nature of such intersubjective affirmations could count against their plurality. For that reason, he might stand by his incompatibility comments.

I will offer a fuller critique of the nature of epistemological relativism towards the end of this chapter. In the next section, I consider the various arguments offered by epistemological relativists to defend their position. First, we will look at how Mosteller, himself a non-relativist, characterizes a possible defense offered by epistemological relativists. Second, we will consider another defense for epistemological relativism offered by Stephen Lane, also a non-relativist. Third, we will look in greater detail at an argument for epistemological relativism offered by Gordon Kaufman, a philosophical theologian but also a relativist, as already noted. I will then proceed to the promised critique of epistemological relativism at the end of the chapter.

MOSTELLER'S DEFENSE OF EPISTEMOLOGICAL RELATIVISM

Let me begin by highlighting a defense of epistemological relativism presented by Mosteller. I note, first, that Mosteller locates two different types

22. Luper, "Epistemic Relativism," 272.
23. Luper, "Epistemic Relativism," 273.

of argument for epistemological relativism, which I will call ER. The first, ER_1, can be stated in summary as follows: no neutral standards by appeal to which competing knowledge claims can be adjudicated exist. If such neutral standards by appeal to which competing knowledge claims can be adjudicated exist, then epistemological relativism follows. Therefore, epistemological relativism follows.[24] This argument commits an informal fallacy by denying the antecedent. By that move alone, it should be rejected, but Mosteller launches his review and subsequent critique of the argument from an entirely different approach. Mosteller quickly notes that neutral standards of the sort alluded to in the premises of the argument may be unavailable, but neutral standards in the weaker sense that they do not unfairly prejudice any particular live disputes may exist. For this reason, Mosteller charitably disambiguates the first premise by rewording it: no globally neutral standards by appeal to which competing knowledge claims can be adjudicated exist.[25]

What should we make of the argument presented in this way? Following Harvey Siegel, Mosteller finds the first premise false specifically because locally neutral standards by means of which one can evaluate competing knowledge claims do, in fact, exist. In other words, although competing standards for evaluating particular knowledge claims may exist, some standards considered locally neutral by parties making specific claims may also exist, and the laws of logic often function as such locally neutral standards.[26]

Mosteller notes how such laws themselves need not always be considered locally neutral, since knowledge claims about them may also be disputed. In Mosteller's view, in cases where the laws of logic are being considered true or false, appealing to the laws of logic as locally neutral arbiters in the dispute would perhaps not be the way to go because competing knowledge claims about the laws of logic may, in fact, exist. In this case, the laws of logic cannot function as a locally neutral standard.[27]

Still, even if the relativist gives very persuasive reasons against the availability of local neutrality, relativism does not follow for at least one reason: when the relativist claims that local neutrality is impossible, either the claim itself is neutral or it is not. If it is a locally neutral claim, then the claim itself is false, for it claims local neutrality is impossible. If the law is

24. Mosteller, *Relativism*, 12.
25. Mosteller, *Relativism*, 12.
26. Mosteller, *Relativism*, 12.
27. Mosteller, *Relativism*, 12.

not locally neutral, then non-neutrally persuasive reasons for asserting that claim is impossible. For this reason, the assertion remains ineffective in the argument for the conclusion epistemological relativism seeks to establish.[28] These critiques by Siegel and also by Mosteller seem essentially correct.

Mosteller offers a second argument, ER_2, for epistemological relativism: one cannot globally transcend all perspectives. If one cannot globally transcend all perspectives, then epistemological relativism obtains. Therefore, epistemological relativism obtains. The anti-relativist might agree with the first premise, according to Mosteller, but he or she would add that some local perspectives can be transcended. For example, children do transcend their local perspectives of not being able to grasp the concept of fractions by eventually grasping those very concepts. They transcend the local perspective that some things remain invisible to the naked eye by eventually confirming the existence of such things using a microscope. In each case, argues Mosteller, the person in the first local perspective simply moved into an improved perspective. From these examples we find no reason to think that epistemic agents are trapped in or bound by their perspectives such that those perspectives remain impervious to critical scrutiny.[29]

I now turn to Luper's characterization of the defense of epistemological relativism. In recognition of the fact that relativism has the subjective element and the pluralist element, Luper proposes ways in which each element could be defended. He begins, first, by considering subjectivist relativism: an assessment of the epistemic merit of a point of view can be made only against the backdrop of an authoritative standard. If none exists, then no view is defensible. Neither can any view be condemned as irrational.[30] This conclusion places all views and beliefs on par with one another with respect to the causes of their credibility. This fact represents the pluralist element.[31]

Luper formulates a more extended defense for relativism: he notes, first, that an argument for relativism amounts to an argument against absolutism. For this reason, to engage with their absolutist opponents, relativists must argue on grounds absolutists take seriously. According to Luper, absolutists will reject as question-begging the assertion, supposedly from relativists, that epistemic merit can be assessed subjectively. They will also

---

28. Mosteller, *Relativism*, 13.
29. Mosteller, *Relativism*, 13–14.
30. Luper, "Epistemic Relativism," 273.
31. Luper, "Epistemic Relativism," 274.

reject the idea that this assertion can be defended using subjective considerations, which have no bearing on epistemic merit as the absolutist understands it. Hence, a subjectivist case for subjectivist relativism fails.[32]

Similarly, Luper notes, the absolutists will reject the standards by which pluralism is defensible. For example, suppose that in order to support their view, pluralists point out that it is not self-contradictory. Possibly, by that standard, pluralism remains justifiable. However, absolutists will reject the idea that mere consistency is adequate support for a view. For that reason, a pluralist case for pluralism fails as well. To be sure, the absolutist will not be satisfied with anything short of a non-relativist defense of relativism.[33]

Epistemological relativism understood in this way seems to remain vulnerable to the charge of "untrustworthiness" to preserve truth. Though epistemological in approach, the charge takes a moral appeal. To what extent, for example, should we trust the claim that no view is indefensible? If no view is indefensible, then the view that no view is indefensible is, itself, indefensible. If it cannot be defended, then it cannot be trusted, hence the ethical issue. Moreover, if all views are rational, what do we make of cultic leaders who, because of and based on their teachings, duped their followers into committing mass suicide? The plurality aspect of relativism fails to offer a satisfactory answer to this question. Of course, this idea borders on the livability of epistemological relativism, and unless we gain access to an answer that diffuses this concern, the plurality aspect of epistemological relativism remains unlivable if pushed to its logical conclusion.

In order to get a fuller picture of epistemological relativism, let us turn to one of the most formidable defenses for relativism, which comes from the work of Gordon Kaufman. He presents a summary of epistemological relativism: objective descriptive studies in history and the social sciences seem to reveal wide variations in valuation, judgment, and cognition interculturally and intra-culturally. Also, the kinds of problems investigated by scientists are a function of the interests of scientists; thus, not even the prestige of natural science has preserved it immune from relativistic analysis. These, in turn, vary with all manner of cultural and psychological pressures. Even logic has a history, and some would contend that the structures of human thought itself vary with time and place. Therefore—and this captures

---

32. Luper, "Epistemic Relativism," 279–80.
33. Luper, "Epistemic Relativism," 280.

the central claim Kaufman is trying to make—values and even truth are relative to the historical context or to the individual personality.[34]

After giving this summary, Kaufman responds to four objections raised against relativism, objections he finds based on misconceptions of relativism. The only formidable objection he finds hitherto unmet seems to be the objection of logical inconsistency. After giving snapshot responses to the first three, he spends the major part of his book responding to this objection—a response that seems to be an expansion of the premises for the argument he presents in the summary already considered. For the sake of making a systematic presentation of Kaufman's views, I will proceed in what follows by first showing how Kaufman expands his argument stated earlier and then by highlighting the objections he tries to meet.

In order to demonstrate the acceptability of the relativistic worldview, Kaufman appeals to the utility of epistemological relativism in the following way: relativistic thinkers contend that a relativistic perspective actually frees human beings from subjection to uncritical dogmatisms, thereby enabling humans to develop broader and all-encompassing knowledge of themselves and of the world. Citing Karl Manheim, also a relativist, Kaufman tries to show how relativism provides a more comprehensive framework for understanding and interpreting the experience of human beings than any absolutistic system. He concurs with Manheim that relativism not only frees us from regarding our own insights as necessarily true. It also frees us from thought, which is based on an absolutistic model of truth. Thus, we get empowered to grasp certain kinds of truth not otherwise comprehensible.[35] What these truths entail, Kaufman does not exactly say, though a closer look at his explication will reveal some pointers, such as his version of the emergence of consciousness.

However, expanding on this very notion of a non-absolutist conception of truth, Kaufman agrees with Manheim's contention that certain sociohistorical "truths" are apprehensible only from certain sociohistorical perspectives such that if this contention is true, a static absolutistic model of truth is no longer tenable. Kaufman finds the process of evaluating and refuting relativistic theories of truth via logic quite illegitimate.[36]

In order to clarify his vantage point, Kaufman distinguishes between what he calls "external relativism" and "internal relativism," both of them,

---

34. Kaufman, *Relativism*, 3.
35. Kaufman, *Relativism*, 4.
36. Kaufman, *Relativism*, 5.

presumably, epistemological. According to Kaufman, external relativism finds its basis on the results of "objective" and "descriptive" analysis of various historical periods, of various cultures, or of differing social movements or individuals within a given culture or historical period. Thus, in this version of epistemological relativism, anthropological, historical, and psychological descriptions of the "values" and "truths" accepted from different perspectives may all be introduced as evidence in support of the view that value itself and truth itself are relative to the concrete situation.[37]

Kaufman finds this conclusion hardly satisfactory based on the evidence specifically because our conceptions of what we value and what we regard as true are related to our awareness of what ought to be the case and not simply of what is the case. However, according to Kaufman, descriptions of what is the case in different cultures or persons or what has been the case in the past can give us no answer to the question of what ought to be valued or regarded as true. Hence, the external relativism based merely on such description cannot stand up under analysis. For this reason, Kaufman thinks that relativists of this stripe remain unable to account for the claim to truth of the truth of their own standpoint, owing to the fact that such claims to truth are themselves based on certain norms or criteria of validity and not on descriptive analysis at all.[38]

Internal relativism, however, remains unfounded on this kind of objective description, Kaufman thinks, and for this reason, it remains immune to the absurdities of external relativism. In what way is it immune? First, internal relativism, according to Kaufman, grows out of the investigator's attempt to "get inside" the strange culture, historical period, or person he or she is studying to the extent that the strangeness of the customs and ways of thought of the subject are overcome. Eventually, the perspective from which the strange culture views reality gradually becomes a perspective the investigator himself or herself can assume with increasing sympathetic sensitivity—apprehending the norms recognized from that perspective as norms. Rather than being simply concerned with what other people say they value and think to be true, the attempt is made actually to assume completely the perspective and outlook of the position being investigated.[39]

Moreover, the more the historian sympathetically enters the situation she is studying, the more she understands, according to Kaufman, what is

37. Kaufman, *Relativism*, 14.
38. Kaufman, *Relativism*, 14.
39. Kaufman, *Relativism*, 15.

being attempted and thought and valued in that situation. One comes to apprehend these norms in the same way that one recognizes the norms under which one is constantly working and with which one remains familiar by noting and experiencing the subjective normative tension they exert. Hence, one becomes aware of the multiplicity of norms, values, and standards, each related to its own peculiar situation. If one were to carry out this sympathetic interpretation to perfection, Kaufman argues, one would feel the real need and drive and value of headhunting to the headhunter, for example, and would be able to sympathize with the obligation of the headhunter to perform this act.[40]

Kaufman notes how we adequately apprehend and portray the life of other people only insofar as we achieve such a sympathetic analysis and understanding. He notes how impossible it was in the nineteenth-century historical studies to gain understanding of positions other than our own unless we were able to reenact or relive, imaginatively, the experiences out of which those positions grew. Kaufman concludes that this insight and the important consequences resultant upon applying it to the history of thought remain the real basis for relativism, epistemological or otherwise, and the possibility of seeing what individuals in a given situation saw and understanding the questions and problems they were attempting to deal with exists only when we get inside that situation. Only then, Kaufman says, do we find ourselves in a position to understand why such individuals gave the answers of the sort we find in them. This reality makes it apparent that philosophers with viewpoints other than one's own could not be viewed simply as living in error that needed explanation. Each different viewpoint represented in the history of thought appeared, from within its own situation, to be in fact nothing other than truth itself, for the simple reason that no philosopher or theologian worthy of the name holds to a position he or she finds erroneous. Hence, the position at which philosophers find themselves in their work is the nearest approximation to the truth they find themselves able to attain. For this reason, Kaufman concludes, when viewed from within the philosophers' perspectives, the position they have developed appear true and other positions appear either as outright errors or, at best, as relative truths that have been taken up in their own positions.[41]

Kaufman remains fully aware of the mutual exclusivity of various worldviews in certain crucial aspects despite the fact that these worldviews

---

40. Kaufman, *Relativism*, 16.
41. Kaufman, *Relativism*, 16–17.

overlap in other areas. He has worldviews such as logical empiricism, atheistic existentialism, Buddhism, and Christianity in mind. He finds them inconsistent with one another in their ultimate institutions of reality, truth, and value judgments. He also believes each may be fully consistent with itself and may have what appears to be, from within, a completely adequate interpretation of all the facts with which the others are concerned. Just the same, they remain mutually incompatible at practically every point because of the radically different ways in which they order and interpret the facts in question.[42]

How, then, does one account for the differences in perspective? According to Kaufman, one does so by appealing to something other than abstract thought if, by definition, one believes that completely universal laws of logic govern abstract thought. Kaufman believes non-logical and non-rational factors must be operating within the process of knowing itself, leading it sometimes in one direction and sometimes in another. More accurately, thinking must be a function of the concrete historical and psychological situation in which it emerges as well as of certain norms of truth and error.[43]

How does Kaufman account for this contention? Consider, for example, the emergence of consciousness. According to Kaufman, factors other than the categories of consciousness must be involved in the genesis of consciousness in the human organism. Consider how infants lack knowledge of the proper causes of their pangs of hunger or discomfort, yet they still respond when the breast is given them.[44] For Kaufman, our knowledge of the external world emerges first in the encounters of will and feeling with that world. Withdrawal occurs spontaneously with the occurrences of a feeling of pain. Attraction, however, occurs with the feelings of pleasure. Out of this encounter, consciousness of both self and world gradually develops in us.[45] We spontaneously intend an act by our drives, which push us forward or outward blindly and begin to effect it. Instead of the realization of the intention, a sensation of pressure and resistance arises within us. This sensation, in turn, gives rise to a kind of rudimentary awareness of limitation

---

42. Kaufman, *Relativism*, 18.
43. Kaufman, *Relativism*, 20.
44. Kaufman, *Relativism*, 29.
45. Kaufman, *Relativism*, 30.

or unfulfillment of the original drive. An awareness of the original drive itself subsequently appears.[46]

Kaufman finds any ascriptions of universally true norms to thinking vulnerable to and guilty of what he calls "the rationalistic error," and any ascriptions of only the concrete historical and psychological situation to thinking seems vulnerable to the error of external relativism, which he rejects. Only in internal relativism do we find a way out, says Kaufman: it attempts to understand from within and to appreciate fully the claims to truth of alternative philosophical positions.[47]

These considerations complete our overview of epistemological relativism. The question we must ask, at this point, is whether epistemological relativism can be held consistently as a theory of truth and whether it withstands rational muster. In order to answer this question, we will merely revisit the arguments already outlined by Mosteller, Luper, and Kaufman and test them for consistency. No argument was given for relativism except for a brief definition. For this reason, no critique of relativism in general seems necessary at this point, though I am sure a formidable critique can be made. For now, however, let me begin my evaluation of epistemological relativism.

A BRIEF EVALUATION OF RELATIVISM IN GENERAL

Consider our definition for relativism in general, earlier stated as follows: for any statement S and for any person P, S is true for P if and only if S seems either subjectively true for P, or S expresses a viewpoint subscribed to by persons other than P, or both. When we arrived at a formulation of this definition, I promised to determine whether or not the overview captured by this definition remained consistent.

Syntactically speaking, the statement seems contingent by the rules of logic; hence, it is not a necessary truth. Neither is it a necessary falsehood. What we must do with the statement, then, is to evaluate it semantically. When we claim that S expresses a viewpoint subscribed to by persons other than P, we imply the pluralistic aspect of relativism. I noted earlier, in my attempt to diffuse Luper's contention that pluralism remains inconsistent with subjectivism, how intersubjectivity can be construed in a way consistent with pluralism. More specifically, I noted how different individuals

46. Kaufman, *Relativism*, 31.
47. Kaufman, *Relativism*, 20.

or cultures could have identical subjective viewpoints, thus attesting to the possibility of intersubjectivity. I pointed out the possibility of Luper responding by suggesting that identical subjective viewpoints no longer remain pluralistic specifically because they really are congruent rather than diverse. Luper would seem correct in this appraisal of relativism. If epistemic relativism insists on the plurality of ideas while, simultaneously, subscribing to their subjectivity, it will find itself vulnerable to a *reductio ad absurdum* of a certain kind specifically because, semantically speaking, it will encounter divergent viewpoints, some of which will seem contradictory. In that sense, if my characterization of relativism is correct, then relativism, by definition, runs the risk of internal inconsistency.

AN EVALUATION OF EPISTEMOLOGICAL RELATIVISM

After presenting an argument for epistemological relativism, Mosteller outlines various reasons why he thinks those arguments fail. Appealing, once again, to Harvey Siegel, he presents an argument against epistemological relativism: if a standard exists by which epistemological relativism is judged to be false, then epistemological relativism is false. Therefore, epistemological relativism is false. Let me call this response "rebuttal C_1 against epistemological relativism" and merely refer to it as C_1 henceforth.

According to Mosteller and, of course, Siegel, in order to deny premise 1 of ER_1, the relativist must deny that the falsity of ER_1 follows from it being judged to be false. This sort of move remains impossible for the relativist because going by the very definition of relativism, all propositions, including epistemological relativism, are true or false just in case they are judged to be so. Hence, to deny the first premise, the relativist must deny the very thing asserted in the definition of epistemological relativism, namely, that truth (or, for that matter, falsity) is relative to standards. Hence, in maintaining that epistemological relativism is true, the relativist must allow that epistemological relativism is false if a standard judges it to be false.[48] This implication of C_1 will henceforth be referred to as C_1^*.

Possibly, a context-specific argument for epistemological relativism could be advanced: if a standard exists in a particular context by one or more individuals by which epistemological relativism is judged false, then epistemological relativism is false. A standard exists in a particular context by one or more individuals by which epistemological relativism is judged

48. Mosteller, *Relativism*, 15.

to be false. Therefore, epistemological relativism is false.[49] As with C_1, let me call this criticism "rebuttal C_2 against epistemological relativism" and C_2 for short. Notice that implication C_1^* applies just as cogently to C_2 as it does to C_1.

Another interesting argument against epistemological relativism comes from Siegel: if epistemological relativism is rationally justifiable, then there must be some non-relative, neutral framework or ground from which we can make that judgment, that is, that epistemological relativism is rationally justifiable. However, according to the definition of epistemological relativism, no non-relative, neutral framework or grounds exist. Therefore, epistemological relativism is not a rationally justifiable position.[50] Let me call this criticism "rebuttal C_3 against epistemological relativism" and C_3 for short.

Mosteller then asks us to suppose the relativist takes issue with the first premise of the argument. The relativist must then claim that epistemological relativism is rationally justifiable and that the claim that a neutral framework is required is false. Nevertheless, whatever rational justification a relativist has for the affirmation of the antecedent and the denial of the consequent of the first premise, it cannot be a justification that remains neutral since the relativist seems to be denying the possibility of any such neutrality. The very notion of the rightness of truth of a proposition seems undermined in the very definition of relativism. For this reason, if epistemological relativism is true, it would be false because we would find no neutral ground from which to assess the rational justifiability of any claim, including epistemological relativism itself.[51] As with other objections to epistemological relativism, I will call this implication C_3^*.

Mosteller and Siegel offer extended arguments against epistemological relativism. For example, they try to show that epistemological relativism results in solipsism as a logical conclusion. Briefly stated, their argument runs something similar to the following formulation: if you and I are not the first-person relativist in question, then the truth about me and about the friends and the spouse of the first-person relativist is, for the first-person relativist, simply a function of his or her own dispositions to believe.

---

49. Mosteller, *Relativism*, 16.
50. Mosteller, *Relativism*, 16.
51. Mosteller, *Relativism*, 17.

Owing to the fact that the antecedent of this claim is true, the consequent must also be true.[52]

Mosteller could say more about this contention, and he does. For our purposes, however, C_1, C_2, and C_3 will suffice, along with their attendant implications. What we find from these criticisms is the consensus that something self-stultifying afflicts the motif of epistemological relativism if Mosteller and Siegel interpret the claims of epistemological relativism correctly. What we have not hitherto ascertained is whether Luper thinks across similar lines, and we now turn to his critique.

Luper summarizes the epistemological relativist argument: to defend their view successfully, relativists must honor the no-deadlock principle that each side in a dispute must argue on the basis of claims acceptable to the opposing side. If they argue on relativist grounds, they cannot meet this principle, so a relativist case for relativism is no case at all.[53]

How might a relativist respond to this characterization of epistemological relativism? To be fair to the relativist, Luper thinks the relativist might defeat the first premise as follows: absolutists must apply the no-deadlock principle to themselves as much as to everyone else. No one can defeat relativism or defend absolutism on the grounds acceptable to determined relativists, Luper notes. For this reason, absolutists must conclude that neither relativism nor absolutism is defensible. As for relativists, they do not face this difficulty because they need not rely on the no-deadlock principle in a relativist case for relativism. Similarly, Luper adds, the absolutist is not positioned to show that relativists have to honor the no-deadlock principle. This fact remains because absolutists must, by that very principle, argue on grounds acceptable to relativists. However, relativists find that principle antithetical to their case and reject anything it supports. Thus, according to Luper, if the absolutists accept the no-deadlock principle, the acceptance bars them from insisting that relativists should follow suit.[54]

In addition, Luper notes how, in arguing for anything, subjectivist relativists get greatly hobbled by their view that no standard is authoritative. Suppose they are correct in their view. We find no authoritative point of view from which to defend any view, including the assertion that no standard is authoritative. Just the same, claims can be supported subjectively in the same sense that assertions of taste and related matters are

---

52. Mosteller, *Relativism*, 20.
53. Luper, "Epistemic Relativism," 280.
54. Luper, "Epistemic Relativism," 280.

defensible. However, by their own admission, the subjectivist's defense of a view A does not show that it is preferable to an alternative position B, for proponents of B can easily "support" B and "criticize" A subjectively. In particular, subjectivist-style grounds cannot be adduced to show that subjectivist relativism is better than absolutism because absolutists can easily "support" their view subjectively, say on the grounds that people who deny absolutism are irritating.[55]

Similarly, Luper continues, pluralist relativists can offer a relativist defense of their view: if each standard, applied in exclusion to others, is authoritative, or if many are, then whether a view is defensible depends on the standard in play, and pluralism is defensible relative to standards that support it. Still, pluralists must admit that a pluralist-style defense of a view A does not show that it is preferable to an alternative B whose advocates might defend B and attack A relative to their own standards. Hence, a pluralist defense of pluralism does not show it is superior to absolutism.[56]

Luper continues, saying absolutists will be ready to reject a relativist defense of subjectivism as well as a relativist case for pluralism upon concluding that both violate the no-ties principle: a "defense" of relativism that does not contend, let alone establish, that relativism is superior to absolutism is not a defense at all. Notice how relativists will not have the same response because they reject the no-ties principle:[57] if the defense of the authoritativeness of standard T is not better than the defense of the authoritativeness of an alternative to T, then there are inadequate grounds for accepting the authoritativeness of T.[58]

Hence, the relativists will admit that, from their viewpoint, relativism is not justifiable by some "valid" standards. For people who embrace those standards, relativism is indefensible, but there are also "valid" standards by which relativism can be supported. For anyone who accepts the no-ties principle, relativism *is* indefensible. Luper thinks some "valid" standards exist by which relativism can be supported, and for anyone accepting the no-ties principle, relativism is indefensible. This fact does not show how, for the relativist, relativism cannot be supported.[59]

---

55. Luper, "Epistemic Relativism," 280.
56. Luper, "Epistemic Relativism," 281.
57. Luper, "Epistemic Relativism," 281.
58. Luper, "Epistemic Relativism," 276.
59. Luper, "Epistemic Relativism" 281.

Luper's conclusions here might be warranted if we look at relativism syntactically. Just the same, if we focus on the deeper semantic contentions made by relativists such as Kaufman, we see a different story. Kaufman makes a powerful claim concerning the reality of pluralism, a claim that tries to explain custom variations among people groups. According to Kaufman, objective descriptive studies in history and the social sciences seem to reveal wide variations in valuation, judgment, and cognition inter-culturally and intra-culturally. Notice that this inter-cultural and intra-cultural variation affects both science and logic. This claim finds its basis in a certain presupposition on Kaufman's part: the existence of an objective standard according to which the epistemologist determines that a certain claim p varies distinctly from another claim q in its truth value or that a given entity E presents itself to individual X in one way and to individual Y in another way. Kaufman would not make this claim consistently if he did not presuppose the existence of this objective standard, for he would have no way of knowing that p is distinct from q or that E appears to X in one way and to Y in another way. Strangely, this presupposition of the existence of such a standard is the very thing Kaufman seems to take pains to reject. Moreover, if we find wide variations in valuation, judgment, and cognition inter-culturally and intra-culturally, what reason do we have to suppose, as Kaufman does, that the studies in history and social sciences revealing these wide variations are themselves objective and, therefore, immune to these variations? Kaufman seems unaware of this possibility.

What do we make of Kaufman's contention that relativistic thinkers find their views quite liberating from uncritical dogmatism, enabling human beings to develop broader and more comprehensive knowledge of themselves and of the world? We can say several things about this observation. First, it rests on a confusion on Kaufman's part between the acquisition of facts and the evaluation of those facts. Anyone can gain cognitive access to some facts, whether the person is a relativist or an absolutist. Presumably, both have the ability to gather comprehensive information about themselves and about the world. The distinguishing factor, therefore, is not whether or not they have comprehensive knowledge. Rather, the distinguishing factor is how they classify the knowledge they acquire: do they find the information true or false, bad or good, correct or incorrect? Apparently, for Kaufman, this distinction seems invisible.

Of course, Kaufman could offer a rejoinder here by showing how judging a true statement false implies a lack of knowledge on the part of the epistemologist just as much as it would be for the same epistemologist to judge a false statement true. Whereas this rejoinder remains essentially correct, Kaufman still suffers from the confusion alluded to previously, and here's why: he rejects the existence of the very basis used to judge one claim true and another false. Since that basis remains nonexistent in Kaufman's epistemology, knowledge, for Kaufman, whether true or false, remains confined to the exercise of acquisition of facts.

Kaufman finds relativism free from the problem of uncritical dogmatism. This finding on Kaufman's part, I argue, presupposes an unstated objective principle of the epistemological wrongness of uncritical dogmatism, an objective principle Kaufman is taking pains to avoid. Moreover, his presentation encounters a similar oddity when he finds the process of evaluating and refuting relativist theories of truth via logic illegitimate. Once again, this finding presupposes another unstated objective rule on Kaufman's part: the illegitimacy of refuting relativistic theories of truth via logic. Stated more distinctly, he would suggest that the exercise of refuting relativistic theories of truth via logic is epistemologically illegitimate. This seems to presuppose the existence of a universal objective principle according to which one determines the illegitimacy of such a move.

Just as curiously, Kaufman claims that value itself remains relative to the concrete situations. This claim, as with the others already noted, presupposes an objective principle on the basis of which Kaufman launches it while, simultaneously, denying the existence of that principle itself. To see this, Kaufman needs his readers to see that the claim itself universally applies to all persons. If it does, then it is objectively launched. If it does not, then one need not be committed to its demands, which, presumably, Kaufman is getting his readers to do. Also, if relativism does have a basis that Kaufman identifies as history, then that basis must exist objectively, which is what Kaufman is trying to deny.

Kaufman also rejects the notion of the absolutist conception of truth. Truth, for him, is relative. Consider his agreement with Manheim: a static absolutistic model of truth is no longer tenable. I find this claim very difficult to sustain for one simple reason. I suspect Kaufman assumes this claim is absolutely true in the sense that it cannot be false. If the claim is absolutely true, then it represents an absolutistic model of truth, which he rejects. However, if an absolutistic model of truth no longer exists, as Kaufman contends, then that claim, which seems a species of that very absolutistic model, no longer exists as well. In short, the claim is self-defeating.

We still find more interesting claims in Kaufman's explication of internal epistemological relativism. Consider his example of a historian sympathetically entering the situation he or she is studying and thereby seeing specific norms and values. According to Kaufman, he or she remains familiar with these norms and is working constantly with them. He or she comes to apprehend them in the way they are recognized. He or she then becomes aware of the multiplicity of their values and standards. Kaufman did suggest that some of these norms might actually be internally consistent in themselves even if they remain mutually exclusive with each other. Moreover, if one were to carry out this sympathetic interpretation to perfection, one would feel the need and drive and value of headhunting to the headhunter and would sympathize with the obligation of the headhunter to perform his or her act.

Whereas Kaufman's observation here may work in certain situations, I find it doubtful it would work in all situations. I already mentioned the case of mass poisoning, such as the one by Reverend Jim Jones and his followers in Guyana. I wonder how Kaufman would attest to the truth and validity of such norms. Would Kaufman sympathize, for example, with cultures that seem to thrive on indigenous tenets such as female circumcision? Whereas this practice remains highly valued in some cultures, not every member of those cultures delight in the practice. To be sure, a majority do not, 72 percent to be exact, based on specific research done in a select group of cultures.[60] Or take the question of cannibalism. Some cultures do eat their neighbors.[61] Would a historian working in such a culture sympathize with the obligation of the headhunter to perform this act? I find this notion extremely difficult to sustain. To be sure, we may understand why clitoridectomy surgeons do what they do or why cannibalism prevails in some quarters; however, just because we understand them in an epistemological sense does not necessarily entail the acceptance of those acts on our part. I suspect the historian would fear for his or her life upon having an in-person encounter with such cultures! Additionally, I suspect Kaufman would find both cases, and many more not mentioned here, quite difficult to embrace if not impossible. The reason for this is simple: we have an intuitive sense of both moral and epistemic truths—truths we cannot abandon.

Kaufman, however, rejects the view that logical or rational factors operate within the process of knowing itself. In his view, some non-logical

---

60. Horowitz and Jackson, "Female Circumcision," para. 45.
61. Murano, "10 Most Chilling Stories," paras. 5–6.

and non-rational factors must be the ones operating within the process of knowing. For Kaufman, thinking remains the function of the concrete historical and psychological situations in which it emerges.

If what Kaufman says here is true, we find ourselves afflicted with some form of uncertainty. How else does one reliably know that a given state of affairs obtains except through the use of one's rational process? Surely, one's rational faculties play a crucial role in the process of knowing. Assuming one's cognitive faculties fail to function as they were designed, to what extent would they reliably convey useful information? If, for example, Kaufman abandoned his reasoning process and opted for a less rational form of locution in his writings, we would not find his written work meriting much attention. If logical and rational factors cannot be appealed to as important aspects of the process of knowing, the deliberations contained in Kaufman's work remain untrustworthy. Obviously, Kaufman would want us to trust the deliberations contained in his work. This possibility means logical factors must be appealed to as an important aspect of the process of knowing. Kaufman himself denies this conclusion.

We find ourselves, therefore, countenancing a paradox in this work. Based on what Luper, Mosteller, and Kaufman say concerning epistemic relativism and based on our findings so far, we determine no specific reason to subscribe to epistemological relativism as a reliable expression of important truths about our world. It seems completely inadequate as a theory of truth and, for that reason, should be abandoned.

Additionally, it fails to account for the problem of truth's preexistence alluded to at the beginning of this work. Truth on a relativistic reading remains fundamentally dependent on a person's perspective; the absence of that person necessarily implies the absence of truth. Therefore, prior to the arrival of humans onto the scene and given the suppositions of methodological naturalism, truth, from a relativistic vantage point, did not exist, for truth would have to be contingent upon the existence of the human person perceiving states of affairs. Theologically, the Judeo-Christian vantage point suggests the existence of infinite truth in the person of an omniscient God. Hence, theologically speaking, truth did exist as an omniscient being in the person of the Judeo-Christian God. The issue of truth not existing prior to the arrival of humans presents no problem to the Judeo-Christian thinker. It does present a problem to the methodological naturalist as well as to the relativist. Thus relativism, in its explication of truth, seems both philosophically inadequate and theologically false.

3

Pragmatism as a Theory of Truth
Peirce and James

HAVING CATALOGUED THE RELATIVISTIC THEORY of truth, including possible criticisms dissenting epistemologists could plausibly raise against it, I move to another non-objectivist version of a theory of truth, namely, pragmatism. A serious and careful look at various versions of pragmatism will somewhat show its affinities with postmodernism—a view we will examine in a later chapter. James Smith suggests one should view pragmatism as postmodernism but with an American accent. He sees pragmatism as something somewhat more straightforward and somewhat less mercurial than its postmodernist French counterpart.[1] Smith also thinks pragmatism is a radical critique of the project of modern philosophy.[2]

According to H. S. Thayer, pragmatism was the most influential philosophy in America in the first quarter of the twentieth century. Today it stands out as a philosophical movement that has evolved energetically, best understood as, partly, a rejection of what we find in much of traditional academic philosophy and, partly, a move to ground some non-negative goals.[3] Thayer finds pragmatism the most distinctive and major contribution of America to the world of philosophy. It has influenced notable philosophers such as Georg Simmel, Wilhelm Ostwald, Edmund Husserl,

---

1. Smith, *Postmodernism*, 17–18.
2. Smith, *Postmodernism*, 18.
3. Thayer, "Pragmatism," 430.

Hans Vaihinger, Richard Muller-Freienfels, Hans Hahn, Giovanni Papini, Giovanni Vailati, Henri Bergson, and Edouard Le Roy.[4]

Owing to the scope and purpose of this chapter, a detailed analysis of each of these thinkers will, perhaps, take us too far afield. Therefore, I will focus on the thoughts of the prominent forerunners of pragmatism as well as its champions in the American arena, beginning first with Charles S. Peirce and then proceeding to William James who, arguably, was one of pragmatism's most formidable defenders. We will then examine the work of more recent pragmatists such as Richard Rorty and, surprisingly, Hilary Putnam. The reason I begin with Peirce stems from the fact that he was the first thinker to develop pragmatism. I will then outline James's view because he revived pragmatism and reformulated it as a theory of truth.[5] Rorty and Putnam, however, take pragmatism to epistemological destinies quite possibly unintended by either James or Peirce, and I intend to highlight just how they made such moves.

How should we understand pragmatism? What tenets characterize this view? In what ways does it present itself as a theory of truth? I intend in this chapter to answer these questions in order to determine its sufficiency as a theory of truth. Let me begin with a very brief definition, which will then give us an idea of what pragmatism entails. Subsequently, I will try to highlight how various thinkers in this field arrived at the definition.

A DEFINITION OF PRAGMATISM

As with relativism, a unified, agreed-upon definition of pragmatism may be difficult to find. According to Thayer, for example, Peirce and James often gave very different accounts of what they understood by *pragmatism*. The explanation for this difference stems from the possibility that James distorted and perhaps misunderstood Peirce's ideas. This fact prompted Peirce to rename his view as *pragmaticism* because Peirce found the new appellation unattractive enough to keep it safe from potential kidnappers.[6]

Owing to the uncertainties concerning exact entailments of pragmatism, I will merely present an approximation of what different pragmatists tend to accept as important tenets of this view. Norman Geisler, for example, tries to offer an overarching view of pragmatism. He finds all pragmatists

4. Thayer, "Pragmatism," 430–31.
5. Thayer, "Pragmatism," 431.
6. Thayer, "Pragmatism," 431.

contending that truth is something we can discover by attempting to *live* it rather than *think* it or *feel* it. More accurately, truth must be seen as something experientially workable rather than something consistent or empirically adequate.[7]

I note, also, that our definition of pragmatism as a system of philosophy helps to provide a general but somewhat sketchy understanding of pragmatism as a theory of truth. We noted earlier the variant definitions of pragmatism itself, arising from the different theories of pragmatism available, which according to Reuben Abel, presents itself in various ways. He says the main idea in these loose formulations seems to be an emphasis on the human activity of verifying, or for that matter, *making* true. Thus, for pragmatism, the truth of a proposition finds entailment not from the notion of its correspondence with reality or from the notion of its coherence with other propositions. Rather, its truth is entailed by its *becoming* true only when acted upon.[8]

The usefulness of this way of characterizing pragmatism remains to be seen in what follows. Notice, however, Geisler's observation concerning the practical aspect of pragmatism, namely, that the truth of a given notion or statement finds confirmation in its workability or, for that matter, the practical and useful results that follow the stipulations contained in that statement. Having offered this brief sketch, let me begin by adumbrating the pragmatic theory of truth as generally presented by different pragmatists.

THE PRAGMATISM OF CHARLES S. PEIRCE

In one of his famous articles entitled "How to Make Our Ideas Clear," Charles S. Peirce makes a claim quite significant in specifying the pragmatist's motif.[9] According to Peirce, the rule for attaining clarity of understanding a given notion N consists, fundamentally, not merely of the process of familiarity with N or the definition of N but also of the process of considering the possible practical effects we perceive N to have.

How does Peirce arrive at this rule? First, consider the Cartesian notion of *clarity* (used in Descartes's famous phrase "clear and distinct") as a way of arriving at indubitable certainty. According to Pierce, the clarity requirement of a given notion N, if understood merely as familiarity with N,

---

7. Geisler, *Christian Apologetics*, 101.
8. Abel, *Man Is*, 77.
9. Peirce, "How to Make," 1–32.

remains inadequate as a rule for certainty. Equally inadequate, Peirce says, is the postulation of *distinctness*, understood as a definition of *N*. Peirce finds both postulates inadequate because they belong to the extinct philosophies of Rene Descartes and Gottfried Leibniz. Descartes, for example, failed to distinguish between an *apparently* clear idea and an *actually* clear idea. Leibniz, on his part, failed to see that the human mind can only transform knowledge and that it can never originate knowledge. Instead, Leibniz reduced the first principle of science into two classes: those that cannot be denied without self-contradiction and those that result from the principle of sufficient reason. Above all, abstract definitions played a great part in his philosophy. Peirce thinks nothing new can ever be learned by analyzing definitions.[10]

Second, Peirce argues, if the two rules of clarity (implying familiarity) and distinctness (entailing definitions) remain inadequate by themselves, the epistemologist has a right to demand that logic should teach us how to make our distinctions clear. This process entails a knowledge of what we think. For example, when questions arise in our minds, they signify the occurrences of doubt. Doubt, however, involves what Peirce calls "the irritation of thought." This activity excites one's thought process, an excitement involving a rapid flow of images through consciousness. The flow ceases only when we find ourselves decided as to how we should act under the circumstances occasioning our hesitation to decide or, for that matter, occasioning our doubt. In other words, this cessation comes about once we attain belief. Therefore, the "soul meaning" of thought entails the production of belief. More accurately, thought in action has the attainment of thought at rest for its only possible motive, and whatever fails to refer to belief cannot belong to the thought itself. Therefore, Peirce finds three properties in belief. First, belief is something we remain aware of. Second, belief appeases the irritation of doubt, and, third, belief involves the establishment, in our nature, of a rule of action or habit. In other words, the essence of belief is the establishment of habit. Conclusively, Pierce considers the exercise of volition the final upshot of thinking.[11]

Third, Peirce uses several examples to illustrate the veracity of his claims. He argues how, in addition to the first two rules of clarity and distinctness, we need a third rule determining the practical effects we might find conceivably arising from the effect of our conceptions or ideas. Take,

---

10. Peirce, "How to Make," 5.
11. Peirce, "How to Make," 12.

for example, the conception of hardness. According to Peirce, the whole conception of this quality of hardness lies in its conceived effects. When we call a thing hard, Peirce argues, we mean such a thing will remain unscratched by many other substances. When a hard thing and a soft thing remain untested, we find absolutely no difference between them. To be sure, until all hard things are tested, we find no falsity in the mode of speech contending that all hard things remain perfectly soft. Such modes of speech would entail a change in our current use of language with respect to the terms *hard* and *soft* but not their semantics.[12]

Under this very reason, consider the example of weight. Weight is force, and what we mean by force itself is completely involved in its effects. To say a body is heavy simply implies that in the absence of opposing force, the body will fall. According to our rule, we must begin by asking what the immediate use is of thinking about force. In thinking about force, we account for the changes in motion. If bodies were left to themselves without the intervention of forces, every motion would continue unchanged both in velocity and in direction. The idea excited by the word *force* has no other function than to affect our actions, and these actions have no reference to force other than through its effects. Consequently, if we know what effects of a force are, we are acquainted with every fact implied in saying that a force exists, and there is nothing more to show.[13]

Peirce's fourth reason for his central claim is the idea of reality. He notes how the sense of familiarity renders the notion of reality quite clear; even a child would understand it. Moreover, with respect to the second rule, most epistemologists would find the process of defining reality quite a puzzling exercise. However, when we apply the third rule, the following definition obtains: reality, like every other quality, consists in the peculiar sensible effects that things partaking it produce. The only effect that real things have is to cause belief specifically because all the sensations they excite emerge into consciousness in the forms of beliefs, and true belief, or belief in the real, is distinguished from false beliefs, or belief in fiction, through the experiential method of settling opinion. A person arbitrarily choosing the propositions he or she will adopt can use the word *truth* only to emphasize the expression of his or her determination to hold on to that individual choice. The followers of science, however, are animated by the hope that the process of investigation, if only pushed far enough, will give

12. Peirce, "How to Make," 18.
13. Peirce, "How to Make," 24.

one specific solution to each question to which they apply it. According to Peirce, in scientific research, different minds may set out with the most antagonistic views. However, the progress of investigation carries them by force outside of themselves to one and the same conclusion. Peirce observes how this activity of thought, by which we are carried, not where we wish, but to a foreordained goal, is like the operation of destiny. For Peirce, no modification of a point of view taken can enable a person to escape the predestinate opinion. This great hope is embodied in the conception of truth and reality. The opinion fated to be ultimately agreed to by all who investigate is what is meant by truth, and the object represented in this opinion is the real.[14]

What do we make of Peirce's pragmatic view of truth? First, we note how, in his criticism of Descartes's and Leibniz's rationalistic approaches to truth, he seems essentially correct for several reasons. First, the Cartesian and Leibnizian rationalistic methods, though valuable in many ways, seem to find their basis on an invalid move from thought to reality. The thinkability of a given entity E does not entail E's actual existence. Thinkable things seem to furnish the mind only with the realm of "the possible" without necessarily entailing the realm of "the actual."[15] To be sure, no strictly rational proofs seem available for the existence of anything. The existence of any triangle T, for instance, entails the necessity of T's three-sidedness without necessarily entailing, in a logical sense, that T exists anywhere. These considerations lead us to find Peirce's criticisms of Descartes and Leibniz quite on target.[16]

The story seems somewhat different when we look at Peirce's second reason for his second claim. Consider his contention that the sole meaning of thought entails the production of belief and that the essence of belief is the establishment of habit. What does he mean by "the establishment of habit"? Perhaps he means the following: once we gain awareness of certain facts and believe them, we find ourselves acting on those beliefs. Could this meaning be the sort Peirce wishes to express? Whereas this observation by Peirce may be true of some particular instances—in the sense that they entail a reliable report of the facts they express, it does not seem universally true. Consider a state of affairs where repeated scientific confirmation highlights the dangers of certain habits. Armed with such knowledge, an

---

14. Peirce, "How to Make," 30.
15. Geisler, *Christian Apologetics*, 42.
16. Geisler, *Christian Apologetics*, 43.

individual's habit still remains unchanged, exposing himself or herself to those scientifically confirmed dangers. If this state of affairs seems to be what Peirce is trying to describe, one may find it hardly consistent with Peirce's overall goals of finding practical effects following certain notions. Exposing oneself to consequential dangers arising from stipulated notions or ideas seem hardly practical.

A defender of Peirce may find this outcome too strong—way beyond Peirce's intentions. Such a defender may propose or opt, instead, for a weaker version of that expression: the moment we gain some awareness of certain facts and believe them, we at once find ourselves knowing how we should act even if we choose not to act in those ways. This interpretation may, perhaps, be truer to Peirce's intentions. However, the expression seems afflicted with the naturalistic fallacy. The naturalistic fallacy, according to G. E. Moore, famously warns us against defending the goodness of a thing based on its natural predisposition or criticizing a thing for its badness based on its "unnatural" disposition.[17] Logicians also instruct us on how value judgments cannot be logically derived from statements of fact. For example, we cannot validly derive the moral claim "humans ought to eat ice cream" from the premise "most humans get pleasure from eating ice cream." The reason for this rule's rational acceptability seems plain: the *ought* in the conclusion does not follow logically from the *is* in the premise.[18]

Asking whether Peirce's claims remain vulnerable to this fallacy seems appropriate here. His contention, in this second reason for his second claim, seems to be as follows: the essence of belief entails the establishment of habit. Suppose, then, I believe that eating ice cream gives me pleasure. I should, consequently, eat ice cream. The belief that eating ice cream gives me pleasure establishes the habit of actually eating ice cream. This pattern of argument seems suspiciously identical to the pattern of argument reflective of the naturalistic fallacy.

Finally, contrary to the conclusions of later pragmatists, Peirce's pragmatism seems to subscribe to some form of absolutism rather than to a non-absolutist version of truth. His determinate allusion to the inescapability of "the predestinate opinion" fated to be agreed upon ultimately by all who investigate seems to point to a realist conception of truth rather than to an anti-realist one. Also, his contention that reality is independent of what you or I or any finite member of humans may think about it seems

---

17. Moore, *Principia Ethica*, 45.
18. Baronett, *Logic*, 553.

reminiscent of objectivity. He does, however, seem to think that reality is not necessarily independent of thought in general. Peirce adds that though the object of the final opinion depends on what that opinion is, what that opinion is does not depend on what any humans think. Further, he postulates that if after the extinction of our race, another should arise with faculties and dispositions for investigation, that true opinion must be the one they will ultimately come to. In this sense, one could correctly label Peirce an objectivist with respect to truth. Gertrude Ezorsky seems to concur. According to Ezorsky, by defining truth as absolute fixity of belief, Peirce set it apart from the fixed opinion of the scientific community, which is all that inquiry really yields.[19] At any rate, the available evidence in this piece suggests a realist conception of truth on Peirce's part. Overall, the reasons make Peirce's conclusion only likely rather than foregone and the vulnerability of his argument to the naturalistic fallacy seems to render his view quite suspect.

THE PRAGMATISM OF WILLIAM JAMES

In a work entitled *Pragmatism: A New Name for Some Old Ways of Thinking*, William James sets forth his practical understanding of pragmatism. According to James, the pragmatic method is primarily one of settling interminable metaphysical disputes and interpreting each notion in the dispute by tracing its respective practical consequences. For James, pragmatism tries to determine the difference a notion would make if that notion or one contrary to it were true. Absent the target difference, the alternatives mean practically the same thing.[20]

According to William James, the term *pragmatism* gets its derivation from the Greek word *pragma*, meaning action. Our English words *practice* and *practical* come from the same word. James notes how Peirce introduced the word in philosophy. According to Peirce, James reports, in order to develop a thought's meaning, we need only determine what conduct that thought or meaning is fitted to produce. For us, that conduct is the thought's sole significance. Moreover, at the root of all thought distinctions, the tangible fact remains that all of them consist in a possible difference of practice. Therefore, a thought's perfect clarity entails a consideration of

---

19. Ezorsky, "Pragmatic Theory," 427.
20. James, "What Pragmatism," 120–21.

what practical effects the object may involve.[21] The aforesaid recapitulates for us a Jamesian version of Peirce's central claim in his work.

Meanwhile, James continues to observe how the number of philosophical disputes collapsing into insignificance remains astonishing once the epistemologist subjects those disputes to the simple test of tracing a concrete consequence. Any difference anywhere makes a difference everywhere. A difference in abstract truth, notes James, must express itself in a difference in concrete fact as well as in conduct arising as a consequence of that fact. The whole function of philosophy should be to find out what definite difference it will make to you if a given world formula is the true one.[22]

Interestingly, James notes how we find nothing new in the pragmatic method. According to him, Aristotle and Socrates used this method though only as preluders of pragmatism. Moreover, he adds, Locke, Berkeley, and Hume made momentous contributions to it. For James, pragmatism represents a perfectly familiar attitude in philosophy, namely, the empiricist's attitude. However, it represents this disposition in a more radical form and in a less objectionable one than seventeenth-century empiricism.[23]

We also find additional tenets within pragmatism itself. A pragmatist forsakes a lot of inveterate habits dear to professional philosophers, such as abstractions, insufficiency, fixed principles, closed systems, and pretended absolutes and origins. According to James, the pragmatist embraces concreteness and adequacy toward facts, actions, and power, which imply possibilities of nature as against dogma, artificiality, and the pretense of finality in truth.[24]

One might wonder why James adopts this system of philosophy as opposed to other rival systems available in his day. According to James, metaphysics has usually followed a very primitive kind of quest wherein the universe has always appeared to the natural mind as a kind of enigma of which the key must be sought in the shape of some illuminating or power-bringing word or name. For James, that word names the universe's principle, and to possess it entails the fashion to possess the universe itself. "God," "Matter," "Reason," "The Absolute," and "Energy" are some of so many solving names.[25]

21. James, "What Pragmatism," 121–22.
22. James, "What Pragmatism," 122.
23. James, "What Pragmatism," 122.
24. James, "What Pragmatism," 122.
25. James, "What Pragmatism," 122.

By contrast, James finds the pragmatic method quite different. According to him, if you follow it, you cannot look at any such word as closing your quest. You must bring out of each word its practical cash value and set it at work without the stream of your experience. In this way, theories become instruments in which we can rest rather than becoming enigmas. We then move forward, James suggests, and remake nature over on occasion, rather than lie back upon those words.[26]

Pragmatism, according to James, unstiffens all our theories, limbers them up, and sets each one at work. He thinks pragmatism harmonizes with many ancient philosophic tendencies. For instance, it agrees with nominalism in ways appealing to particulars. It agrees with utilitarianism in ways emphasizing practical aspects. It agrees with positivism in its disdain for verbal solutions and metaphysical abstractions. It is fully armed and militant against rationalism as a pretension of thought even though it stands for no particular result at the outset. According to James, pragmatism lies in the midst of our theories like a corridor in a hotel with innumerable chambers out of it. In one chamber you will find an atheist, in another a theist, in another a chemist, in another an idealist metaphysician, and still in another a non-metaphysician, and all of them are engaging in their disciplines while embracing pragmatism. To be sure, notes James, they must use pragmatism if they want a practical way of getting in or out of their respective norms. The pragmatic method implies only an attitude rather than results of orientation. It implies looking away from first principles and looking toward last things, fruits, consequences, and facts.[27]

Having given a brief outline of pragmatism in general, James presents his understanding of the pragmatic theory of truth, a theory he derives from Schiller and John Dewey. According to James, both Schiller and Dewey present truth as meaning the same thing it means in science: the ideas that themselves are parts of our experience become true if and only if they help us get into a satisfactory relation with other parts of our experience. The idea that will carry us prosperously from any part of our experience to another part, working securely, simplifying and saving labor, is an idea we must regard as true instrumentally. The instrumental view of truth in our ideas implies their power to work.[28]

---

26. James, "What Pragmatism," 122.
27. James, "What Pragmatism," 122.
28. James, "What Pragmatism," 123.

According to James, Dewey, Schiller, and their allies, they have only followed the example of geologists, biologists, and philologists in reaching this conception of truth. These sciences are successful because they always take some simple process, actually observable in operation, and then generalize it, making it apply to all times and producing great results by summarizing its effects through the ages. The observable process, according to James, is the one by which any individual settles into new opinions by meeting new experiences that put his old stock of opinions to a strain. He tries to escape the strain by modifying the old opinions. At last, some new idea comes up that he can graft upon the ancient stock with a minimum disturbance of the latter. This new idea is then adopted as the true one, preserving the older stock of truths with a minimum of modification.[29]

New truths, James continues, marry old opinion to a new fact in order to show minimum jolt and maximum continuity. This leads James to the following central statement: we hold a theory true just in proportion to its success in solving this problem of maximum and minimum. However, success is a matter of approximation in this context, James is quick to add. For example, we say that a theory solves a problem on the whole more satisfactorily than another theory. Nevertheless, that expression refers to "more satisfactorily to ourselves." Note that individuals will emphasize their points of satisfaction differently. The influence of older truths is absolutely controlling, and loyalty to them remains the first principle and, in most cases, the only principle. According to James, therefore, a new opinion counts as true as it gratifies the individual's desire to assimilate the novel idea in his experience to his beliefs in stock.[30]

What, then, does James have to say about objective truth? According to him, purely objective truth is nowhere to be found. The reason we call things true, in James's view, stems from the fact that individuals can marry previous parts of experience with newer parts. Admittedly, incorrigible and independent truth no longer malleable to human need exists superabundantly or is supposed to exist. However, such truth, according to James, "is the dead heart of a living tree."[31]

Such truths are quite plastic, according to James. In other words, they change. How plastic even the oldest truths really are has been vividly shown in our day by the transformation of logical and mathematical ideas. It is

---

29. James, "What Pragmatism," 123–24.
30. James, "What Pragmatism," 124.
31. James, "What Pragmatism," 124–25.

a transformation that seems to be invading even physics. The pragmatist clings to facts and concreteness, observes truth at its work in particular cases, and then generalizes. Truth, for the pragmatist, becomes a class name for all sorts of definite-working values in experience. When the pragmatist undertakes to show in detail just why we must defer, the rationalist is unable to recognize the concreteness from which his or her own abstraction is taken. He or she accuses the pragmatist of denying truth, whereas the pragmatist has only sought to trace exactly why people follow it and always follow it.[32]

James argues that the concreteness and closeness to facts of pragmatism follows the example of the related sciences, interpreting the unobserved by the observed. It converts the absolutely empty notion of "correspondence" between our minds and reality into that of a rich and active commerce between particular thoughts of ours. If theological ideas prove to have a value for concrete life, they will be true for pragmatism in the same sense of being good for so much. According to James, a good pragmatist ought to call the absolute "true in so far forth." By this expression the pragmatist means that owing to the fact that the absolute finite evil is overruled already, so we may treat the temporal as if it were potentially eternal and be sure we can trust its outcome.[33]

James also observes how certain ideas are not only agreeable to think about but are also helpful in life's practical struggles. According to him, if any life is really better, we should lead it. Moreover, if any idea that, if believed in, would help us lead that life, then it would be really better for us to believe in that idea unless belief in it incidentally clashed with other greater, vital benefits. Thus, James maintains, "what would be better for us to believe" sounds very like a definition for truth because it comes very near to saying we ought to believe. What is better for us to believe *is* true unless the belief incidentally clashes with some other vital benefit. The greatest enemy of any one of our truths may be the rest of our truths, James says. Truths have, once and for all, this desperate instinct of self-preservation and of desire to extinguish whatever contradicts them.[34]

According to James, with respect to truth, pragmatism asks what the cash value of truth must be in experiential terms and what concrete difference its being true will make in anyone's actual life. The moment

---

32. James, "What Pragmatism," 125.
33. James, "What Pragmatism," 125.
34. James, "What Pragmatism," 127.

pragmatism asks these questions, James notes, it sees the answer: true ideas are those we can assimilate, corroborate, and verify. False ideas are those we cannot. This fact entails the practical difference of having true ideas. The truth of an idea is not a stagnant property inherent in it. According to James, truth happens to an idea. The idea is made true by events, and its verity is an event, a process.[35]

James, however, sees the need to explicate his understanding of "verification" in this context. The words *verification* and *validation* in pragmatism signify certain practical consequences of the verified and validated idea. According to James, the ordinary agreement formula is a phrase that best characterizes these consequences. The ideas lead us through the acts and other ideas that they instigate. This function of agreeable leading is what we mean by an idea's verification. The possession of true thoughts means the possession of invaluable instruments of action and our duty to gain truth can account for itself by excellent practical reasons.[36]

From James's perspective, we live in a world of realities that can be infinitely useful and infinitely harmful. Ideas that tell us which of them to expect count as true ideas in the sphere of verification. The pursuit of such ideas is a primary duty. If I am lost in the woods and starved and find what looks like a cow path, of utmost importance for me must be to think of human habitation at the end of the cow path. If I do so and follow it, I will save myself. The practical value of true ideas is thus primarily derived from the practical importance of their objects to us.[37]

James also notes the obvious advantage of having a general stock of extra truths of ideas that shall be true of merely possible situations. According to James, they may become practically relevant to one of our emergencies. They pass from cold storage to do work in the world. Thus, our belief in the world grows active. We say of such truths that they are useful because they are true and vice versa. True is the name of whatever idea starts the verification process. Useful is the name for its completed function in experience.[38]

James also cites two reasons for the possibility of waiving complete verification in the usual business of life. First, consider that our thoughts and beliefs pass so long as nothing challenges them. For example, we assume Japan to exist without ever having been there, and we make this

35. James, "What Pragmatism," 129.
36. James, "What Pragmatism," 129.
37. James, "What Pragmatism," 129.
38. James, "What Pragmatism," 129.

assumption because doing so works. Making this assumption leads to no frustration or contradiction in James's view. Second, when we have once directly verified our ideas of one specimen of a kind, we consider ourselves free to apply them to other specimens without verification. We do so because all things exist in kinds and not singly. Indirectly or only potentially, verifying processes may thus be true as well as full verification processes.[39]

Finally, James turns to the notion of agreement in pragmatism. According to James, agreement turns out to be essentially a useful affair of leading because it moves us into quarters that contain objects that are important. True ideas lead us into useful verbal and conceptual quarters as well as directly up to useful termini. They lead to consistency, stability, and flowing human intercourse. In the end and eventually, all true processes must lead to the face of directly verifying experiences somewhere that somebody's ideas have copied.[40]

In James's view, the absolutely true, meaning what no further experience will ever alter, is the ideal vanishing point toward which we imagine all our contemporary truths will someday converge.[41] Meanwhile, we have to live today by what truth we can get today and be ready to call it falsehood. Consider that Ptolemaic astronomy, Euclidean space, Aristotelian logic, and Scholastic metaphysics were expedient for centuries. However, human experience has boiled over those limits, and we now call these things only relatively true within those borders of experience. *Absolutely* they are false, for we know that those limits are casual and might have been transcended by past theorists just as they are by present thinkers.[42]

AN EVALUATION OF WILLIAM JAMES'S PRAGMATISM

This extended explication completes our survey of the pragmatic view of William James in a way that allows us to offer a fair critique of his position. It does have some beneficial ideas, including the idea of pursuing what we think will work in a given situation. Of course, the challenge, in this notion, entails the ability to determine what would work prior to pursuing it. Confronted with two courses of action or two ideas to adopt, knowing the ideal course of action or the ideal idea to be adopted may provide specific

---

39. James, "What Pragmatism," 130.
40. James, "What Pragmatism," 130.
41. James, "What Pragmatism," 132.
42. James, "What Pragmatism," 133.

challenges both to the epistemologist and to the ethicist. In some cases, the result of a given course of action remains unknown prior to pursuing the action. Whereas pursuing a workable course of action or idea does, indeed, sound scientifically noble, we have no way of figuring this out when dealing with unknown cases.

Consider, for example, the very complex scenario of negotiating with a psychopathic bank robber holding customers of a certain bank hostage in the bank's building. Police officers normally find themselves confronted with a host of options, none of which present immediate promising successes once followed. If they try to storm into the building, they have no way of knowing whether the gunman will surrender or whether he or she will begin shooting hostages at random. They may not even be sure whether or not the gunman will shoot a negotiator if they send one into the building. Admittedly, in some cases, such contingencies seem knowable based on effective negotiations with perpetrators of such crimes. However, this state of affairs does not always obtain in other situations, and for that reason, factors that help make the sort of difference James talks about may not even be available.

This reality is one of several others afflicting the pragmatism of James. Let me focus on them. Notice, for example, how James contends that when there is a difference in abstract truth, that difference must express itself in a possible difference in concrete fact as well as in conduct that arises in consequence of that fact. Let's call this statement P. As we noted concerning Peirce's view, we also note, here, how P remains vulnerable to the naturalistic fallacy. P seems to draw an *ought* from an *is* by urging the epistemologist cum ethicist to honor an obligation to conduct his or her life in a certain way based on certain observable facts countenanced by the epistemologist in question.

The second thing I wish to highlight about P is the following anomaly. P does not seem to pass its own test and, for that reason, appears vulnerable to self-stultification: if P is true in the Jamesian sense, in what concretely factual way does P express itself and what sort of conduct arises as a consequence of the fact of P's expression? Stated differently and more generally, does P meet the standards it lays out for other truths, and would its failure to do so then attest to the falsity of P? James does not seem to answer this question in his presentation.

Notice, also, how James's deviation from Peirce's pragmatism finds expression especially when he forsakes a lot of compulsive favorite habits among professional philosophers. What habits might James be referring to here? The answer to that question is readily available: fixed principles, pretended absolutes, and origins. James pits his pragmatism against what he calls "dogma" and against "artificiality" and against the pretense of "finality in truth." Peirce did affirm the possibility of arriving at some form of finality in truth, the very thing James rejects. Also, notice how James's method seems to break its own rules. By presenting pragmatism as a view that forsakes the absolutist views of professional philosophers, he does the very absolutist thing he urges us to forsake. He presents his pragmatic idea almost as the final truth, as if truth cannot be arrived at through a view other than pragmatism. Other theories of truth outside pragmatism do use pragmatism in their pursuits of reliable information about the world, he says. However, if pragmatism has the final say, then surely it runs the risk of presenting itself as objectively true, the very thing James takes pain to avoid.

Additionally, notice how James's pragmatism spirals into epistemological relativism in spite of the fact that he anchors it, unconsciously, on an absolutist assumption. When he shows how pragmatism can be harmonized with many ancient philosophies, we find this very tendency toward relativism. For example, he shows how an atheist and a theist can both engage in their disciplines while embracing pragmatism. This only serves to show how pragmatism is really a tool, an instrument of attaining certain goals, rather than a way of arriving at a reliable knowledge about the world. James presents this instrumental view of truth as a virtue.

Several problems face this view. First, telling the truth can yield undesirable results.[43] Suppose a woman dear to you, clad in a newly bought dress she seems excited about, asks for your honest opinion regarding her aesthetic appearance. More specifically, she wants to know whether her dress makes her look beautiful. In your honest opinion, the dress is not at all flattering. Based on similar situations in the past, you know how crestfallen she would be if you expressed your honest opinion. You go ahead, however, and convey to her your verdict. Consistent with your expectations, your opinions fail to settle well with your precious friend. She walks away deeply wounded by your truthful comments. Thus, telling the truth can, sometimes, yield undesirable results, contrary to the claims of pragmatism.

Equally contrary is the second unsurprising example illustrating the fact that telling a lie can, sometimes, yield desirable results. Consider the

---

43. Geisler, *Christian Apologetics*, 113.

scenario where your fourteen-year-old nephew has a piano recital and has asked you to attend. Being musically talented in such situations, you willfully agree. During the performance, you find yourself in utter disbelief at the lack of musicianship displayed by your nephew, even though you knew he had been preparing for this recital for at least twelve months. You find the musical phrases, the notes, and the overall performance quite below your expectations. Your nephew, however, seems unaware of these mistakes and is quite proud of his accomplishments. With deep sincerity and hoping to hear a positive remark from you, your nephew asks for your honest opinion. Based on your previous experience with him, you remain absolutely sure how crushed he would be should you present your honest criticism of his work. Not wishing to crush your nephew's feelings and against your personal opinion, you express to him how good his performance was and how you think he is a great musician. Your nephew finally walks away with his ego intact and with his morale significantly boosted.

The first-case scenario refutes pragmatism by showing how truth can sometimes yield undesirable results. In such a scene, telling the truth would work, contrary to pragmatic views. The second-case scenario refutes pragmatism by showing how telling a lie can sometimes yield desirable results. In such a scenario, telling a lie works, once again, in a way contrary to James's pragmatism.

To be fair, James tries to solve the difficulty posed by these two scenarios. Apparently, he seems somewhat aware of the difficulties his view might pose to the epistemologist if pursued to its logical conclusions in its application. To avoid such pitfalls, James advises us to believe what seems better to believe unless the belief clashes incidentally with some other vital benefit. Hence, if you believe that telling the truth would hurt someone more than telling a lie, telling a lie would be more beneficial. In addition, if you believe telling a lie would help the person rather than hurt the person, telling a lie would be more beneficial. This state of affairs seems consonant with James's alternative definition for the pragmatic view of truth: the affairs describes as that which would be better for us to believe sounds like a definition for truth. If applied to both cases, James would say something similar to the following remark: believing that telling a lie is better than telling the truth would, in fact, be better for us. This act of telling a lie would be a definition of truth. This expression, of course, sounds rather odd and paradoxical. Telling a lie as if that lie was the truth really is profoundly misleading.

Closely related to the second example is the fact that James's pragmatism, if followed through to its logical conclusion, upholds a certain variety of behavior one might find immoral. Suppose, for example, a thief intends to gain access into a safe full of money, and the only way to gain entry is to pick the lock. If the thief has the skill to pick a lock, doing whatever works would entail picking the lock and gaining access to the safe.

Finally, I note how James's pragmatism found inspiration from a situation of an epistemological dilemma in which one scenario experienced by observers seemed to warrant two counterfactual explanations. In instances of epistemic distance of this sort, James tried to determine the difference each claim would make if one were true and the other false. For James, this difference counted as the deal-breaker of sorts. Whereas room for such epistemological maneuvers seem certainly available and, perhaps, even desirable in specific instances, applying the principle to every scenario as we have observed in the three adumbrated cases seems counterproductive.

Also, this theory of truth remains vulnerable to the critique that the Judeo-Christian account overcomes. The pragmatic theory casts truth in a way that makes it contingent upon human statements or, for that matter, propositions. Hence, truth, in this view, would not be existent prior to the arrival of humans onto the scene. On this view, then, one would not even know the truth behind the process of humans coming into existence—a process quite near and dear to the scientific enterprise. In short, William James's pragmatic theory of truth seems inadequate if followed to its logical conclusion. Not only is it self-defeating in its postulates; it fails to show how some undesirable outcomes can be avoided when we express certain truths. Moreover, it warrants specific instances of behavior deemed unethical, including the act of telling lies. For this reason, this form of pragmatism needs to be rejected.

4

Pragmatism as a Theory of Truth
Rorty and Putnam

RICHARD RORTY'S PRAGMATISM

Richard Rorty's pragmatism presents a variant, rather than a deviant, version of pragmatism when compared to William James's version. According to Rorty, we need to replace the objectivist correspondence theory of truth with a pragmatic understanding of truth,[1] namely, truth understood as solidarity in the sense of tolerance, respect for divergent views, and a willingness to listen to those views.[2] How does Rorty defend this claim?

He begins, first, by noting how our epistemological peers should be satisfied that they have no better way of digging out our inner states than from our reports. For this reason, they need not know what lies behind our making those reports. Rorty says we know, quite sufficiently, how our peers have their acquiescent attitudes, and that fact alone seems sufficient for that inner certainty about our inner states. According to Rorty, the society justifies these reports. If the society justifies these reports rather than the character of the inner representations they express, then we find no point in attempting to isolate privileged representation. This state of affairs, according to Rorty, expresses what he calls "epistemic behaviorism"—the process of explaining rationality and epistemic authority by reference to

---

1. Rorty, "Dismantling Truth," 546.
2. Rorty, "Dismantling Truth," 544.

what society lets us say. Moreover, epistemic behaviorism requires we understand the rules of the language game. It also requires we understand all we can possibly understand about why moves in that language game are made.[3]

Second, according to Rorty, the pragmatic view of truth involves treating the nature of the study of human knowledge just as the study of certain ways in which human beings interact. The view of truth takes the claim "S knows that P" as a remark about the status of S's report among S's peers and not as a remark about the relationship between the subject S and an object O. Herein, and somewhat of an echo of William James, philosophy can straighten out pointless quarrels between commonsense and science. However, philosophy will not, in this regard, contribute any arguments of its own for the existence or nonexistence of something. Here, then, truth entails "what is good for us to believe,"[4] echoing William James again,[5] rather than "truth as contact with reality."[6]

Third, having used the notion of "science," "rationality," "objectivity," and "truth" synonymously, our culture (supposedly, American culture) tends to think of the rational sciences as paradigms of rationality. According to Rorty, a secularized culture in which the scientist replaces the priest seems characterized by worries about "cognitive status" and "objectivity" wherein the scientist keeps humanity in touch with something beyond itself. Truth is then thought of as the only point at which humans are responsible for something. One result of this, argues Rorty, seems to be that any academic discipline desiring a place at the trough but is unable to be scientific must pretend to imitate science in some way or find a way of obtaining "cognitive status" without the necessity of discovering the facts.[7]

Practitioners of these disciplines, according to Rorty, must either affiliate themselves with this quasi-priestly order by using terms such as "behavioral science" or else find something other than "fact to be concerned with." Notice that people in the humanities typically choose the latter strategy, namely, the strategy of value and not of facts. The distinction between objective and subjective was designed to parallel the one between fact and value. These distinctions entail an awkward and clumsy way of knowing

3. Rorty, "Dismantling Truth," 542.
4. Rorty, "Dismantling Truth," 542–43.
5. See James, "What Pragmatism," 127.
6. Rorty, "Dismantling Truth," 543.
7. Rorty, "Dismantling Truth," 543.

because they create more difficulties than they resolve. Rorty, therefore, suggests we start afresh by finding another vocabulary, namely, a new way of describing the natural sciences, of ceasing to see them on the model of the priest, and ceasing to see them as the place where mind confronts the world.[8]

Fourth, Rorty tries to accomplish his suggestion by distinguishing between two senses of rationality. The first sense entails the notion of being methodical, and the second sense is more akin to "sanity" or "reasonableness." The first sense involves a prior stipulation of the criteria for success in arriving at truth. Under this rubric, the natural sciences would be paradigms of rationality, thereby ruling out the humanities. Humanities seem concerned with ends rather than means. We have no way of evaluating their success in terms of prior criteria. The second sense of rationality names a set of moral virtues such as "tolerance," "respect for the opinions of those around one," and being "willing to listen." In this sense, rational means something similar to "civilized."[9]

Thus, according to Rorty, to be rational in this second sense entails discussing any topic in a way eschewing dogmatic, defensive, and righteous indignation. For Rorty, we should try to eradicate the sort of hankering characteristic of the humanists and the public who yearn for rationality in the first stronger sense of the term—one associated with objective truth, correspondence to reality, method, and criteria.[10]

Fifth, Rorty draws from Thomas Kuhn, who asked whether imagining that one, full, objective, and true account of nature exists seems helpful and whether the proper measure of scientific achievement is the extent to which that achievement brings us closer to the ultimate goal. According to Rorty, pragmatists quote such statements in an effort to enlist Kuhn in the campaign to drop the objective-subjective distinction altogether and blur those distinctions. For Rorty, owing to the fact that truth is a univocal term, applying equally to the judgment of lawyers, anthropologists, physicists, philologists, and literary critics, pragmatists like to put all cultures on an epistemological level.[11]

Sixth, Rorty admits that a reason exists in assigning degrees of "objectivity" or "hardness" to such disciplines because the presence of unforced

---

8. Rorty, "Dismantling Truth," 543–44.
9. Rorty, "Dismantling Truth," 544.
10. Rorty, "Dismantling Truth," 545.
11. Rorty, "Dismantling Truth," 545.

agreement in all of them gives us everything in the way of "objective truth" that one could possibly want, namely, intersubjective agreement. The pragmatic view endorsed here espouses a specific brand of relativism, namely, the ethnocentric view. In this view, we find nothing to be said about either truth or rationality apart from descriptions of familiar procedures of justification that a given society (ours) uses in one or another area of inquiry. This brand of relativism, notes Rorty, rejects the self-refuting version that finds every belief as good as every other. It also rejects the brand of relativism that finds truth equivocal, having as many meanings as there are contexts of justification.[12]

Seventh, Rorty observes how pragmatists do not have a theory of truth, much less a relativistic one. According to Rorty, we would be better off without the traditional distinctions between knowledge and opinion construed as the distinction between truth and correspondence to reality and truth as a commendatory term for well-justified belief. Rorty finds nothing to be said about truth except what each of us will commend as true those beliefs we find good to believe. As partisans of solidarity, therefore, the pragmatist account of the value of cooperative human enquiry has only an ethical base rather than an epistemological base. The gap between truth and justification is the gap between the actual good and the possible better. To say that what is rational for us to believe now may not be true is simply to say someone may come up with a better idea.[13]

Also, according to Rorty, pragmatists drop the idea that enquiry is destined to converge to a single point and that truth exists out there waiting for humans to arrive at it. Rorty believes that all we find worth preserving of the claim that rational inquiry will converge to a single point is the assertion that we must be able to explain why false views were held in the past and thus explain how we go about educating our benighted ancestors. To be sure, our ability to trace such a direction and tell such a story does not mean we have come closer to a goal that is out there waiting for us. Rather, we should relish the thought that the sciences as well as the arts will always provide a spectacle of fierce competition between alternative theories, movements, and schools. The end of human activity is not rest but richer and better human activity. Rorty says we should think of human progress as making it possible for humans to do more interesting things and be more

---

12. Rorty, "Dismantling Truth," 545.
13. Rorty, "Dismantling Truth," 545–46.

interesting people, not leading toward a place that has somehow been prepared for us in advance.[14]

The upshot of this entire consideration, according to Rorty, seems to entail we drop the criterial idea of rationality in favor of the pragmatist conception, which, in turn, entails giving up the idea of truth as something to which we are responsible. Instead, we should think of true as a word that applies to those beliefs upon which we are all able to agree as roughly synonymous with "justified."[15]

Rorty's attempt to get society to arrive at some form of solidarity as a way of attaining justified beliefs seems rather desirable and, perhaps, even commendable. How this state of affairs might be achieved, however, remains a challenge for Rorty in spite of the fact that he makes a few suggestions that, hitherto, seem not to have worked. A deeper look into his views might help us see why this state of affairs seems to fail.

Rorty makes several ambitious claims, some of which I recall here. First, according to Rorty, the best way to dig out information about our inner states is through the reports we give of those states, and those reports get their justification from society. Stated differently, Rorty's view of truth finds expression as follows: S knows that P entails a remark about the status of S's report among S's peers and not a remark about the relationship between the subject S and an object O. Moreover, we need to do away with the notion of objectivity characteristic of rationalistic science—a view that eventually succeeded the priestly model of, for example, Judeo-Christianity as a custodian of truth. Rorty hopes to replace this view of truth with an alternative model of rationality, one characterized by ideas such as "tolerance," "respect for the opinions of those around one," and "civilized."

AN EVALUATION OF RORTY'S VIEW

Rorty seems to bequeath society with the responsibility of deciding the truth or falsity of reports made by individuals in that society. More specifically, society remains, for an individual, the custodian of truth. The problem with this way of reasoning can be located in a variety of places. First, society, as a whole, may be mistaken with regard to the process of justification. Rorty may not know this fact, but consider a case scenario where an individual P postulates how he or she intends to raid a neighboring village to capture a

14. Rorty, "Dismantling Truth," 546.
15. Rorty, "Dismantling Truth," 546.

certain human being *H* for food. Suppose *P*'s host culture, call it *C*, remains well-known for its cannibalism, and *P* reports to *C* that he harbors an intense desire to raid the neighboring village to capture *H* for food. Given *C*'s propensity toward cannibalism, *C* will more than likely find *P*'s desire quite justified based on Rorty's explication. More generally, Rorty's observation concerning a culture justifying an individual's inner state reports seems open to the endorsement of practices deemed universally immoral even if those practices may seem moral on a particular culture's readings.

Moreover, this very consideration by Rorty seems to warrant the question "what society is he talking about?" Is the society he is referring to inclusive of Jim Jones's—one that morally justified the inner state of its individual leader and whose members proceeded to take the poison on a massive scale? Is it inclusive of David Koresh's society? Or is he referring to some cannibalistic society in some remote location somewhere in the two-thirds world? Once we begin to ask such questions, problems begin to emerge in Rorty's reasoning.

With respect to replacing objectivist forms of reasoning with more tolerant ones, he seems merely to be replacing with one hand what he took away with the other hand. If pressed hard enough as to why he would value "tolerance," "respect for the opinion of others," and "civility," Rorty would, perhaps, have a hard time denying the view that such values seem desirable or even ideal. The reason they seem so, however, might just be because they meet a certain standard Rorty presupposes, consciously or unconsciously. This standard might be the sort that plays the role of a point of reference for Rorty, one he uses to embrace "the tolerant" and to forsake the "intolerant." Stated differently, the reason Rorty would value tolerance and respect over intolerance and disrespect seems to hinge on the possibility of a presupposition, on his part, of the existence of a standard, so to speak, that urges him to do exactly that. This standard would, quite easily, fit as an objective way of deciding between truth and falsehood or, for that matter, right and wrong.

Quite possibly, Rorty either appeals to this standard without qualification, or he appeals to some form of a relativistic standard. Assuming he appeals to this standard without qualification, we find ourselves led to the conclusion that he presupposes, in his explication, the existence of some form of objective absolute standard as a point of reference—the very thing he urges us to abandon. If he appeals to some form of a relativistic standard, such as the justification of an individual's report by the individual's society, then his views expose themselves to the problems I have already alluded to here, namely, the problem of finding no way to determine whether the society's way of justifying S knows that P is itself justifiable and, if so, by what means.

As already noted, this move is what Rorty, in fact, makes quite repeatedly. He sees the standard of truth as entailing familiar procedures of justification a given society uses in one area of inquiry. In pursuing this line of thought, Rorty remains unrelenting. The line of thought, however, does not seem applicable in many situations. A simple illustration should prove my point.

Consider, for example, a society that upholds the view implicating spiritual entities in certain varieties of illnesses prevalent in that culture, one of them entailing some form of serious incontinence. The medicine person in that culture informs members of the society that, from practice as a medicine person, he or she has access to some kind of cure believed to eliminate the illness, a cure that can be actualized by performing certain kinds of rituals, including drinking water from a well situated next to the culture's communal outhouse. The more the villagers drink the water, however, the sicker they get. A village council convenes to settle the matter in the Rortian sense. They all agree that the pandemic can be resolved by drinking more of the water from the well. However, the more they drink it, the sicker they become. The fact that the water may, likely, be the source of the epidemic does not seem to occur to them specifically because, out of their solidarity, they lack countermeasures to keep them from taking the water. Nothing, following Rorty's view, seems to keep this state of affairs from unfolding, especially when he advocates placing all cultures on the same epistemological footing.

Recall also Rorty's claim contending how better off we would be without the traditional distinctions between knowledge and opinion—construed as the distinction between truth as correspondence to reality and truth as a commendatory term for well-justified beliefs. Rorty's view is misleading here. His allusion to the view that we are better off without these distinctions leads us to ask, "Better off with respect to what standard or whose standard?" What if the state of affairs Rorty considers "better off" by individual P entails the exact opposite (i.e., worse off) of what individual Q finds? This state of affairs is not farfetched. From P's perspective, some cultures eat their neighbors, and this seems better off for P but worse off for Q. From Q's perspective, some cultures love their neighbors, and this seems better off for *Q*, though for *P* we really do not know! At any rate, an oddity exists here, one Rorty may need to explicate further.

From Rorty we turn to Hilary Putnam, a contemporary philosopher whose views on this very issue experienced radical transformation from what Putnam called Realism with a capital *R* to realism with a small *r*. His other name for his view is "conceptual relativism" or, as he himself termed it, "pragmatic realism."

THE PRAGMATISM OF HILARY PUTNAM

Hilary Putnam adopts a conceptual relativist position, one he calls pragmatic realism.[16] By adopting this position, he rejects the dichotomy characterizing absolutist epistemologies along with their analogues, wherein specific absolutes (understood as having objectively intrinsic "thing-in-itself" properties) remain characterized as existing apart from what he calls subjective non-absolutist realism.[17] How does Putnam arrive at this central claim?

First, Putnam gives us an argument from solidity, wherein he gets his cue from a simple scientific illustration. He notes, for example, that the person on the street visualizes a table as mostly solid matter. However, physics has discovered that the table is mostly empty space. The distance between the particles is immense in relation to the radius of the electron or the nucleus of one of the atoms of which the table consists. According to Putnam, this view illustrates the fact that Realism with a capital *R* does not always deliver what the innocent expect of it. The only wholly legitimate appeal of Realism is the appeal to the commonsense feeling that, of course, there are tables and chairs. The realist promises common sense to rescue it from its enemies, namely, the idealists, the Kantians, the neo-Kantians, and the pragmatists. These enemies want to deprive common sense of the belief that the table is solid and that it is really there. But the scientific realist breaks the news that what common sense will get is not the table. Rather, all that exists is what science will say exists.[18]

Second, Putnam's argument appeals to the non-uniformity of the origin of color and the subjectivity of our judgments about color. According to Putnam, we often find certain claims to the effect that color is simply

16. Putnam, "Pragmatic Realism," 597.
17. Putnam, "Pragmatic Realism," 600–601.
18. Putnam, "Pragmatic Realism," 591.

the disposition of an object to selectively absorb certain wavelengths of incident light and reflect others. However, Putnam observes how recent research has shown that this account is much too simple. Reflectance itself does not have one uniform physical explanation. A red star, a red apple, and a reddish glass of colored water are red for quite different physical reasons. According to Putnam, an infinite number of different physical conditions may well exist that could result in the disposition to reflect red light and absorb light of other wavelengths. A dispositional property, argues Putnam, whose underlying dispositional explanation is extremely nonuniform remains simply incapable of being represented as a mathematical function of the dynamic of variables.[19]

With respect to subjectivity, Putman's argument rests on how hues turn out much more subjective than we thought. To be sure, any shade on the color chart in the green part of the spectrum will be classed as standard green by some subject, even if it lies at the extreme yellow-green end or extreme blue-green end. In sum, no characteristic recognized by this way of thinking corresponds to such a familiar property of objects as red or green. Hence, the idea that a property exists that all red objects have in common and a different one exists that all green objects have in common is a kind of illusion on the absolutist objectivist view we have come to take for granted since Descartes and Locke's time.[20]

Putnam considers how both Locke and Descartes provided a sophisticated substitute for our pre-scientific notion of color. This substitute involves the idea of sense datum. For example, the red sweater I see is not red in the sense I thought it was, but it does have a disposition to affect me in a certain way. It has a disposition to cause me to have certain sense data. These data do truly have a simply uniform non-dispositional sort of redness. This picture, argues Putnam, captures the dualism of the physical world and its primary qualities on the one hand and the mind and its sense data on the other. Edmund Husserl and William James, according to Putnam, highlight the disastrous nature of this picture. The wrongness finds its accent on the fact that solidity is in much the same boat as color. If objects do not have color as they naively seem to, Putnam argues, they do not have solidity as they naively seem to. Moreover, to the objection that this picture works because our acceptance of it is an inference to the best explanation, Putnam responds by noting how an explanation involving connections of

19. Putnam, "Pragmatic Realism," 592.
20. Putnam, "Pragmatic Realism," 592–93.

a kind we do not understand at all and concerning that which we have not even the sketch of a theory seems to be an explanation, though something more obscure than the phenomenon explained.[21]

Also, Putnam shows how William James and others find every single part of the sense datum story to be a supposition and a theory of the most peculiar kind. The epistemological role "sense data" are supposed to play by traditional philosophy required them to be what we remain absolutely sure of independently of scientific theory. Putnam notes how the scientific realism of the seventeenth century has not lost all its prestige yet, but it has saddled us with a disastrous picture of the world. According to Putnam, sense data remain the visible symptoms of a systemic disease. He finds the deep systemic root of the diseases lying in the notion of an "intrinsic property"—a property something has in itself apart from any attribution made by language or mind. This notion remains extremely robust, judging by its appeal to different kinds of philosophers. All the strains of philosophy that accepted the seventeenth-century circle of problems adopted the distinction even if they disagreed over its application. Hence, notes Putnam, a subjective idealist would say that there are only sense data and that *red* is an intrinsic property of these objects while persistence is something we project. A dualist would say the *external* objects have persistence as an intrinsic property, but red is, in their case, something we project. However, Putnam urges us to note how all of these philosophers have the distinction. Except for Berkeley, we may say that the remaining philosophers all accepted the account of redness and solidity hitherto described.[22]

However, and this functions as the third reason for Putnam's central contention, Putnam contends that these are not intrinsic properties of external things we ascribe them to; rather, they are dispositions to affect us in certain ways in the case of external things. They affect us by producing certain sense data in us. The idea that these properties are in the things themselves as intrinsic is a spontaneous projection. According to Putnam, the Achilles heel of this story is the notion of a disposition. In order to see this contention, Putnam distinguishes between a strict disposition—the disposition that something has to do something no matter what—and "other things being equal" disposition—the disposition to do something under normal conditions. The disposition of sugar to dissolve in water is not a strict disposition. Sugar placed in water already saturated will not dissolve.

21. Putnam, "Pragmatic Realism," 593.
22. Putnam, "Pragmatic Realism," 593–94.

However, what we say is that under normal conditions, sugar will dissolve if placed in water. The problem of causality emerges here, similar to what we observed in connection with color and solidity. If the *intrinsic* properties of *external* things are the ones we can represent by formulas in the language of fundamental physics by suitable functions of the dynamic variables, then solubility is also not an intrinsic property of any external thing, and similarly, neither is the "any other things being equal" disposition.[23]

Projection is thinking of something as having properties it really does not have, but we can imagine without being conscious that this is what we are doing. Therefore, projection is a species of thought. Descartes intended to say that the objectivist picture has something to tell us about thought. His view was that there are two fundamental substances—mind and matter—not one. Therefore, there should be two fundamental sciences: physics and psychology. However, according to Putnam, we have ceased to think of mind as a separate substance at all. Contrary to Descartes's hopes, a fundamental science of psychology that explains the nature of thought never came to existence. Therefore, to explain the features of the commonsense world, including color, solidity, and causality, in terms of projection is to explain just about every feature of the commonsense world in terms of thought.[24]

Fourth, Putnam urges us to note what seems to be happening as a result of this fact, namely, that so far as the commonsense world is concerned, the effect of what is called "realism" in philosophy is to deny objective reality, to make it simply thought. The problem seems to be that thought itself has come to be treated more and more as a projection by the philosophy that traces its pedigree to the seventeenth century. The reason is clear: we have not succeeded in giving content to the theory that thought is just a primitive property of a mysterious substance called mind. If we insist on sticking to the fundamental *objectivist* assumptions, the only line we can take is that mental phenomena must be highly derived physical phenomena in some way. Modern objectivism has simply become materialism, and the central problem of materialism is explaining the emergence of mind. Ironically a fundamental objectivist assumption is that a clear distinction exists between the properties things have in themselves and the properties that we *project* and the assumption that fundamental science, physics, tells us what properties things have in themselves. If reducing color, solidity,

---

23. Putnam, "Pragmatic Realism," 594.
24. Putnam, "Pragmatic Realism," 594–95.

or solubility to fundamental physics seems impossible, why should this vastly more ambitious program prove tractable? Putnam believes good arguments do exist to show that mental states are not only compositionally plastic but also computationally plastic. Physically possible creatures who believe there are a lot of cats in the neighborhood may have an indefinite number of different programs. The hypothesis that a necessary and sufficient condition exists for the presence of a given belief in computational terms seems unrealistic in just the way that the theory that a necessary and sufficient condition exists for the presence of a table in phenomenalistic terms is unrealistic. Such a condition would have to be infinitely long and not constructed according to any effective rule.[25]

Fifth, the key to working out the program of preserving commonsense realism while avoiding the absurdities and antinomies of metaphysical realism seems to be something called "internal realism" or pragmatic realism. According to Putnam, this realism is just the insistence that realism is not incompatible with conceptual relativity. One can be an internal realist and a conceptual relativist. Internal realism is a view that takes our familiar commonsense scheme as well as our scientific, artistic, and other schemes at face value without helping itself to the notion of the thing in itself. Conceptual relativism is different from relativism because it has none of the "there is no truth to be found." *True* is just a name for what a bunch of people can agree on the implications of relativism.[26]

For a simple example, Putnam asks us to consider a world with three individuals, namely, X_1, X_2, and X_3 as its only members. On a Carnapian interpretation,[27] that world has only three members. But on a Polish logician's interpretation, that world has at least seven members, namely, X_1, X_2, X_3, (X_1+X_2), (X_1+X_3), (X_2+X_3), and $(X_1+X_2+X_3)$.[28] The fact that metaphysical realists cannot recognize this phenomenon is no accident. Given a version, the question "how many objects are there?" can be answered in a specific way, namely, "three," in the case of the Carnapian version and "at least seven," in the case of the Polish logician's version. Once we make clear how we are using *object*, the question "how many objects exist?" has an

---

25. Putnam, "Pragmatic Realism," 595–96.

26. Putnam, "Pragmatic Realism," 598.

27. I use *Carnapian* to denote a method used by Rudolph Carnap as depicted by Putnam.

28. The parentheses used here are not members of this three-object world. I use parentheses merely to help the reader individuate the members visually.

answer that is not at all a matter of convention. Hence, this program does not support radical cultural relativism. If this is right, Putnam argues, then it may be possible to see how what is in one sense the "same" world can be described as consisting of "tables and chairs" in one version and consisting of "space-time" regions, particles, and fields in other versions. To require that all of these must be reducible to a single version is to make the mistake of supposing that the question "which are the real objects?" makes sense independently of our choices of concepts.[29]

Sixth, some philosophers assume we can make the distinction between what is simply true and what has only conditions of assertability or the cut between what is already true or false and what is an *extension* of previous use, or between what is a *projection* and what is an independent and unitary property of things in themselves epistemically. According to Putnam, the attempt to draw these distinctions has been a total failure. Philosophers often take perfectly sensible continua and get in trouble by trying to convert them into dichotomies, such as the relatively subjective and the relatively objective, as follows:

1. Being very amusing
2. Being a region of space containing at least one hydrogen atom
3. Being soluble
4. Being a single case of counterfactual conditional (i.e., "the match would have lit if it was struck at a certain time")
5. Meaning "do you speak French?"

The average person might rank these predications as follows:

1. Being amusing
2. Being a single case of counterfactual conditional
3. Meaning "do you speak French?"
4. Being soluble
5. Being a region of space containing at least one hydrogen atom

However, as soon as we are asked to turn this ranking into a dichotomy, we find that there is no agreement at all in our philosophical intuitions. The point at which subjectivity ceases and objectivity with a capital *O* begins

---

29. Putnam, "Pragmatic Realism," 597–98.

has proven chimerical. If this is right, argues Putnam, then a number of other famous dichotomies must be abandoned, such as projection/property of thing in itself and power/property of thing in itself.[30]

Seventh, Putnam argues that the line of thinking that hoped science will give us a better substitute now looks tired. Science is wonderful at destroying metaphysical answers but is incapable of providing substitute ones. It takes away foundations without providing a replacement. Whether we want to be there or not, science has put us in the position of having to live without foundations. Moreover, Putnam notes that the phenomenon of conceptual relativity has become pervasive in contemporary science. The fact that ways exist of describing the same facts that are equivalent but also in some way incompatible is a strikingly nonclassical phenomenon. Putnam rejects these dichotomies because they have become distorting lenses that prevent us from seeing real phenomena and their full extent and significance. The dichotomy between what is human projection and what is in the things themselves tends to undermine realism rather than be constitutive of it.[31]

Also, Putnam rejects the dichotomy between the claim that a statement possesses only conditions of assertability versus the claim that a statement possesses conditions of truth. Speaking with the vulgar, Putnam believes we can know, for example, the truth of the claim that the water would have boiled if one had turned on the stove without having the slightest idea whether this truth is "realist" truth or only an idealization of "warranted assertability." However, Putnam is quick to note that resisting the dichotomy within kinds of truth in the commonsense world is not the same as saying anything goes.[32] We can and should insist that some facts are there to be discovered, and this claim remains to be said when one has adopted a certain way of speaking—a language, a conceptual scheme.[33]

The upshot of Putnam's contention in this article is as follows: internal realism says we do not know about things in themselves, and *that* fact implies that the dichotomy between intrinsic properties were supposed to be just those properties things have in themselves. The thing in itself and the property the thing has in itself belong to the same circle of ideas, and it is time to admit that what the circle encloses is worthless territory.

30. Putnam, "Pragmatic Realism," 600–601.
31. Putnam, "Pragmatic Realism," 601–2.
32. Putnam, "Pragmatic Realism," 602.
33. Putnam, "Pragmatic Realism," 604.

This extended sketch gives us an idea of Putnam's pragmatism. What remains for us is to determine whether his view can be construed as an adequate theory of truth. In order to present a realistic critique of Putnam's position, we need to bear certain issues in mind, brought to our attention by some of his critics such as William Alston. Alston notes two preliminary issues important to consider for anyone attempting to criticize Putnam. First, Putnam seems to have what Alston calls a fondness for offering brief presentations of view a number of times, instead of giving a more extended exposition.[34] Second, Putnam's thought seems to be in more or less a continuous flux such that currently he finds himself rejecting a position he espoused in the late seventies and early eighties. At that time, notes Alston, Putnam argued for non-realist views. Moreover, defending his "internal realism," determining just what he meant by that expression, remains a difficult task.[35]

At any rate, a possible critique of Putnam could be formulated in what follows. Before doing so, however, I point out my indebtedness to Alston for the insights contained in this critique. How then, should we proceed? Consider, first, Putnam's contention that since we find no possibility of any objective rational settlement of the conflict characterizing certain ontological positions, the best diagnosis is that these differences are in the conceptual frameworks used for representing reality rather than disagreement as to what that reality is like. What Putnam claims concerning these conflicting views seems to be what everyone recognizes as far as many surface incompatibilities are concerned. Familiar cases abound wherein what seems to be incompatible statements reflect different ways of representing them rather than differences in the facts themselves.[36]

A few examples should help shed light on this notion. Suppose I travel a certain distance, call it *D*, and an observer reports how far I traveled. For the sake of mathematical precision, he denotes the distance traveled as follows: $D=10$. Another statistician happens to have been observing the distance I traveled and denoted it: $D=16$. Both expressions denote the same thing, namely, the distance I traveled. However, the enumerations remain different. The problem gets easily solved when we discover that my first observer covered the distance in miles and the second observer covered the distance traveled in kilometers. A more accurate denotation, therefore,

---

34. Alston, *Realist Conception*, 133.
35. Alston, *Realist Conception*, 133.
36. Alston, *Realist Conception*, 165–66.

would be $D=10$ miles for the first observer and $D=16$ kilometers for the second. Analogously, I could use the concept of time to illustrate this idea further. Suppose a teleconference is scheduled to begin at 7 p.m. Eastern Standard Time. Attendees of the conference in the western part of the United States would miss the conference if they joined it at 7 p.m. Pacific Time. In order for them to be at the conference, they will need to show up at 4 p.m. Pacific Time. In other words, we have different ways of reporting the same facts.[37]

Alston notes how, in a certain sense, Putnam seems to employ a fairly rigorous example of a reality we routinely find familiar in certain cases, such as those I have highlighted here. The problem with Putnam's view, as Alston correctly sees it, involves his assumption that this state of affairs obtains in every example or that, to use Alston's depiction, this rubric applies to all cases. According to Alston, Putnam drops all neutral ways of specifying the fact being represented in different ways. If everything we say reflects some replaceable mode of representation, we remain completely and fully blurred from arriving at a pure and unadulterated specification of the objective fact itself.[38]

An ontological realist might find issues with Putnam's rejection of the possibility of finding a rational, objective way of deciding between ontological conflicts of the sort in question. Suppose, the ontological realist might argue in each case a possible way of demonstrating how one of the contending parties is right and the other wrong. Then Putnam's argument becomes innocuous. Recall how the plausibility of his position finds its basis in the contention that we have no way of deciding between the alternatives. How then do we decide on this matter that Putnam is right and the ontological realist is wrong? In other words, how do we decide whether settling the ontological conflict to which Putnam appeals is wrong? We have no way of doing so.[39]

Plenty of ontological disagreements still exist to which Putnam can appeal as evidence for the veracity of his contention. However, the ontological realist can still argue how this fact does not demonstrate that conclusive reasons have not been presented by one or the other and that none will be offered in the future. Granted, unanimity among those who consider the matter thoroughly may certainly be a good reason for deciding the matter

---

37. Alston, *Realist Conception*, 166.
38. Alston, *Realist Conception*, 166.
39. Alston, *Realist Conception*, 168.

in question. However, unanimity of this sort is neither a necessary condition for the settlement of the matter nor the only good reason, as we shall see shortly.[40]

According to Alston, the first step in recognizing a valid argument is to comprehend the importance of deciding upon an idea *de jure* rather than *de facto*. A number of components can interfere with a person's understanding of an argument's significance, including not regarding how all the pieces of an argument fit together and maintaining long-held prejudices or opinions from environmental influences.[41] Moreover, grasping some truths remain beyond the capacity of some people. Such factors seem to prevent a general consensus, even if a conclusive case exists for one of the contending parties.[42]

In addition, the possible nonexistence of a conclusive case in the present remains an insufficient reason for the contention that a case will not be developed in the future. According to Alston, the future of any intellectual endeavor remains notoriously impossible to predict. To be sure, the idea that one may predict a fundamental or other theoretical advancement seems inconsistent. If one were to succeed in predicting a fundamental theory of science, one would have developed that theory already and the prediction would no longer be a prediction; it would be an accomplished fact. For this reason, to be justified in supposing that a real possibility of a decisive case exists for one of the contending parties in the ontological disputes on which Putnam's argument finds its basis seems difficult if not impossible.[43]

We can recast another response a realist might give as follows. The realist can agree with Putnam that we find no real possibility of demonstrating which of the dissenting groups holds the correct way of how to construe the world. He or she can then maintain that a unique fact of the matter exists as to whether, for example, things such as rabbits endure as substance or societies of Whiteheadian actual occasions. Truth always remains distinct from epistemic status. Even Putnam and Dummet agree that a possibility for truths we are capable of recognizing exist as such. They are "evidence transcendent." For this reason, the hard-nosed ontological realist would wonder why he or she should be moved by even the strongest

---

40. Alston, *Realist Conception*, 169.
41. Alston, *Realist Conception*, 169.
42. Alston, *Realist Conception*, 169.
43. Alston, *Realist Conception*, 169.

arguments for ontological relativity that seem based on the premises of affirming the existence of questions about whether p or not-p is true that we remain incapable of decisively answering. The realist sees no reason to be moved by this consideration to deny that the world really is such that either p or not-p, but not both, is true in this case.[44]

A third response to Putnam might run as follows: suppose we agree with Putnam that no sufficient rational basis exists for selecting between various vantage points on this issue, ranging from Putnam's no mereological sum (recall his X_1, X_2, X_3, example) to all possible sums. Suppose, however, we also maintain that we find no genuine issue here just because we find no rational bar to accepting the existence of any of the contending candidates. We find no reason for denying the existence of a composite entity consisting of my computer, the Taj Mahal, or even the number sixteen. To be sure, the composite does no harm. It takes up no room that is not occupied. Making an issue out of whether we find such an object as that mereological sum or not resembles overscrupulous nit-picking. We find no reason to object if someone cares to refer to this object. More so, we rarely find ourselves referring to such entities. However, if someone takes on the task of singling out these entities, why should we say anything against it?[45]

As these three objections show, Putnam's view seems porous enough for the epistemologist to locate its weak points. This fact seems crucial in helping us decide whether or not we could adopt Putnam's view. Alston, admittedly, locates a few conciliatory objections that might allow one to see how Putnam's argument might have some merit, in spite of the weaknesses adumbrated by the absolutist. However, a realist need not adopt Putnam's view if, in fact, the objections raised against his conceptual relativism can be seen to have some merit, and they do.

Since Putnam's pragmatic realism is a form of relativism, it remains vulnerable to the same concerns I raised against relativism in the second chapter of this work. Putnam's rejection of absolutist epistemologies in favor of conceptual relativism is, itself, a move based on absolutist assumptions, hence risking self-stultification. Putnam has to presuppose a standard S on the basis of which to determine or decide or find absolutist epistemologies problematic, on the one hand, and conceptual relativism unproblematic, on the other. I imagine, though, that Putnam would want his audience to see the rational acceptability of S. This possible desire on Putnam's part

44. Alston, *Realist Conception*, 169–70.
45. Alston, *Realist Conception*, 171.

seems to come dangerously close to an objectivist or absolutist epistemology, which he rejects.

Also, since his view seems human-dependent, it fails to show how truth would have existed prior to the arrival of humans on the scene. If we are the producers of truth via the statements we make to describe reality, then truth was nonexistent before humans inhabited this world. The significance of this conclusion gets underscored by the fact that, on a pragmatist reading of human origins, reliable knowledge specifying our arrival into the world will remain elusive to us. On a Judeo-Christian reading, though, God put us here, and that truth comes to us promulgated by omniscience.

5

Postmodernism as a Theory of Truth
Lyotard, Foucault, and Derrida

HAVING LOOKED AT THE PRAGMATIC position espoused by Rorty and Putnam, I now turn to the postmodern view espoused by Jean François Lyotard, Michel Foucault, and Jacques Derrida. I limit my overview to these three thinkers because philosophers widely regard them as the key proponents of postmodernism even though other thinkers such as Friedrich Nietzsche seemed to have played a part in its advent, in which case Nietzsche would be seen as a forerunner of this view.

Beginning with Lyotard, we find pragmatic motifs quite reminiscent of Rorty's view. This fact could prompt the keen reader to conclude, justifiably, that pragmatism and postmodernism are different sides of the same coin. As already noted about Rorty, some philosophers consider him a postmodernist.[1] Owing to the fact that Lyotard's postmodernism seems to possess vestiges of pragmatism, I focus on his views in this chapter. I will then focus on Foucault's view of truth followed by Derrida's.

LYOTARD'S OVERALL VIEW OF POSTMODERNISM

How does Lyotard define postmodernism? He defines it as incredulity toward metanarratives.[2] Some thinkers believe that by metanarrative, Lyotard rejects the notion of the existence of what we would call objective truth—a

1. Sire, *Universe Next Door*, 221.
2. Lyotard, *Postmodern Condition*, xxiv.

transcendental, nontemporal standard of truth external to us by which we determine whether a given statement S is true or false. The motivation spearheading this interpretation of Lyotard finds its basis on his aversion toward scientific truth, which seems, in Lyotard's view, to assume the privileged position of deciding what is true or false for any given statement. For example, he makes specific references to the view that thinks of science as the grand narrative. He defines *modernism* as the view that legitimates itself with reference to a meta-discourse, making an explicit appeal to some grand narrative such as the hermeneutics of meaning.[3] We find this interpretation of Lyotard in the works of James Sire and James K. A. Smith. Whether or not this interpretation of Lyotard is correct remains to be seen in what will come later. For now, however, I will assume, without trying to justify the assumption, that this scientific view of metanarratives is indeed what Lyotard seems to attack.

Lyotard begins his argument by noting that the condition of knowledge in the most highly developed or advanced societies is postmodern.[4] This postmodern state of affairs followed from some kind of social metamorphosis afflicting scientific discourse; thus, Lyotard uses the term postmodernism to refer to the sort of skepticism he has about the kinds of metanarratives caused by progress in the sciences. Broadly speaking, Lyotard offers what I will call a negative defense and a positive defense of postmodernism. In his negative defense, he attacks a view of truth represented by modern empiricism—a view empiricist epistemologists commonly term the correspondence theory of truth, which we will examine in a later chapter. In his positive defense, Lyotard demonstrates the plausibility, not only of postmodernity in general but also of the postmodern understanding of truth in particular. His presentation of this two-pronged defense of postmodernism demonstrates the inadequacy of the correspondence theory of truth commonly found in modern science. Lyotard does not use that expression. However, his characterization of the sciences strongly suggests he is criticizing this very theory. Let me begin with Lyotard's attack of the scientific understanding or the correspondence view of truth.

---

3. Lyotard, *Postmodern Condition*, xxiii.
4. Lyotard, *Postmodern Condition*, xxiii.

Rejection of Merely Scientific Knowledge

Even though Lyotard may seem to find value in denotative utterances (i.e., utterances purporting to provide reliable factual information of the external world), he thinks, by themselves, they fail to account for the whole story with respect to knowledge in general. He uses the term *modern* to denote any science that justifies itself with reference to a meta-discourse P, thereby making an explicit appeal to some grand narrative such as what he calls "the hermeneutics of meaning."[5] What we find in denotative scientific knowledge, from Lyotard's view, is the scientific requirement that the utterer should speak the truth S about a given referent R by proving his or her statements and by refuting contrary statements about R. In turn, the listener should give or refuse his assent validly to S.[6] Moreover, R should be expressed by a statement corresponding to what is. Hence, the scientific metanarrative view seems to hold that as long as I can produce proofs for S, thinking reality is the way I say it is should be quite permissible. Moreover, the epistemologist countenancing R cannot, upon investigating R, provide a plurality of inconsistent proofs. According to Lyotard, scientific knowledge gives the language game of denotation the privileged position of functioning as the flag bearer of truth while excluding other language games such as prescriptive and performative ones. One is learned if and only if one can produce a true statement S about R. This state of affairs sets scientific knowledge apart from language games that combine to form the social bond. A statement of science S, therefore, gets taught only if S is still verifiable through argumentation and proof.[7] This understanding of science seems to demonstrate Lyotard's rejection of the existence of an objective overarching truth. Consider how he builds his case for rejecting the adequacy and primacy of the scientific view of truth.

First, Lyotard notes that the rule of consensus of a statement S with truth value is deemed acceptable among interlocutors in a dialogue if the interlocutors cast S in terms of a possible unanimity between rational minds. Moreover, Lyotard observes how science has always been in conflict with narratives of the sort he highlights. The yardsticks of science, Lyotard contends, render a majority of the narrative false. However, he rejects this way of viewing the acceptability of narratives specifically because even

---

5. Lyotard, *Postmodern Condition*, xxiii.
6. Lyotard, *Postmodern Condition*, 23.
7. Lyotard, *Postmodern Condition*, 25.

science itself remains obligated to justify the rules of its own game.[8] Moreover, empirical scientific knowledge fails to represent the totality of knowledge specifically because it has always existed alongside and in competition with narrative knowledge. Lyotard believes the model he presents of narrative knowledge portrays a dynamic of internal balance and friendliness, the likes of which remain poorly portrayed in the scientific epistemology.[9]

Second, the central problem of legitimation, according to Lyotard, seems to receive an impact from the demoralization of the scientist. Reminiscent of Plato, the right to decide what is true seems contingent upon the right to decide what is just, irrespective of whether or not the statements consigned to those two authorities differ in nature. Consider that an empirical statement must, as a rule, fulfill a stipulated set of conditions in order to find acceptance in the scientific community. The scientist, as a legislator, gets authorized, then, to prescribe the stated conditions determining whether or not the statement in question should be included in the discourse for consideration in the scientific community. This observation leads Lyotard to conclude that a strict linkage exists between the language of science and the language of ethics and politics.[10] Whereas science by itself cannot determine this fact, Lyotard would seem to argue that narrative knowledge would hold no qualms about its acceptability in light of its tolerant stance.

Third, not only do we find truth interlinked with justice in the Platonic sense, according to Lyotard. We also find that knowledge and power are juxtaposed as two sides of the same question concerning the determinant of the nature of knowledge, as well as who knows the identity of the determinant. The determinant of what counts as knowledge, of course, is a knowledge question. The knower of the identity of the determinant is a power question. Ergo, knowledge and power remain juxtaposed as two sides of this question, which Lyotard calls the question of double legitimation.[11] Quite possibly, Lyotard finds this notion of double legitimation invisible to science specifically because scientific knowledge remains limited only to denotative utterances while the issue of power seems to belong to the category of performative utterances.

8. Lyotard, *Postmodern Condition*, 25.
9. Lyotard, *Postmodern Condition*, 7.
10. Lyotard, *Postmodern Condition*, 8.
11. Lyotard, *Postmodern Condition*, 9.

POSTMODERNISM AS A THEORY OF TRUTH

Fourth, Lyotard believes that the blossoming of techniques and technologies since World War II caused the notion of the grand narrative to lose its credibility.[12] The speculative apparatus we have demonstrates that the reduplication of knowledge seems to be its legitimation. This reduplication happens when knowledge cites its own statements in a second-level discourse that actually does the legitimation. However, this discourse seems to belong to a pre-scientific form of knowledge. If so, then the discourse demotes knowledge to the lowest rank. In order to illustrate his point, Lyotard draws attention to the following claim: a statement of science is knowledge if and only if that statement can take its place in a process of engendering that is universal. Let's call this statement K. K is real knowledge if and only if K can pass its own test. Lyotard thinks it does pass its own test if it presupposes that the process of engendering exists and K is, itself, an expression of that process. This presupposition, then, is indispensable to the speculative game. Without it, the language of legitimation remains illegitimate.[13]

The problem with this presupposition is that it defines the set of rules (call them D) one must accept in order to play the speculative game, which, in turn, assumes that we accept the view that the positive sciences represent the general mode of knowledge. Additionally, it assumes that language implies certain formal axiomatic presuppositions of the kind it must always make explicit. This process of legitimation, Lyotard observes, seems fueled by the demand for legitimation[14]—a demand prescriptive in nature. According to Lyotard, this form of legitimation has no way of proving that if a statement S describes a real situation R is true, a prescriptive statement based upon S will be just. Stated differently, we have no way of inferring, as a consequence, the imperative to open the door from a possible antecedent denotative claim that the door in question is closed.[15] For this reason, we face a crisis of scientific knowledge, Lyotard argues, and it is a crisis that represents an internal collapse of the legitimacy principle of knowledge. With an apparent notion of triumph, Lyotard finds erosion at work inside the speculative game of science, and for that reason, he calls into question the classical dividing lines between various fields of science.[16]

---

12. Lyotard, *Postmodern Condition*, 37.
13. Lyotard, *Postmodern Condition*, 38.
14. Lyotard, *Postmodern Condition*, 39.
15. Lyotard, *Postmodern Condition*, 40.
16. Lyotard, *Postmodern Condition*, 39.

Therefore, Lyotard finds science to be a language game with its own special sets of rules. However, it lacks the calling to supervise the praxis aspect of society, and for that reason, cannot be given the privileged position it erroneously enjoys. It remains at par with other forms of knowledge. It plays its own game. It remains inadequate, Lyotard argues, in its attempt to legitimate other types of utterances such as the language games of prescription. Most fatally, for Lyotard, science remains incapable of legitimating itself, even though it erroneously assumed it could.[17]

Fifth, as if dealing a deathblow to the notion of metanarratives, Lyotard notes how scientists play by the rules of the narrative game when they appeal to un-epic knowledge to justify their findings.[18] Hence, Lyotard thinks the scientist inevitably makes a recourse to narrative knowledge to the extent that scientific discourse desires to present its postulates as truth, on the one hand, while, on the other, fails to provide the necessary resources for legitimating the truths of those very statements. Absent this maneuver, Lyotard insists, science would beg the question by presupposing its own validity, the very thing science says should not be done.[19] However, in the absence of modern science, Lyotard leaves behind what he calls a metaphysical search for a first legitimation of some kind of transcendental authority that assumes the privileged position of determining the conditions of truth. This state of affairs leaves Lyotard to conclude, additionally, that the rules of the game of science do not transcend the boundaries of an already scientific debate but remain confined within those boundaries.[20]

These five reasons capture Lyotard's rejection of scientific knowledge as the metanarrative given the privileged position of legitimating other types knowledge. Lyotard, as noted, believes that scientific knowledge should be placed on the same playing field as other types of narratives in light of the rise of different languages brought about by major advancements in science and technology. If scientific knowledge can be rejected in this manner, the postmodern view seems promising, especially in its rejection of the nature of an overarching metanarrative, such as the reality of objective truth. Lyotard defends the postmodern tradition not only by showing how it should be construed, or by showing how scientific knowledge fails to undercut it. He also makes a push for the postmodern tradition by appealing

---

17. Lyotard, *Postmodern Condition*, 40.
18. Lyotard, *Postmodern Condition*, 27–28.
19. Lyotard, *Postmodern Condition*, 29.
20. Lyotard, *Postmodern Condition*, 29.

to its broad-based nature of accounting for other uses of language. Let me give it a fuller explication.

Rationale for Postmodernism

The first thing to note, according to Lyotard, is the fact that the status of knowledge undergoes some kind of evolution when societies and cultures find themselves arriving into the postindustrial age or, for that matter, the postmodern age.[21] To illustrate, Lyotard draws our attention to the fact that empiricism has been forced to deal with new languages such as phonology, theories of linguistics, theories of algebra, cybernetics, and informatics. Moreover, the mercantilization of machines seems to be directly impacting and changing how learning gets acquired, categorized, accessed, and used.[22] Lyotard believes that the possibility exists that eventual results of research being translatable into computer language will dictate the direction of the research in question. The result seems inevitable—producers and consumers of knowledge will be forced to acquire new ways of translating their inventions. They will be forced to learn these languages.[23]

Second, Lyotard contends that knowledge ought not to be limited merely to learning. By learning, Lyotard seems to refer to the acquisition of data by the learner in the scientific sense. According to Lyotard, knowledge entails acquiring the ability to form good denotative, prescriptive, and evaluative utterances. Hence, learning is not limited only to uttering good denotative statements such as those we find in the sciences.[24] What makes an utterance good, whether it falls under the denotative or prescriptive or evaluative category, is the fact that the utterance conforms to the relevant standard accepted in the social circle of the epistemologist's statements. In other words, some kind of societal unanimity and consensus plays a crucial role in determining an utterance's acceptability.[25]

Third, Lyotard thinks narration is the ideal form of customary knowledge in several ways. First, consider that popular stories routinely recount the successes or failures a hero experiences in his or her undertakings.[26]

21. Lyotard, *Postmodern Condition*, 3.
22. Lyotard, *Postmodern Condition*, 4.
23. Lyotard, *Postmodern Condition*, 4.
24. Lyotard, *Postmodern Condition*, 18.
25. Lyotard, *Postmodern Condition*, 19.
26. Lyotard, *Postmodern Condition*, 19.

These stories subsequently gain some kind of legitimacy upon social institutions because they function as myths. Sometimes they represent positive or negative models of integration into established institutions.[27] Second, the narrative form of knowledge, unlike the scientific form, lends itself to denotative, deontic, interrogative, and evaluative types of discourse, which Lyotard calls language games.[28] Third, the narration of these languages obeys the sorts of rules unanimously consented by their host societies, thereby defining for themselves a tripartite competence of skills in general, and speaking and listening skills in particular. Lyotard thus believes that the set of pragmatic rules constituting the social bond is what we find transmitted through these narratives.[29] A fourth way Lyotard believes narration is the ideal form of customary knowledge is his observation that narrative knowledge is the artistic-cum-time-defining periods offering specific historic backgrounds in which those stories could be set, thereby giving us a contextual window of understanding those narratives. Fifth, and possibly most importantly for our purposes, narratives carry in themselves immediate justification, which Lyotard calls legitimation. The narratives, according to Lyotard, determine the standards of competence, demonstrating how they can be applied. How exactly do they accomplish this feat? They do so by determining what has the right to be uttered and what has the right to be done in the culture in question.[30]

Fourth, Lyotard finds the denotative aspect of mere scientific knowledge as well as nonscientific metanarrative knowledge woefully inadequate in fostering learning. He notes, for example, that they are both composed of sets of statements. He finds one just as necessary as the other. If such is the case, judging the validity of narrative knowledge on the basis of scientific knowledge seems impossible, and vice versa. Moreover, Lyotard postulates that narrative knowledge does not concern itself as much as science does with the issue of its own justification. It remains content with the methods of its own legitimation without needing to appeal to some kind of argumentation or proof. According to Lyotard, narrative knowledge has a comprehension of the scientific discourse juxtaposed by a certain kind of tolerance.[31]

27. Lyotard, *Postmodern Condition*, 19.
28. Lyotard, *Postmodern Condition*, 20.
29. Lyotard, *Postmodern Condition*, 21.
30. Lyotard, *Postmodern Condition*, 22.
31. Lyotard, *Postmodern Condition*, 27.

Fifth, for Lyotard, since no transcendental authority for determining the condition of truth exists, the people within a given society hold the right to decide for society through consensus. To be sure, Lyotard would argue, consensus among the people ought to be seen as a sign of legitimation. It helps decide what is true or acceptable. They do so in the same way the scientific community decides the truth and falsehood of a statement. Stated differently, the people accumulate civil law analogously to how scientists accumulate empirical laws, and where necessary they perfect their principles of consensus analogously to how scientists think of new paradigms to help them revise the rules of their discoveries.[32] Lyotard believes that humanity functions as validator of knowledge and that the validation of knowledge is not internally locatable in knowledge itself. Humanity, the practical subject, is the validator of knowledge.[33] Those laws do not conform to some nature external to humans either but through the autonomy of the human will. This mode of legitimation creates a totally different aspect of language invisible to the scientific discourse, namely, the prescriptive aspect. For Lyotard, the important thing is not only to justify denotative utterances pertaining to the truth but also prescriptive utterances pertaining to justice. This way of viewing knowledge renders it the servant of the human subject rather than rendering it the subject itself, for its only legitimacy makes the reality of morality possible.[34]

In short, the reason postmodern narrative knowledge is preferable and enriching for the epistemologist as opposed to a metanarrative such as the one we find in scientific discourse is the facticity of its broad-based approach to the notion of learning. The scientific kind of knowledge confines itself only to denotative utterances—those limited only to what is either true or false. Postmodern knowledge, however, extends beyond mere truth and falsity into the realm of what is morally right and morally wrong. Moreover, it embraces additional types of utterances in its scheme of learning, such as prescriptive utterances and evaluative utterances. What I have highlighted in this section is not the only reason Lyotard offers for the plausibility of postmodernism's view of truth, or for that matter, language. I offer an outline of his understanding in the next section.

---

32. Lyotard, *Postmodern Condition*, 30.
33. Lyotard, *Postmodern Condition*, 35.
34. Lyotard, *Postmodern Condition*, 35.

Mercantilization, Performativity, and Truth

According to Lyotard, knowledge will be produced in order to be sold. It will become a major stake in the worldwide competition for power.[35] The argument for this view is long and tenuous. First, consider, by way of example, that the methods used by scientific research possess demonstrative properties that challenge classical reason specifically because of their pragmatic nature—the kind invisible to scientific reason. It uses language subject to a pragmatic condition by formulating its own rules and then *petitioning* the addressee to accept them. It then defines axioms and symbols commonly called *well-formed formulas* in standard logic texts. The axioms, however, ought to be defined by a metalanguage that specifies formal conditions that ought to be satisfied by the standards of decidability, syntactic completeness, and independence of the axioms. In this way, it defines the properties it requires of the scientific method.

The main problem with this view, notes Lyotard, is the fact that all formal systems have internal limitations, and this applies to logic as well.[36] For example, Gödel has demonstrated that a proposition exists in mathematics that is neither demonstrable nor refutable within the arithmetic system.[37] This fact entails that even in arithmetic, we find certain propositions that fail to satisfy the condition of completeness. Moreover, logic uses natural, everyday language as its metalanguage—a language clearly universal owing to the fact that we can translate all other languages into it. The problem following this reality is the fact that the language allows for the formation of paradoxes. Moreover, other sciences owe their status to the existence of a language whose rules of functioning cannot be demonstrated. Ironically, the rules of functioning of those sciences are themselves the object of a consensus of experts.[38]

Here, then, is the problem this conundrum creates. We immediately face a state of affairs where statements remain unverified for lack of proof following the use of a scientific device that, in many cases, is designed to optimize performance of the human body for the purpose of proof production! For this reason, such a device requires additional expenditures. If the money to buy such pieces of equipment is unavailable, we lack not just

---

35. Lyotard, *Postmodern Condition*, 4.
36. Lyotard, *Postmodern Condition*, 45.
37. Lyotard, *Postmodern Condition*, 41–42.
38. Lyotard, *Postmodern Condition*, 43.

the proof but also the means of verification of statements, which, in turn, entails the absence of truth.[39]

Second, Lyotard argues that the production of proof falls under the control of a language called performativity. The goal here, then, is not truth. Performativity turns out to be the best possible input-output equation. By this definition, Lyotard seems to think of performativity as the most preferrable result that succeeds technologically. In this sense, he seems to take the pragmatic bent. If this interpretation is the case, then the state sponsoring a given technological goal must justify the new goal of performativity and abandon the idealist and humanist narratives of legitimation. Hence, scientific technicians and instruments get purchased in order to augment power rather than to find truth, and the question will be to determine what comprises the discourse of power.

Lyotard also notes that human sensation, arguably, is deceptive and the range of its powers of discrimination remains limited. Therefore, technology comes to the rescue of the human organs that receive data as their function. The technological equipment follow the principle of optimal performance of maximizing output and minimizing input. Moreover, he argues, technology is a game pertaining to efficiency rather than to the true, the just, or the beautiful and a technical move is good when it works better or expends less energy than another. In other words, performativity increases the ability to produce proof that, in turn, increases the ability to be right.[40]

One can master all the language games, Lyotard argues, by mastering reality. Technology does precisely this. For this reason, he believes that if one reinforces technology, one reinforces reality. Moreover, he continues, one's chances of being right and just increase accordingly. Also, if one has access to scientific knowledge and decision-making authority, technology gets reinforced more effectively. Interestingly, Lyotard holds that legitimation by power follows this very dynamic. Power is not only good performativity but also effective verification and good verdict. Power legitimates science and the law. It does so on the basis of their efficiency. It also legitimates this very efficiency on the basis of science and law.[41]

---

39. Lyotard, *Postmodern Condition*, 45.
40. Lyotard, *Postmodern Condition*, 46.
41. Lyotard, *Postmodern Condition*, 47.

Usefulness of Language

Language, for Lyotard, seems to be the vehicle for anchoring truth, not in the correspondence or coherence understanding but in the pragmatic understanding. He emphasizes the pragmatic aspect of language by showing how it has many characteristics, ranging from the merely denotative ones to the declarative and prescriptive ones. A denotative utterance, for example, positions the speaker as a custodian of knowledge, that is, a knower. It positions the listener as receiver of the knower's postulates in a way that the receiver can accept or reject those very postulates. Moreover, it positions the referent as something demanding a correct identification by the statement referring to it.[42]

By contrast, a declaration such as "I now declare you husband and wife," pronounced by a minister, seems invisible to the specifications of the denotative aspect of language specifically because its performative utterance coincides with the enunciation of the referent. A man and woman become husband and wife because the minister has declared them husband and wife. According to Lyotard, this reality is not subject to verification by the receiver of the declaration, and the speaker must be vested with the relevant power to make the declaration.[43] In addition, utterances such as "give money to the university" fall under the category of prescriptions and can be recast as orders, commands, requests, and prayers. In this case, the speaker seems placed in a position of authority because he or she expects the listener to perform the action in question.[44]

This view of language leads Lyotard to make three further observations: first, he thinks their rules do not carry their own justification within themselves. Rather, the rules are the object of a contract between the players. Second, Lyotard thinks that if no rules exist, no games exist. In addition, a slight alteration of the rules alters the nature of the language game. Third, every utterance should be thought of as a rule in a game.[45]

Important also for Lyotard is his contention that language is the social bond. Each person is always located at a position through which different kinds of messages pass, placing him or her at the post of speaker and receiver with respect to a referent. Language has certain features set as the

---

42. Lyotard, *Postmodern Condition*, 9.
43. Lyotard, *Postmodern Condition*, 9.
44. Lyotard, *Postmodern Condition*, 9.
45. Lyotard, *Postmodern Condition*, 10.

minimum relations needed for any society to exist.[46] Notice how the usefulness of language as a social bond helps to facilitate the overall functioning of the society, according to Lyotard. He thinks that the true goal of the system is the organization of the global relationship between performativity of input and output. This goal is the reason why the society, presumably through the use of language, programs itself like a computer.[47]

MICHEL FOUCAULT ON TRUTH

Having looked at Lyotard's view of truth, we can arrive at a fuller understanding of postmodernism when we consider the view of one more postmodern thinker, namely, Michel Foucault. Foucault does not believe truth lies outside of power; neither does it lack power. Moreover, truth is not the privilege of individuals who succeed in liberating themselves. For Foucault, truth is produced only by virtue of multiple forms of constraint, thereby inducing regular effects of power. He believes each society has its regime of truth, which Foucault calls a society's "general politics" of truth. A general politics of truth involves the types of discourse a society accepts and makes that function as true. For him, these types of discourse entail the mechanisms and instances that enable an individual to distinguish true statements from false ones, the means by which each statement gets sanctioned, and the valuation of techniques and procedures in the process of acquiring truth. Moreover, it entails the status of individuals charged with stipulating what counts as true.[48]

Foucault finds five important traits characterizing the political economy of truth in a society. First, truth is placed on the form of scientific discourse and institutions producing it. Second, it is subject to constant economic and political incitement. By this observation, Foucault believes a demand for truth exists as much for political discourse as it does for political power. Third, truth remains the object, under diverse forms, of immense diffusion and consumption. In other words, it circulates through the apparatuses of education and information whose extent is broad, relatively speaking, in the social body. Fourth, if not exclusively, truth is dominantly produced and transmitted under the control of a few great political and economic apparatuses such as the university, the military, the printed page,

---

46. Lyotard, *Postmodern Condition*, 15.
47. Lyotard, *Postmodern Condition*, 11.
48. Foucault, "Truth and Power," 252.

and the media. Finally, truth is the subject of a whole political debate and social confrontation.[49]

Almost analogously to Lyotard's view, Foucault apparently contends how one must not take "the bearer of universal values" into account with respect to truth. Rather, what one must take into account is the person occupying a specific position, and that person's specificity must be linked to the general functioning of an apparatus of truth. Foucault does have intellectuals in mind when he makes this assertion based on what he says next, namely, intellectuals possess a threefold specificity. First, they possess the specificity of their class position, whether as petty bourgeois in the service of capitalism or the proletariat. Second, they possess the specificity of their conditions of life and work linked to their condition as intellectuals, such as a field of research or their position in the laboratory. Third, they possess the specificity of the politics of truth in their societies. With this third aspect, the intellectuals' position can take on a general significance and their local specific struggle can have implications beyond merely professional or sectoral.[50]

Foucault believes the intellectual can operate and struggle at the general level of the regime of truth essential to the structure and functioning of the society. He notes that a battle for or around truth exists. This battle does not mean the ensemble of rules according to which the true and the false are to be separated and specific effects of power attached to the true. It is not a battle on behalf of the truth; rather, it is a battle of the status of truth and the economic and political role it plays. Foucault believes we should think of the political problems of the intellectual in terms of truth and power rather than in terms of science and ideology. We understand truth, he says, as a system of production, regulation, distribution, and operation of statements.[51] Whereas this observation may lead one to conclude erroneously that Foucault subscribes to some form of coherent theory of truth, his next comments speak differently. He thinks truth is linked in a circular relation with systems of power that produce and sustain it and to effects of power it induces and that extend it. He calls this relation "a regime of power."[52]

---

49. Foucault, "Truth and Power," 252.
50. Foucault, "Truth and Power," 252.
51. Foucault, "Truth and Power," 252–53.
52. Foucault, "Truth and Power," 253.

For Foucault, this regime was a condition of the formation and development of capitalism and was not merely ideological or superstructural. Moreover, it is subject to certain modifications in its operation in the socialist countries. The essential political problem for the intellectuals, according to Foucault, is that of determining the possibility of constituting a new politics of truth. It is not the problem of criticizing the ideological contents supposedly linked to science. Neither is it that of assuring his own scientific practice is accompanied by a correct ideology. The problem for Foucault involves changing the political and economic institutional regime of the production of truth rather than that of changing people's consciousness. For Foucault, truth is already power. For this reason, it cannot be emancipated from every system of power.[53] From Foucault, I move to the third prominent postmodern thinker whose views various philosophers term deconstructionism.

DERRIDA'S POSTMODERN REJECTION OF OBJECTIVE TRUTH

Having examined the views of Foucault and Lyotard, I now turn to Jacques Derrida. Before delving deeper into Derrida's take on truth, let me admit that my treatment of Derrida will not be a summary of his entire work *Of Grammatology* for two reasons: first, a summary of this work will take us far afield and certainly beyond my goals in this section; second, his work is too enormous to be summarized in this section. I will, therefore, focus on why he thinks subjective interpretation and expression of our experiences through the exercise of writing lack constitutive meaning even though that is all we have in demonstrating our knowledge of the world around us.

In his prominent work *Of Grammatology*, Derrida defends the claim I have alluded to by making the observation that the history of metaphysics is one that has always assigned the origin of truth to the Greek concept of logos. As if trying to characterize the concept of this kind of objective truth negatively, Derrida argues that this history has been the debasement and repression of writing outside of full speech.[54] Later in that work, Derrida argues that all the metaphysical determination of truth seems more or less immediately inseparable from the instance of the logos coterminous with reason. To be sure, this reason has been thought to remain within the

---

53. Foucault, "Truth and Power," 253.
54. Derrida, *Of Grammatology*, 3.

lineage of the logos in whatever sense one understands it. Within this logos, Derrida contends, the original and essential link to phonetic language has never been broken. For him, the essence of phonetics would be immediately proximate to that which, as logos, relates to meaning within thought.[55] According to Derrida, the rationality that governs a writing enlarged and radicalized beyond mere phonetics no longer issues from a logos. It inaugurates the *deconstruction* of all the significations that have their source in that of the logos, particularly the signification of the truth.[56]

Second, Derrida argues that the development of the practical methods of information retrieval teaches us that phonetic writing, widely regarded as the medium of the great metaphysical, scientific, technical, and economic adventure in the West, is limited in space and time. It limits itself even as it remains in the process of imposing its laws upon cultural areas that seemed invisible to it. This development vastly extends the possibilities of the message to the point where it is no longer the written translation of language or, for that matter, the conveyance of a certain referent that could remain spoken of in its integrity.[57]

Third, Derrida thinks that over the years, the concept of science, which has always been determined as logic, has always been a philosophical concept. This fact has remained consistent even when the practice of science has constantly challenged its imperialism of the logos by invoking, for example, non-phonetic writing. Peculiarly for each epoch, however, science can no longer be satisfied with phonetic writing especially at the time when phoneticization of writing begins to lay hold on world culture.[58]

Fourth, everything that for at least some twenty centuries tended toward being successfully classified under the name of language is, according to Derrida, beginning to allow itself to be transferred to the name of writing. Apparently, the concept of writing is beginning to go beyond the extension of language. Writing comprehends language, but it describes the movement of language.[59] What we call language could have been in its origin and in its end a species of writing. It merges with a history that has associated technics and logocentric metaphysics for nearly three millennia. Apparently, however, it is approaching its own exhaustion, what Derrida

---

55. Derrida, *Of Grammatology*, 10.
56. Derrida, *Of Grammatology*, 10.
57. Derrida, *Of Grammatology*, 10.
58. Derrida, *Of Grammatology*, 3.
59. Derrida, *Of Grammatology*, 3.

calls the "death of the book," manifesting itself through a convulsive proliferation of the libraries. This death of the book announces nothing but the death of speech.[60]

Fifth, Derrida thinks the concept of writing exceeds and comprehends that of language, presupposing a certain definition of language and of writing. For some time, Derrida notes, we have been saying "language for action," or "language for movement," or "language for reflection." Now, however, we replace *language* with writing and say language for all that and more in order to designate the totality of what makes it possible. Notice, Derrida says, that writing for all that to an inscription in general is alien to phonetics such as cinematography and choreography, even if what it distributes in space is not alien to phonetics. Further, it is alien to pictorial, musical, and sculptural writing. Derrida adds that one might also speak of athletic writing.[61]

Sixth, Derrida thinks all these describe not only the system of notation secondarily connected with these activities but the essence and the contents of these activities themselves. Also, in this sense, the biologist speaks of writing and program in relation to the most elementary processes of information within the living cell. In addition, Derrida writes that the entire field covered by the cybernetic program will be the field of writing. Moreover, suppose the theory of cybernetics is to oust, by itself, all metaphysical concepts that, until recently, served to separate humans from machines. It must conserve the notion of writing until its own historico-metaphysical character is also exposed.[62]

Seventh, even though not all humans have the same writing or speech sounds, Derrida believes all humans have the same mental experiences. Let me call those experiences M. What humans write and speak about happen to be the primary symbols for M. In other words, for every word W, W is an interpretation or a signifier of M. What has been written, however, is always technical and representative and, according to Derrida, lacks constitutive meaning. You, the reader, would be justified to see how W would remain bereft of any truth value if Derrida is correct in his insinuation that W lacks any constitutive meaning. However, Derrida argues that this derivation is the origin of the idea of the signifier. According to Derrida, the idea of the sign always has within itself the distinction between the signifier and the

60. Derrida, *Of Grammatology*, 8.
61. Derrida, *Of Grammatology*, 8–9.
62. Derrida, *Of Grammatology*, 9.

signified, even if they get distinguished simply as two faces of the same leaf.[63]

Eighth, the difference between the thing signified, call it T, and W, belong in a profound and implicit way to the totality of the great epoch covered by the history of metaphysics and more narrowly to the epoch of Christian creationism. Still, as modern structured thought has realized, language is a system of signs, and linguistics is part and parcel of the science of signs. Thus, the constitutive mark of any linguistic sign in particular is its twofold character—one sensible and the other intelligible.[64]

In order to understand the implications of Derrida's distinction between the sensible and the intelligible, an exegesis of both terms would be helpful. With respect to his use of the word *sensible*, he seems to have the human five senses in mind, namely, the sense of sight, sound, smell, taste, and touch. Also, his use of *intelligible* seems to refer to a mental experience M of T, and T is the thing in the external world that humans perceive. W is, therefore, an expression of M, as already noted, since W is the attempt to put in writing one's mental contents. Moreover, Derrida speaks of the distinction between sensible and intelligible as being between the signifier and the signified.[65] Derrida would therefore say that the subject affects itself and is related to itself in the element of ideality.[66]

Ninth, Derrida seems to say the entire world is a text. Since we use texts to list our experience of the world and language is the means by which we experience our world, our interpretation of the world seems to be on the basis of language.[67] Quoting from Galileo and Karl Jaspers, among others, he advances this very claim. Thus, Galileo said the book of nature is written in mathematical language. Jaspers said the world is the manuscript of an *other*, inaccessible to universal reading, which only existence deciphers.[68]

According to James Smith, what Derrida is really saying is that the world, as text, is subject to interpretation. Interpretation brings in presuppositions that are, in turn, informed by our beliefs of the world. According to Smith, Derrida believes all reality is interpreted and that uninterpreted realities do not exist. We see the world through interpretive lenses governed

63. Derrida, *Of Grammatology*, 11.
64. Derrida, *Of Grammatology*, 13.
65. Derrida, *Of Grammatology*, 13.
66. Derrida, *Of Grammatology*, 12.
67. Smith, *Postmodernism*, 34.
68. Derrida, *Of Grammatology*, 16.

by ultimate beliefs. More specifically, we already see the world through a worldview, and this reality holds true for everyone.[69]

Finally, as if to strike a conciliatory tone with the idea of the logocentric aspect of truth characteristic of biblical Christianity, Derrida acknowledges its usefulness. He also argues that the thematics of the sign have been the agonized labor, for about a century, of a tradition that professed to withdraw meaning, truth, presence, and the idea of being from the movement of signification. For Derrida, no linguistic signs existed before writing. He argues elsewhere for the nonexistence of phonetic writing by contending that what we call phonetic writing can only function by incorporating nonphonetic signs.[70] Therefore, according to Derrida, the exterior nature of the signifier is really the exterior nature of writing. Without that exteriority, Derrida adds, the very idea of sign falls into decay. Our entire world and language would collapse with it. Its evidence and its value keep an indestructible solidity.[71]

Derrida provides additional reasons to demonstrate the inadequacy of logocentric phonetic writing when compared to writing that goes beyond it. What I have selected here seems sufficient for the purpose of this work, namely, to show how postmodernism remains hesitant to acknowledge the adequacy of the concept of objective truth. I now turn to an evaluation of postmodernism.

EVALUATION OF LYOTARD'S POSTMODERNISM

Lyotard seems right in his observation that denotative utterances remain woefully inadequate in determining the usefulness of declarative and pragmatic utterances. However, in order to advance this claim, Lyotard apparently anchors his argument on a standard of argumentation that seems properly evaluative. Stated differently, in order to cast doubt in the existence of a metanarrative, in order to find any metanarrative incredulous, the epistemologist skeptical of Lyotard's musings could justifiably ask Lyotard how he bases his aversion toward metanarratives. Consciously or unconsciously, Lyotard seems to presuppose the existence of a standard, a metanarrative, so to speak, that furnishes him with the frameworks for finding metanarratives incredulous! His position, therefore, risks self-decimation.

69. Smith, *Postmodernism*, 54–55.
70. Derrida, "Différance," 225–40.
71. Derrida, "Différance," 14.

Also, Lyotard seems correct when he observes that the scientist is a legislator authorized to prescribe stated conditions determining whether or not a scientific statement S should be included in the discourse for consideration in the scientific community. To be sure, in light of the community's assumption as to what counts as scientific, the ought-ness of the scientific legislator to promulgate the conditions in question remains invisible to the science. Science does not seem to have the capacity to legislate this sort of ought-ness.

However, an epistemologist as well as an ethicist would seem inclined to wonder to what basis of ought-ness Lyotard appeals. Lyotard, as already noted, rejects the idea of a metanarrative; he is incredulous with respect to this idea. Therefore, suppose an ethical objectivist believes, as he or she should in light of the postulates of objectivism, in the existence of an objective moral standard by which humans determine the moral rightness or wrongness of a specific moral claim. Upon admitting Lyotard's claim of finding metanarratives incredulous, the ethical objectivist will be required by Lyotard to render moral objectivism incredulous. This possible state of affairs would then leave the moral objectivist with the option of abandoning his or her objectivist position for a nonobjectivist one.

Second, Lyotard seems concerned that scientific knowledge cites its own statements in a second-level discourse that actually does the legitimation and that his second-level discourse belongs to a pre-scientific form of knowledge, thereby demoting knowledge to the lowest rank. Some aspects of knowledge may seem vulnerable to this charge. Still, other aspects of knowledge seem to remain invulnerable. Some aspects of knowledge have internal features of self-legitimation. I refer here, for example, to statements commonly deemed necessarily true. The truth of these statements are such that their denial entails a self-contradiction. In some cases, such statements seem self-evidently true. Consider, for example, statements such as "all triangles are three-sided figures" or "no one is taller than himself," or others such as the law of noncontradiction, claiming a statement p cannot be simultaneously true and false with respect to its referent. The truth of these statements seem self-evident; the attempt to deny their truth will yield epistemological absurdities. A variety of scientific knowledge of the sort Lyotard finds problematic may very well fuel his worry. However, a different variety of such knowledge exists that remains immune to this worry. They proceed on the assumption that statements of the sort I have cited are reliably true. Their truth need not be ascertained by appealing to a second-level discourse external to them. One of the moves Lyotard thinks scientists make in order to legitimize their own language game is to appeal to un-epic narrative knowledge. I argue that certain principles whose truth scientists know *a priori* help to ground the assumptions of their scientific enterprise.

Third, scientists may admit that denotative utterances describing their empirical enterprise may be limited only to the exercise of reporting the facts of science. Moreover, they would have no problem admitting that their enterprise seems unequipped to legislate states of affairs that would ground prescriptive utterances by failing to derive a given sense of oughtness from an existing state of affairs. Such an admission does not imply for scientists that they lack prescriptive utterances in their fields. If it did, then the whole exercise of prescribing medicine in the field of medical science would not only be absent but deadly in some cases. Scientists in the medical field know the value of offering prescriptions for human well-being. The whole exercise of evaluating a patient's health condition and making a health conclusion based on that condition seems clearly evaluative. Moreover, in order for the physician to acquire this kind of knowledge, the requisite skills are inescapable.

Apparently, the scientist would imply what in philosophical circles has been termed a hypothetical imperative following the ethical philosophy of Immanuel Kant.[72] The structure of such an imperative would run as follows: if you desire x, you need to do y. An instance of such a statement could take the following format: if you desire the well-being of your patients, you need to prescribe the relevant medicine for them. Notice that even if the consequent of this imperative does not follow from the antecedent with strict necessity, it does follow obligatorily. Hence, Lyotard's ascription of the tripartite competence only to narrative knowledge without acknowledging that scientists also value this kind of knowledge seems rather narrow. Based on their experience, they would know the value of technical skills requisite for their scientific enterprise.

Fourth, Lyotard also believes, as already noted, that the people within a given society have the right to decide for society through consensus specifically because no transcendental authority for determining the condition of truth exists. This belief may sound both noble and attractive. Just the same, certain aspects of vulnerability afflict it. First, the question of adjudicating between intersocietal conflict remains elusive. Conflicting societies

---

72. See Kant, *Practical Reason*, I.1.20.

will not appeal to an authority external to them to adjudicate between those conflicts. If Lyotard is correct in his view here, and a given society, call it B, decides through some form of consensus to develop weapons of mass destruction with the intention of obliterating a rival society, call it C, no transcendental authority exists beyond B and C that C would appeal to for help.

A second aspect of vulnerability can be seen in the following consideration. Lyotard's suggestion here seems to collapse into cultural relativism. For this reason, all the problems afflicting relativism in general seem to afflict Lyotard's view in particular. One such problem, besides the one mentioned already, is the problem of self-decimation. Lyotard already appeals to a metanarrative to anchor his claim that for any society H of humans, the people within H hold the right to decide for H through consensus. Presumably, Lyotard believes this suggestion applies to all existing human societies. If it does, then he inadvertently casts it as a transcendental authority determining the conditions of moral truths—a metanarrative of sorts. Lyotard therefore embraces and depends on the very thing he rejects to anchor a rival position.

Fifth, Lyotard also argues that other sciences owe their status to the existence of a language whose rules of functioning cannot be demonstrated. Recall that he uses Gödel's demonstration as proof of his point that a proposition p exists in mathematics that is neither demonstrable nor refutable within the arithmetic system. Admittedly, this attack is perhaps one of the most forceful ones Lyotard advances. He raises a point here that should cause anyone skeptical of his view to pause and appreciate its force. To be sure, I cannot think of a possible rebuttal to Lyotard except for one that has some promise, and it could be formulated as follows.

The fact that other sciences owe the legitimacy of their status to the existence of a language whose rules of functioning cannot be demonstrated implies, for Lyotard, that he has in his presupposition a way of determining that the rule in question cannot be demonstrated. This presupposition takes us back to what is now becoming rather familiar, namely, to the presupposition of the existence of a metanarrative, the very thing Lyotard is taking pains to reject. Lyotard's way of determination could function as a standard for deciding on the completeness or, for that matter, on the rules of the sciences in question. Stated differently, Lyotard inescapably resorts once again to a meta-standard for determining whether the language legitimating the rules of science is itself legitimated.

Fifth, Lyotard also draws our attention to the question of performativity of technological equipment that follow the principles of optimal performance, namely, maximizing output and minimizing input. Technology, therefore, has efficiency rather than truth as its goal, and performativity increases the ability to produce proof, which, in turn, increases the ability to be right.

Whether the ability to be right refers to moral rightness or factual rightness is not clear from Lyotard. If he implies factual rightness by that phrase, then he seems to subscribe to a pragmatic theory of truth, whose weakness we have already examined. Perhaps then he refers to moral rightness, thereby subscribing to some form of consequentialism given its dependence on outcomes. Notice, however, that in order for performativity to produce the desired outcome, it has to follow a certain principle. The question Lyotard must answer is whether this principle is the result or product of a consensus among the players of the language game or if it issues from facts about our world. If it is the result of a consensus, then for any players of the language game to arrive at this principle *a priori* and by consensus must be an extremely difficult venture indeed. The difficulty is accentuated by the fact that knowing what results will follow the performance of a given machine *a priori* is extremely difficult without first testing to see if the machine will perform as designed. On the other hand, if the principle is a discovered law already existing in the metaphysical fabric of our world, then it undercuts Lyotard's incredulity toward metanarrative, specifically because that principle is itself just such a metanarrative. In short, the principle of optimal performance to which Lyotard appeals undercuts rather than promotes his postmodern epistemology. From Lyotard, I turn to Foucault.

EVALUATION OF FOUCAULT

I begin with Foucault's contention that a general politics of truth involves the types of discourse a society accepts and makes, which, in turn, function as true. Foucault repeats the same idea differently in his fivefold characterization of truth traits when he says truth is dominantly produced and transmitted under the control of a few great political and economic apparatus such as the university, military, printed page, and media.

An interesting assumption implicit in Foucault's characterization of truth is his claim that the society makes a certain set of discourse, call it *D*, and that this discourse is not only accepted but also functions as true. This assumption should strike the reader as interesting because it puts forward the idea that truth is a product of the society. Therefore, different societies may have different types of truth. Stated differently, what may be regarded as true in one society based on the discourse that society makes may also be deemed false by a different society.

As with Lyotard, then, cultural relativism seems to be at play here. This setup does not sound appealing. Indeed, it seems vulnerable to the charge that it is unworkable. A culture that upholds cannibalism as true specifically because cannibalism is part of the discourse it made will not be helpful for a neighboring culture upholding the golden rule. If the society is the producer of truth, and society is composed of humans, then humans are the producers of truth. The instability of human subjectivity should function as a reason to distrust the truth of our discourse if indeed we, as humans, are producers of truth. Moreover, if humans are producers of truth, then truth did not exist before the arrival of humans.

Second, Foucault seems to reject the notion of truth's universality. More specifically, he contends that one must not take the bearer of universal values into account with respect to truth. Based on what he says about truth as a human product, he would seem to reject, as Lyotard does, the existence of an overarching objective truth universally transcending the boundaries of human societies. As we have seen with Lyotard, such a denial or rejection may actually be innocuous to the existence of truth because deniers of the existence of objective truth will always assume that their denials are objectively true. Foucault, for example, would not think his claim is false, namely, that one must not take the bearer of universal values into account with respect to truth. He must assume that this very claim is, in fact, objectively true. Otherwise, no one would take him seriously

Third, Foucault contends that truth is power. In light of the context of this statement, Foucault seems to suggest the idea that truth is a product of human institutions of power. Possibly he means humans must do the bidding of the regime of truth because the regime of truth is indeed a regime of power. The problem with this view is its failure to take into account the idea of unjust power. It fails to answer the question of whether unjust power is still true even when its victims do its bidding. In Plato's *Republic*, Socrates takes Thrasymachus to task for subscribing to the view that might is right.[73] One fails to see how Foucault would be unaware of this Socratic objection to the "might is right" ideology.

---

73. Plato, *Republic*, 338.

One could object to this evaluation of Foucalt by noting that Foucault is talking about nonmoral power. Socrates was raising an objection to moral power. The objection, however, seems to fall short specifically because Foucault does not seem to qualify the meaning of his use of power in this context. To be sure, the context strongly suggests the fact that Foucault has political power in mind. If so, then the issue of moral power may not, after all, be ignored. Besides, we can easily see the philosophical decimation attending the claim that a given state of affairs is true because powerful human institutions produce it. The same charge I raised earlier applies here. What if the produced state of affairs establishes frameworks oppressive to a certain population—the sort of oppression that would, with time, cause a revolution within the oppressed population, which will, eventually, oppose the framework-producing institution?

For these reasons, I find Foucault's view of truth both inadequate and impractical. Admittedly, however, I will acknowledge the claim that, generally speaking, truth has power—a kind of authority. I will qualify this claim later in this work that the power of truth can be seen in the metaphysical authority it brings to bear on humans. Having offered my evaluation of Foucault, I now turn to Derrida.

EVALUATION OF DERRIDA

Derrida's voluminous work advances the claim that the world is a text and that writing has no constitutive meaning. These two claims are all the ingredients we need to evaluate Derrida's work. Both claims seem to undermine Derrida's entire project, provided we regard both claims central to his goals. Suppose, for example, he truly believes his claim that writing has no constitutive meaning, we are bound to raise two items of concern regarding that very claim.

First, either what Derrida has written, namely, his entire work entitled *Of Grammatology*, has constitutive meaning or it is constitutively meaningless. If it has constitutive meaning, then his claim that writing has no constitutive meaning is false. On the other hand, if what Derrida has written is constitutively meaningless, then the claim itself is nonsensical. Therefore, either his claim that writing has no constitutive meaning is false or it is nonsensical. Obviously, Derrida would not want to believe these conclusions. At any rate, the claim Derrida makes here seems to be self-referentially incoherent.

This observation leads me to the second question about the very claim of constitutive meaninglessness: if writing has no constitutive meaning, are we to conclude from that observation that all writing is false? Stated differently, are we to say no written document functions as a reliable conveyor of truth? If we take what Derrida says at face value, this conclusion seems to be the only one available. However, some writing, quite possibly, possesses constitutive meaning and conveys reliable information about the world. I would imagine, for example, that Derrida certainly wants to believe his readers find his writings reliable.

Having taken the claim into consideration, I now consider his contention that the world is a text and that nothing lies outside the text. James K. A. Smith has made a valiant effort to rescue Derrida from the charge that Derrida believes in the nonexistence of important entities of the external world. However, if Derrida's claim gets juxtaposed with his claim about the meaninglessness of the written text, the logic will run as follows: writing has no constitutive meaning. The world is a text. Therefore, the world has no constitutive meaning. To see the intuitiveness of this logic, we simply need to understand that *writing* and *text* are somewhat synonymous. Hence, we could re-state the first premise as follows: for any x, if x is a text, then x lacks constitutive meaning. The world is a text. Therefore, the world lacks constitutive meaning.

Derrida seems to take such considerations seriously, and this fact seems surprising. Overall, given these findings about Derrida, and in light of my evaluation of Lyotard and Foucault, I conclude that postmodernism's rejection of objective truth falls short and its reasons for advancing such objections remain largely unjustified. What I seem to see is that postmodernism collapses into some form of relativism. Therefore, as already noted, all the shortcomings of relativism afflict it as well. It does not seem adequate as an explication of the nature of truth.

A major flaw with this postmodernist account of truth is how, philosophically speaking, it breaks down before it takes off the ground. With this view, truth remains fundamentally unsustainable, almost nonexistent. If it exists at all, it is more cosmetic than real. It does not exist before humans came onto the scene, and it does not seem to exist after the arrival of humans onto the scene. One could counter this claim by suggesting that it does exist by virtue of its contingency on human utterances. This counterclaim will not do specifically because its subjective nature renders it unlivable, a state of affairs I have already illustrated with cultures or individuals subscribing to contradicting or rival views of what they find subjectively true for them. For this reason, we must seek a more useful account of truth.

6

The Correspondence Conception of Truth

HAVING EXAMINED THREE DIFFERENT CONCEPTIONS or theories of truth, I now turn to what philosophers characterize as the correspondence theory of truth. Most thinkers widely trace the history of the initial articulation of the correspondence theory to Aristotle. In a passage in his work, *Metaphysics*, Aristotle presents one of the earlier versions of the correspondence theory: for Aristotle, one speaks falsely when one says something is the case when that thing is not, in fact the case, and vice versa.[1] He seems to capture the basic motif of the correspondence theory of truth, a motif that continues to furnish contemporary thinkers with ingredients for formulating standard definitions of the theory itself.

Thus, A. N. Prior's entry alludes to Aristotle's formulation in the *Encyclopedia of Philosophy*, but he also observes that the correspondence theory of truth has gained currency largely through the writings of Bertrand Russell.[2] Bertrand Russell thinks that truth consists in some form of correspondence between belief and fact.[3] Russell's student, Ludwig Wittgenstein held a similar view in his earlier writings when he conveyed the idea that statements are true or false only when they are pictures of reality.[4]

Wittgenstein further illustrates the concept of truth as follows: consider a black spot appearing on a white piece of paper. According to Wittgenstein, one can describe the form of that spot in a certain way: by

---

1. Aristotle, *Metaphysics*, 1011b27–29.
2. Prior, "Correspondence Theory," 223.
3. Russell, *Problems of Philosophy*, 107.
4. Wittgenstein, *Tractatus*, 4.06.

stating whether each point of the paper is white or black. A positive fact, Wittgenstein notes, corresponds to the fact that a given point is black. A negative fact corresponds to the idea that a given point is white. Suppose one indicates any point on the plane; the point corresponds to the assumption proposed for judgment.[5]

This definition of the correspondence theory continues to gain acceptance among twentieth-century philosophers as well as contemporary ones. For example, H. B. Acton reiterates a similar understanding of the correspondence theory. He notes, for example, that whenever we believe a proposition P, we apprehend a set of symbols, and our belief that P is true when we use the symbols correctly, having the same structure as the relevant fact. In other words, our belief about P is one that corresponds to the structure.[6] More recently, Alfred Tarski offers a similar idea when he presents the correspondent theory as the view that finds a sentence S true if and only if S describes the existing state of affairs. Tarski draws our attention to a slightly different idea that tries to capture the same motif. For him, a statement is true when it corresponds to reality.[7]

Though not entirely sympathetic to the postulates of the correspondence theory of truth, David Lewis characterizes it as the view that presents truth as correspondence to fact.[8] Gerald Vision, who responds to Lewis's partial skepticism about the correspondence theory, gives a slightly more expanded definition while maintaining its core postulate. For Vision, a general understanding of the correspondence theory holds that a proposition is true if and only if it corresponds to facts. Vision thinks that this general definition seems to capture Lewis's version of the correspondence theory.[9] Patricia Marino also characterizes, in a very general way, the correspondence theory as the view that true sentences, statements, or beliefs correspond to the way things are in the world while false ones do not.[10] Having found this view too general, Marino proposes what she calls a Modest Correspondence Theory, one she finds both plausible and distinctive.[11]

---

5. Wittgenstein, *Tractatus*, 4.063.
6. Acton, "Correspondence Theory," 188.
7. Tarski, "Truth and Proof," 63.
8. Lewis, "Forget About," 275.
9. Vision, "Lest We Forget," 136–37.
10. Marino, "What Should," 416.
11. Marino, "What Should," 447.

As far as the correspondence theory is concerned, three major factors seem to be at play: a state of affairs that obtains in the external world, that is, a fact F, a perceiver or recognizer H of the state of affairs F, and H's interpretation and eventual expression S of F where S could be a verbal or written description of F. How H describes F using S determines the truth or falsity of S. This formulation seems to be the basic motif of the correspondence theory of truth. As we will see in what follows, this characterization of truth may not be as intuitive as it seems to appear. Some philosophers think it fails to account for statements that strike us as intuitively true but have no correspondence to some particular fact in the external world. For example, some thinkers would argue that most philosophers accept the intuitive plausibility of the law of noncontradiction. However, no facts in the external world seem to correspond to that law. As we will see, this objection may not be as forceful as it initially seems though it has some merit. Let me now turn to an explanation of the correspondence theory of truth.

TARSKI'S SEMANTIC THEORY OF TRUTH

According to Tarski, the Aristotelian conception of truth gets widely regarded as the classical conception or the semantic conception of truth. Tarski uses the word *semantics* to denote the division of logic discussing the relations between linguistic objects that get expressed by these objects. Sometimes we speak of the correspondence theory as being based on the classical conception. Tarski's attempt is to offer a more precise explanation of the classical conception that could supersede the Aristotelian formulation while simultaneously preserving its basic intentions.[12]

Tarski begins with a simple problem by considering a sentence in English—a sentence whose meaning remains clear, namely, "Snow is white," and names that sentence S, for short. Tarski then asks what we mean when we say S is true or that S is false. According to Tarski, S is true simply means that snow is white, and S is false means snow is not white, enabling us to arrive at the following formulation, which we will call (1) and express as follows: "Snow is white" is true if and only if snow is white. We express the contradiction of that sentence, which we will call (1'), as follows: "Snow is white" is false if and only if snow is not white. Hence, (1) and (1') provide satisfactory illustrations of the meaning of the terms "true" and "false" when we use them to refer to the sentence, "Snow is white." Therefore, Tarski

---

12. Tarski, "Truth and Proof," 63–64.

believes this formulation provides a partial definition for the terms *true* and *false*. Moreover, (1) and (1') have the form prescribed for definitions by the rules of logic, namely, the form of logical equivalence,[13] also known as material equivalence.

Seemingly (1) might exhibit the flaw of vicious circularity owing to the fact that certain words in (1) occur in both the definiens and the definiendum. However, according to Tarski, these occurrences possess an entirely different character specifically because the word *snow* is a syntactical part of the definiens. The definiens is an entire sentence and the word *snow* is the subject of that sentence. The definiendum is also a sentence expressing the fact that the definiens is a true sentence. An expression enclosed in quotes must be treated grammatically as a single word with no syntactical parts. Therefore, the word *snow* does not occur entirely as a syntactical part. Words that are not syntactical parts of the definiendum cannot create a vicious circle and the danger of circularity dissipates.[14]

Still, Tarski tries another method that he finds just as effective in partly establishing the definition of a true statement. It is a method he characterizes as a letter-by-letter description of an expression. Let me call this formation claim (2), which would run as follows: the string of three words—the first of which is the string of the letter S, the letter N, the letter O, and the letter W, and the second of which is the string of the letter I and the letter S, and the third of which is the string of the letter W, the letter H, the letter I, the letter T, and the letter I—is a true sentence if and only if snow is white. According to Tarski, claim (2) does not differ from (1) in its meaning. Claim (2) has the advantage of the appearance of non-circularity. Both (1) and (2) have the form of claim (3), namely, *p* is true if and only if *p*, where *p* is to be replaced on both sides of (3) by the sentence for which the definition is constructed.[15]

For Tarski, the use of the term *true* in its reference to English sentences then and only then conforms with the classical conception of truth if that use enables us to establish every equivalence of the form (3) in which *p* is replaced on both sides of the biconditional by an arbitrary English sentence. The problem of establishing an adequate use of the term *true* for sentences in English can be solved completely if we succeed in forming an adequate general definition of truth—a definition that will carry all the

---

13. Tarski, "Truth and Proof," 64.
14. Tarski, "Truth and Proof," 64.
15. Tarski, "Truth and Proof," 65.

equivalences of the form (3) as its logical consequences. According to Tarski, a general construction of truth in this way is easy under certain special assumptions,[16] which is outlined in the following text.

For example, suppose we are interested in defining the term *true* for a particular fragment of the English language, which we will call L. If L has precise syntactical rules enabling us to distinguish between a sentence and a non-sentential expression, then *true* does not occur in L and that the meaning of all the words in L is sufficiently clear. Under such an assumption, prepare the complete list of all the sentences in L, assuming L has exactly one thousand sentences and we agree to use the symbols $s_1, s_2, \ldots s_{1000}$, as abbreviations of sentences on that list. As the next step, construct a partial definition of truth for each of the sentences by substituting successively all these sentences for "p" on both sides of the schema (3). Finally, Tarski suggests we form the logical conjunctions of these partial definitions by putting the connective *and* between any two consecutive partial definitions. Tarski suggests we then give the resulting conjunctions a different but logically equivalent form so as to satisfy formal requirements imposed on definitions by rules of logic as follows (5): for every sentence x (in the language L), x is true if and only if either s_1, and x is identical to s_1, or s_2, and x is identical to $s_2 \ldots$, or s_{1000} and x is identical to s_{1000}.[17]

According to Tarski, we arrive here at a statement acceptable as a general definition of truth. Formally, it is correct and adequate because it implies all the equivalences of the form (3) in which "p" has been replaced by any sentence of the language L. However, Tarski notes that this procedure cannot be followed if we are interested in the whole of the English language, specifically because the rules of English grammar do not determine precisely the form of expression we should regard as sentences. Moreover, the set of all sentences in English is potentially infinite. Still, Tarski argues, this state of affairs does not imply that the desired definition of truth for arbitrary English language sentences cannot be obtained in some other way. Just the same, Tarski seems to warn us that if we merely suppose we have an adequate use of the term *true* by any method whatsoever, then that would be a supposition leading to a contradiction.[18]

For Tarski, the simplest statement providing such a contradiction is the antinomy of the liar, which we saw earlier as the liar's paradox. Tarski

---

16. Tarski, "Truth and Proof," 65.
17. Tarski, "Truth and Proof," 65.
18. Tarski, "Truth and Proof," 65.

restates a version of this paradox. Consider the following sentence (6): the sentence printed in red on page 65 of the June 1969 issue of *Scientific American* is false. We agree to abbreviate this sentence *s*. The sentence *s* turns out to be the only sentence printed in red on page 65 of the June 1969 issue of *Scientific American*, and this entails claim (7): *s* is false if and only if the sentence printed in red on page 65 of the June 1969 issue of *Scientific American* is false. We can thus state (8) as follows—*s* is true if and only if *s*, which implies (9), which, in turn, says *s* is true if and only if the sentence printed in red on page 65 of the June 1969 issue of *Scientific American* is false. Of course, this implies the paradoxical conclusion (10): *s* is false if and only if *s* is true. This results in a contradiction in which *s* proves to be both true and false, thereby confronting us with an antinomy.[19]

Tarski then explores various ways in which we can avoid the antinomy. One radical solution he highlights is to remove the word *true* from the English vocabulary or at least to abstain from using it in any serious discussion. This move consists in adopting what Tarski calls the "nihilistic approach" to the theory of truth. In this approach, the word *true* has no independent meaning but can be used as a component of the meaningful expressions "it is true that" and "it is not true that." The meaning ascribed to these expressions is such that one can eliminate them from any sentence in which they occur. Thus, instead of saying, "It is true that all cats are animals," one can simply say, "All cats are animals." In other contexts, however, the word *true* remains meaningless. Thus, if we apply this approach to the antinomy of the liar, *s* changes to, "The sentence printed in red on page 65 in this magazine." From the nihilistic approach, Tarski concludes, this sentence is not meaningful and the antinomy vanishes.[20]

However, many uses of the word *true* are affected by this approach. According to Tarski, we could say that truth-theoretical nihilism pays lip service to some popular forms of human speech while actually removing the notion of truth from the conceptual stock of the human mind. For this reason, Tarski suggests we look for another way out of the predicament of the antinomy—a way that will keep the classical concept of truth essentially intact. Looking for this way out will force us to analyze features of the common language that seem to be the source of the antinomy of the liar. Upon closer scrutiny of this language, we notice one outstanding feature, namely, its all-comprehensive character. It provides adequate facilities

19. Tarski, "Truth and Proof," 65.
20. Tarski, "Truth and Proof," 66.

for expressing everything that can be expressed at all, and it continually expands to satisfy this requirement.[21] In addition, the language contains semantic terms such as *truth*, *name*, and *designation*, which directly or indirectly refer to the relationship between linguistic objects and what those objects express. Consequently, Tarski concludes, for every sentence we formulate in the common language, we can form another sentence in the same language to the effect that the first sentence is true or that it is false.[22]

Moreover, Tarski believes we can construct in that given language a self-referential sentence. In other words, we can construct a sentence S asserting the fact that S itself is true or that S itself is false. Suppose S asserts its own falsity. We are then able to show by a simple argument that S is both true and false, and the antinomy of the liar confronts us again. At any rate, Tarski sees no need to use universal language in all possible situations. For example, in chemistry, its discourse sometimes entails the use of names of certain special objects such as elements, atoms, and molecules but not linguistic objects such as sentences or terms. The language well-adapted to this discussion remains a restricted language and its vocabulary is limited. For this reason, it does not have to be semantically universal.[23]

Tarski believes the same dynamic applies to the language of logic and, more specifically, to the meta-logic and meta-mathematical branches of logic. The question then arises as to whether we can precisely define the notion of truth. According to Tarski, the answer to this question proves to be in the affirmative under certain conditions. The main conditions imposed on this language, Tarski observes, entails the availability of the full vocabulary and syntactical rules of sentences in that language. Moreover, those conditions also entail the precise formulation of other meaningful expressions from words listed in the vocabulary of that language. According to Tarski, the syntactical rules should be purely formal, and the function and meaning of each expression in that language should depend exclusively on its form. Tarski refers to languages satisfying these conditions as formalized languages. He believes the language of interest satisfying these conditions are those we can also translate into natural languages.[24]

Crucially, I think, is Tarski's attempted distinction between what he calls the language which he locates as the object of our interlocution and

21. Tarski, "Truth and Proof," 66–67.
22. Tarski, "Truth and Proof," 67.
23. Tarski, "Truth and Proof," 67–68.
24. Tarski, "Truth and Proof," 68.

the language wherein the definition is to be formed and its implications studied. He terms the former the object language and the latter the meta-language. For Tarski, the meta-language must be sufficiently rich, including the object language as a part. As we will see later, Tarski introduces the distinction between the meta-language and the object language to forestall the possibility of the reappearance of the antinomy, and he believes the maneuver will be successful.[25]

According to Tarski, an adequate definition of truth will imply, as consequences, partial definitions of this notion, that is, all equivalences of form (3). All sentences of the object language must also be sentences of the meta-language. In addition, the meta-language must contain names of sentences of the object language. By defining truth, Tarski suggests, we demonstrate we can introduce semantic terms in the meta-language using definitions. Moreover, Tarski warns that the meta-language, which provides sufficient means for defining truth, must remain essentially richer than the object language. The meta-language cannot coincide with or be translatable into the object-language. Otherwise, both languages would turn out to be semantically universal, and the antinomy of the liar would reappear. However, if the maneuver satisfies all these conditions, the construction of the desired definition of truth will present no difficulties.[26]

Tarski's procedure, therefore, runs as follows. First, take the simplest atomic sentence for consideration. By this suggestion, he seems to refer to a sentence with only one subject and only one verb as its essential parts. Second, define truth directly for this simple sentence. Third, form more complicated sentences from the simpler atomic sentence by the use of syntactical rules. Fourth, extend the definition of truth to the complicated compound sentences.[27]

On the basis of the definition constructed in this way, Tarski believes we can develop an entire theory of truth, deriving from that theory, encompassing all equivalences of form (3), some consequences of a general nature. For example, we can derive the laws of contradiction: no two sentences, one of which is a negation of the other, can both be true. Second, we can derive the law of excluded middle: no two such sentences can both be false.[28]

---

25. Tarski, "Truth and Proof," 76.
26. Tarski, "Truth and Proof," 68.
27. Tarski, "Truth and Proof," 68.
28. Tarski, "Truth and Proof," 68.

Even though we have a definition of truth for a scientific language in place, Tarski admits that this definition does not carry with it a workable criterion for deciding whether a particular sentence in this language is true or false. To see this state of affairs, Tarski asks us to consider, as an example, a sentence in the language of elementary high school geometry alluding to the fact that three bisectors of every triangle meet in one point. Our definition cannot tell us whether or not this sentence is true or false. Only a geometrical inquiry will enable us to decide which is actually the case. In other words, the definition of truth does not provide us with any criterion for deciding the truth and falsity of a sentence. What we need is a procedure that enables us to ascertain or negate the truth of any sentence under consideration. For Tarski, the notion of proof refers to just such a procedure of ascertaining the truths of sentences. The procedure is an essential element of the axiomatic method.[29]

What does the axiomatic method entail? Tarski proposes four cornerstones of this method. First, every discipline begins with a list of a small number of sentences called axioms intuitively evident and recognized as true without further justifications. Second, every discipline accepts no other sentences unless the discipline can prove the sentence with the exclusive help of axioms along with sentences previously proved. Sentences recognizable as true by virtue of these first two principles get categorized as theorems or provable sentences of the given discipline. Third, make an initial list of undefined or primitive terms whose meaning appear to be directly understandable and usable without needing to explain their meanings. Fourth, agree not to use additional terms unless we can explain its meaning by defining it with primitive terms, along with terms previously defined. These four principles, Tarski thinks, stand as cornerstones of the axiomatic method.[30]

However, the concept of the axiomatic method underwent a profound evolution in the nineteenth and twentieth centuries by the introduction of the notion of formal proof, initially proposed by Gottlob Frege. The first step toward supplying a mathematical theory with the notion of a formal proof is the formalization of the language of the theory. The use of formal syntactical rules enables us to distinguish a sentence from a non-sentential expression by merely examining its form. The second step entailed formulating rules of inference that seemed intuitively infallible in the sense that

29. Tarski, "Truth and Proof," 69–70.
30. Tarski, "Truth and Proof," 74.

THE CORRESPONDENCE CONCEPTION OF TRUTH

sentences directly derivable from true sentences using these rules must themselves be true. One such rule, of course, is *modus ponens*. The next step is to apply the rules of proof to axioms and obtain new sentences directly derivable from the axioms. We then apply the same rules to new sentences and obtain further sentences. If, after a finite number of steps, we arrive at a given sentence, we conclude that the sentence has been formally proved.[31]

The question, then, that Tarski confronts is whether the formal proof is actually an adequate procedure for acquiring proof and whether the set of all provable sentences coincides with the set of all true sentences. Tarski refers this problem to the arithmetic of natural numbers. He begins with the vocabulary of the theory, thinking of them as consisting of variables such as m, n, and p, representing natural numbers. They consist of numerals such as 0, 1, and 2, denoting particular numbers. They also consist of symbols such as =, +, <, and >, denoting some familiar relations between numbers and operations on numbers. They finally consist of certain logical terms such as *and, or, if,* and *not* as well as quantifiers.[32]

According to Tarski, taking this language as the object language enables us to construct an appropriate meta-language and formulate it in an adequate definition of truth. More precisely, the definition of truth states that a certain condition formulated in the meta-language is satisfied by all the elements of this set, which are true sentences, and only by these elements. Within the framework of this meta-theory, Tarski believes we can formulate and solve the problem of whether the set of provable sentences coincides with that of true sentences.[33]

We begin by arranging all sentences in an infinite sequence and then number them consecutively. In this way, we establish a one-to-one correspondence between sentences and numbers, which, in turn, leads to a similar correspondence between sets of sentences and sets of numbers. We can, in particular, consider numbers of provable sentences and numbers of true sentences, briefly calling them provable^0 numbers and true^0 numbers. We then reduce our main problem to the following question: are the set of provable^0 numbers and the set of true^0 numbers identical?[34]

Tarski's demonstration may be seen to run as follows: if the set of true^0 numbers could be defined in the language of arithmetic, the antinomy of

31. Tarski, "Truth and Proof," 74–75.
32. Tarski, "Truth and Proof," 75.
33. Tarski, "Truth and Proof," 75–76.
34. Tarski, "Truth and Proof," 76.

the liar could actually be reconstructed in this language. But no expression with an empirical context, such as "the sentence printed in such-and-such place," would occur in the new formulation. This sentence played an essential part in the original formulation of the antinomy of the liar. The antinomy of the liar would, therefore, not be reconstructed in this formulation. Hence, the set of provable^0 numbers is definable in the language of arithmetic, but the set of true^0 numbers is not definable in the language of arithmetic. For this reason, the set of provable^0 numbers does not coincide with the set of true^0 numbers. Furthermore, this result shows that in no domain of mathematics is the notion of provability a perfect substitute for the notion of truth, and so the original triumph of the formal method has been followed by a serious setback. Just the same, proof is still the only method to ascertain the truth of sentences within any specific mathematical theory. The notion of truth remains an ideal limit that can never be reached, but it is a limit we try to approximate by gradually widening the set of provable sentences.[35] This completes our brief survey of Tarski's semantic theory. I will suspend an evaluation of this view to a later section in this chapter. For now, let me turn to a defense of the correspondence theory of truth provided by Patricia Marino.

PATRICIA MARINO'S DEFENSE OF THE MODEST CORRESPONDENCE THEORY OF TRUTH

Patricia Marino defends a version of the correspondence theory, which she calls a Modest Correspondence Theory of Truth, or MCT for short. She locates certain features that function in certain ways in a manner she believes renders her version of the correspondence theory both plausible and distinctive,[36] thus making it immune from collapsing into versions of rival theories. Let me offer an overview of the five features of MCT. The first feature contends that true sentences, statements, and beliefs correspond to the way things are in the world. She calls this feature Correspondence Platitude.[37] The second feature contends that a gap exists between a sentence and the fact it expresses underscored by the fact that worldly conditions that make a sentence S true are not always best expressed by S. She calls

---

35. Tarski, "Truth and Proof," 77.
36. Marino, "What Should," 447.
37. Marino, "What Should," 420.

this feature Cleavage.[38] The third feature holds that truth is a property, suggesting that all true statements have one thing in common. She calls this feature Property-hood.[39] The fourth feature holds that true sentences, if not true in virtue of form, must be true of something. She calls this feature Content-Implication.[40] The fifth and final feature she locates is that of Descriptiveness, which maintains that true sentences function descriptively and in small-scale and wholesale ways that can go wrong. When they succeed, however, we can explain why and how.[41]

Marino defends each of these features throughout her innovative paper and, in the process, provides an overall defense of her version of the correspondence theory. In order to see how she does this, let me begin by outlining her defense of the first feature, which will then be followed by an examination of her defense of the other features.

Marino's Correspondence Platitude

As already noted, Marino presents the feature of Correspondence Platitude as follows: true sentences, statements, and beliefs correspond to the way things are in the world. She notes, however, that the formulation of this feature is common to many views of truth specifically because it can, apparently, be easily reinterpreted. For example, a coherent theory could find the feature acceptable if the expression "corresponds to" means "is appropriately consistent with" and if "the way things are in the world" means "the set of sentences we already believe."[42]

However, correspondence theorists restrict what is meant by "the way things are in the world" to apply only to the "mind-independent, raw, unconceptualized external world." One might add that the correspondence is then a congruence relation or, for that matter, a mirroring relation between a statement and mind-independent world.[43]

Marino also notes how, historically, proponents of the correspondence theory have defined a true sentence as one that corresponds to a fact. Thus, consider a sentence such as "Snow is white and grass is green." Such

38. Marino, "What Should," 424.
39. Marino, "What Should," 427.
40. Marino, "What Should," 430–31.
41. Marino, "What Should," 437.
42. Marino, "What Should," 420.
43. Marion, "What Should," 420.

a sentence is true if and only if both conjuncts are true, and each conjunct is true if a fact exists to which it corresponds. Also, theories associated with the logical atomists follow a similar direction wherein a sentence gets broken down into logically simple pieces called atomic facts. The atomic facts, therefore, are true if and only if a state of affairs exists to which they correspond. The important thing to note is that in each case, truth finds its basis in a correspondence between bits of language and bits of mind-independent, raw, external reality.[44]

Marino, however, thinks the deeper intuition is that correspondence is to "how things are" and that facts are merely introduced to make the theory tidier. She proposes keeping the Correspondence Platitude as it is and taking facts to be only contingently associated with correspondence. For Marino, facts are as they are independently of how we conceptualize them, and the independence relation is special and distinctive.[45] Also, she argues that insofar as the correspondence theorist wants to say that truth consists in a relation between language and world, the theorist should be able to give what Marino calls "a non-trivial explanation" of the connection between a sentence and the worldly conditions that make it true. This suggestion leads her to propose the feature of Cleavage for the correspondence theorist.[46]

Marino on Cleavage

According to this feature, Marino argues, a gap exists between a sentence and the fact it expresses. The gap manifests itself in variation in the sense a sentence S does not always best express the worldly conditions that make S true. The gap also manifests itself in non-repeating truth-conditions in the sense that S always gives its own truth conditions. To illustrate these points, Marino draws our attention to the scientific examples of how scientists determined that the presence of combustion gave air a certain quality, leading them to conclude that the air had absorbed something in the process, which they called phlogiston.[47] The scientists thought that the presence of too much phlogiston impeded combustion and its absence supported it. Later, scientists discovered the error in this theory. What they ascribed to

44. Marino, "What Should," 421.
45. Marino, "What Should," 421–22.
46. Marino, "What Should," 423.
47. Marino, "What Should," 423.

the presence of phlogiston was really due to the absence of oxygen, and conversely.[48]

Marino brings this fact to bear on the correspondence theory. In some cases, we would appropriately say the following: the truth-conditions of "*x* has discharged phlogiston" are best understood as "*x* has taken in oxygen." This serves to show that the sentence itself does not best express its own truth conditions. For Marino, this explanation is a nontrivial way of locating the connection between a sentence and worldly conditions that make it true. Such explanations can also be present when a statement does seem to provide its own truth conditions.[49] These claims outline Marino's take on Cleavage, which seem, in turn, to lead to her third feature, namely, the feature of Property-hood.

Marino on Property-hood

Marino also notes that the insistence of correspondence theorists that truth is a property susceptible to analysis partly characterizes their position. Insofar as the correspondence theorist takes truth to consist in a relation between language and world, the theorist had better acknowledge that other sorts of relations ought not come by the truth label so easily. In a certain sense, Marino contends, the Property-hood of truth matters. If the correspondence theorist wants to stay faithful to his project and avoid collapsing into deflationism, he or she should incorporate the feature of Property-hood into his or her theory.[50]

Marino presents the central tenet of Property-hood with respect to truth as follows: truth is a property, implying that all true statements have one thing in common. Part of what this tenet implies is that different truths cannot be considered in complete isolation or receive unconnected analyses without further comment. Strong Property-hood is the name she gives the contention that all true statements have one thing in common. In contrast to the non-factualism of the ethical skeptic, strong Property-hood suggests one feature of interest among correspondence theorists, namely, that true sentences are either true in virtue of their form (i.e., logically valid) or are true of something. For the correspondence theorists, if true sentences are not true in virtue of form, they must be true of something. Hence, truth and

48. Marino, "What Should," 424.
49. Marino, "What Should," 425.
50. Marino, "What Should," 426.

existence are related, and what we say about truth will have implications for what we say about realism (about debates over what things *really* exist).[51]

This position runs contrary to the ethical skeptic's position who suspects that ethical claims cannot be describing some kind of special ethical reality specifically because he or she believes no such thing exists.[52] However, Marino correctly notes that in practice, we use ethical claims as if they can be true or false, and we do call them true or false. True sentences are true of something. Hence, if ethical claims are true, and they are not true of some ethical realm, we are forced to wonder what realm they describe.[53] For Marino, these concerns pressurize error theorists to respond to the Content Implication feature.[54]

Marino on Content Implication

According to Marino, the Content Implication feature runs as follows: if true sentences are not true in virtue of form, they must be true of something. For this reason, sentences whose subject matter we have doubts over cannot both be true and taken at face value. Either they are true assertions or they are not, or they must be reinterpreted to have different content. The correspondence theory of truth ought to tell us something about how to approach suspected cases of non-factuality. This approach seems to involve linking truth to ontology specifically because we are concerned about the role of the objects involved.

In order to understand what this link entails, consider mathematical statements. Suppose mathematical objects do not exist. We are left wondering what mathematical statements represent. If mathematical objects exist, we must want to figure out how we arrive at our knowledge of them. If they do not exist, we are left wondering what explains their seeming objectivity. We are left wondering how to explain our feeling that something right exists about statements of basic arithmetic such that we would be wrong to deny them.[55]

Moreover, for statements concerning a given subject X to be accepted as straightforwardly true, we must answer the questions of ontology, of

- 51. Marino, "What Should," 427.
- 52. Marino, "What Should," 427.
- 53. Marino, "What Should," 429.
- 54. Marino, "What Should," 430.
- 55. Marino, "What Should," 433–34.

epistemology, of objectivity, and of justification. With respect to ontology, we must answer the question of what the object of *X* is. With respect to epistemology, we must answer the question of how we arrive at our knowledge of the object. With respect to objectivity, we must answer the question of what we are trying to be faithful toward if the object does not exist, and with respect to justification, we must respond to why we reason as if the object exists if, in fact, the object does not exist. According to Marino, Independence-Congruence seems to deliver in its grounding of other features on this perspective: if true statements mirror a mind-independent world, we will not only have immediate ties to features such as Cleavage and Content Implication; we will also recreate similar ties to ontology, epistemology, objectivity, and justification. All we need is just something about the feature of descriptiveness, namely: true statements aim at describing the world.[56] Let me now turn to this feature.

Marino on Descriptiveness

Marino explains the feature of Descriptiveness as follows: true statements function descriptively in small-scale and wholesale ways that can go wrong; when they succeed, we can explain why and how.[57] More broadly, Descriptiveness tells us that a need exists to reconcile surface syntax and semantics with underlying content: true statements aim at describing the world. However, they can go wrong in small-scale and wholesale ways. When they do, we must work to show how we can reconcile surface syntax and semantics with underlying content.[58] Descriptiveness, Marino argues, would explain Cleavage, namely, a gap exists between a sentence and the worldly conditions that make it true. Moreover, Cleavage, together with Propertyhood, would deliver on Content-Implication such that if something fails to function descriptively in the right way, we must find some treatment where we restore descriptiveness.[59] Thus, Marino concludes, scientists erroneously described no-combustibility with the phlogiston case because they confused the absence of oxygen for the presence of phlogiston, causing the epistemologist to use terms that failed to link correctly with the world it

---

56. Marino, "What Should," 434.
57. Marino, "What Should," 437.
58. Marino, "What Should," 435.
59. Marino, "What Should," 435.

described. However, they succeeded in tracking important features of the world.[60]

Hence, Marino argues, with our non-repeating truth-conditions we can locate the actual features of the world that those were and outline the connection between our statements and the facts of our world we seemed unable to describe successfully. In some cases, she notes, we will appropriately say, "The truth conditions of 'x has discharged phlogiston' are best understood as 'x has taken oxygen.'" The treatments that Content-Implication suggests are all ways of restoring proper descriptive function. It tells us that true sentences, if not analytically true or, for that matter, logically true must be true of something. This observation runs contrary to the position held by the ethical skeptic because in this case ethical statements would not be both true and taken at face value. They are either not true, or not assertions at all, or must be reinterpreted to have different content.[61]

According to Marino, when we combine these five features, we formulate MCT. Consider a correspondence theory of this sort based on science. With a theory of this kind, true sentences correspond to how things are. They do so not in a mind-independent objective world but in the ordinary world with which we interact every day as we try to understand it through experiment and observation. Marino thinks such an approach can meet the features of MCT, owing to the fact that the ordinary world with which we interact is what we describe, and our descriptions can go wrong in both small-scale and wholesale ways. A good example for small-scale error is when we thought weight and mass were synonymous. A good example for wholesale error is when we rejected the whole theory of humors as a representation of our basic personality types.[62]

What matters is that in the case of science, our interaction with the world allowed us, apparently, to examine, criticize, and analyze connections, though in a limited, piecemeal way. Moreover, we do not need to insist that all true statements work in the same way. Rather, we acknowledge that statements of science provide a sort of gold standard due to the fact that they are susceptible to examination, analysis, and criticism. They remain paradigmatic for truth because they offer for us a context in which we seem most sure of deciding what consists of truth.[63]

60. Marino, "What Should," 435.
61. Marino, "What Should," 435.
62. Marino, "What Should," 437.
63. Marino, "What Should," 438.

DAVID LEWIS'S OBJECTION TO THE CORRESPONDENCE THEORY

David Lewis raises his objections against two principal versions of the correspondence theory, suggesting that one version does not go beyond the redundancy theory, namely, p is true if and only if p. Neither does it conflict with the coherence, pragmatic, and epistemic theories. The second version, according to Lewis, fails to satisfy its own slogan, namely, truth is correspondence to fact. It also fails to satisfy its claim that it is a theory of truth rather than a bundle of claims having nothing in particular to do with fact.[64]

The first version outlines its commitment to the claim that p is true if and only if p. An example of this would be, "*Cats purr* is true if and only if cats purr." Let me call this claim (1). According to Lewis, saying that cats purr is true remains synonymous with calling it a truth that cats purr. That statement is, in turn, synonymous with calling it a fact that cats purr or with claiming that such a fact as cats purr really exists. According to Lewis, a fact of this usage is nothing other than a true proposition. Similarly, saying that pigs fly is false remains synonymous with calling it a falsehood that pigs fly or with saying that there is no such fact that pigs fly.

On this usage, Lewis admits, truth is correspondence to fact and each truth corresponds to fact by being identical to that fact. Moreover, and this seems to be Lewis's objection, the correspondence theory on this usage remains utterly vacuous. The only work it does is by the redundancy biconditionals we find in its postulates. According to Lewis, the correspondence theory fails to go beyond the redundancy theory on this usage. To be sure, Lewis adds, the correspondence theory does not even go as far as the redundancy theory. Additionally, its claim that truth is correspondence to fact does not conflict with any rival theory of truth. The only conflicting thing is the redundancy biconditionals joined in alliance with the claim, and an adherent of the coherence, pragmatic, or epistemic theory of truth would not deny that truth is correspondence or identical to fact on this usage.[65]

The second version of the correspondence theory may be construed as follows: truth is correspondence to Tractarian facts or a state of affairs. When we make this claim, we get what Armstrong calls the truth-maker

---

64. Lewis, "Forget About," 276.
65. Lewis, "Forget About," 276–77.

principle, which is, indeed, a version of the correspondence theory of truth. Stated formally, it runs as follows: for every truth a truth-maker exists. In other words, for every true proposition, something T exists such that the existence of T implies the proposition in question. According to Lewis, the truth-maker principle is certainly not vacuous though it may be wrong in letter and may stand in need of rearticulation. Moreover, the theory goes beyond the redundancy biconditionals. It also conflicts with the coherence, pragmatic, and epistemic theories specifically because it seems manifestly *a priori*.[66]

However, Lewis finds two problems with this theory. For what reason, he asks, does the truth-maker principle deserve the correspondence theory? He does not see how having a truth-maker amounts to the same thing as correspondence to a fact. If Tractarian facts exist, each of them is a truth-maker at least for the truth that "at least one Tractarian fact exists." However, some things exist that are also not Tractarian facts. For example, if nonfacts exist, each of them is a truth-maker for the truth that at least one nonfact exists. In this case, at least one truth-maker is not a fact.[67]

Second, the reason why the correspondence theory of truth is a theory of truth remains unclear, according to Lewis. It seems to be a theory of all manner of things and not a theory of truth in particular. Whatever we learn about truth does not come from that theory; rather, it comes from the allied redundancy biconditionals. Lewis considers the instance of the truth-maker principle that "it is true that cats purr if and only if T exists such that T's existence implies that cats purr." Let's call this (2).[68] According to Lewis, given the redundancy biconditional of claim (1), (2) is equivalent to a third claim (3): cats purr if and only if something T exists such that the existence of T implies that cats purr.[69]

Notice what remains at stake here, and Lewis points it out: T tells us nothing about truth. Claim (3) is not about the existential grounding of the purring of cats. Similarly, all other instances of the truth-maker principle are equivalent, given the redundancy biconditionals, to biconditionals about the existential grounding of all manner of things rather than about truth. Hence, the truth-maker principle amounts to a bundle of claims,

---

66. Lewis, "Forget About," 277–78.
67. Lewis, "Forget About," 278.
68. Lewis, "Forget About," 278.
69. Lewis, "Forget About," 279.

none of which are about truth at all. For this reason, it should not be called a theory of truth.[70]

Vision, however, disagrees with Lewis's objection. Vision draws our attention to the following claim: saying it is true that cats purr is synonymous with calling it a fact that cats purr. Vision then asks us to assume with Lewis that this statement fails the first two conditions laid out by Lewis. In other words, it should, first, fail to go beyond claim (1): it is true that cats purr if and only if cats purr. Second, it should conflict with the coherence, pragmatic, and epistemic theories. If the satisfaction of these conditions is what a correspondence theory needs to do, Vision argues that no defender of the correspondence theory would want it.[71]

In addition, Vision turns to Lewis's argument against the second version of the Correspondence Theory of Truth. Vision notes how in this argument the fact in question is supposed to be a Tractarian fact, also called states of affairs. Vision finds Lewis's characterization of Armstrong's Tractarian facts very latitudinarian, that is, beyond the fact of it being a worldly item, and he makes this conclusion for the following reason: why even events would not count as facts seems hard to see. According to Vision, Lewis's argument is baffling. Unless one thinks that substituting the right-hand side means truth is no longer an issue as we find in claim (3), Vision can find no grounds for preferring Lewis's deflating inference to Vision's alternative truth-revelatory inference.[72]

Moreover, Vision thinks that the redundancy theory in (3) says more than what (1) says. It adds to the proviso that truth lacks metaphysical implications or a certain sort of implication. Vision thinks that the redundancy theory is a loose collection of views in which this lack includes the claim that "is true" is not a predicate and that truth is not a property. But if it is a property, it is one without a nature; hence, there is no problem of truth. The other alternative seems to be that truth-conditions no longer exist for propositions in which "is true" is predicated on them, and if there are any, they remain deflated in much the same way as the predicate gets deflated. The problem here, though, is that this alternative goes well beyond claim (1) because it is an unforced interpretation of its impact.[73]

---

70. Lewis, "Forget About," 279.
71. Vision, "Lest We Forget," 137.
72. Vision, "Lest We Forget," 138.
73. Vision, "Lest We Forget," 138–39.

Moreover, Vision argues that if we take a phrase such as "a worldly state of affairs" broadly enough to include things such as events, situations, or moments, we would hardly see how a truth could fail to have some worldly states of affairs as its truth maker. Qualifying such states of affairs is reasonable for certain propositions such as "goblins do not exist." Just the same, the state of the world makes such a statement true specifically because truth-makers may include conventional and perhaps even fictional items whose propositions are reducible to truths of distinct ontological kinds.[74]

According to Vision, then, the obvious point is that if Lewis holds that these sorts of truth-makers are required, how we could classify Lewis as a redundancy theorist remains difficult to see. The denial of this sort is precisely what motivates the theory. Hence, if Lewis is not a redundancy theorist, he may not be a coherentist, a pragmatist, or even an epistemic theorist specifically because each of these gets ruled out by his acceptance of claim (1), which he finds incompatible with those views.[75]

A CRITIQUE OF THE CORRESPONDENCE THEORY

The definitional aspect of the correspondence theory of truth seems rather uncontroversial, perhaps even intuitive. Except for one caveat I will locate, I find nothing seriously anomalous with the claim that true statements correspond to facts of the world while false ones do not. Notice the intuitiveness of the first conjunct, namely, that true statements correspond to facts of the world. Thus, the intuitiveness of the claim that "cats purr" is true if and only if cats purr seems too obvious to merit any serious objection. Nor should the falsehood counterpart of this theory lead us to question its intuitiveness, namely, "pigs fly" is false if and only if pigs do not fly. Lewis apparently thinks that this kind of characterization seems widely accepted by pragmatists, deflationists, and epistemic theorists. Lewis, however, finds this fact about the correspondence theory to be rather innocuous against other rival theories, thereby denying the correspondence theorist any claim to some kind of special privilege as a custodian of truth. I will return to Lewis's charge later in this section. For now, let me focus on the apparent intuitive nature of the correspondence theory.

---

74. Vision, "Lest We Forget," 139.
75. Vision, "Lest We Forget," 140.

THE CORRESPONDENCE CONCEPTION OF TRUTH

This theory seems to have the advantage of universal acceptance. Apparently, philosophers and non-philosophers presuppose, consciously or unconsciously, the correspondence theory of truth when verifying statements of ordinary language. For example, if we want to verify the claim that Jack killed Jill on September 10, 1985, we only need to appeal to some kind of testimonial evidence in the external mind-independent world. We will, quite possibly, try to discover the kinds of people who witnessed the murder, the time at which the murder took place, and the method by which Jill was murdered. We will also try to establish which "Jack" we are discussing by appealing to specific descriptions that help us locate the exact person who murdered Jill. In short, the practical aspect that follow the definition of the correspondence theory of truth seems rather intuitive. Denying this fact would seem rather odd. Nothing seems to go awry with the belief that if a statement is true, it will correspond to the external world. Upon closer scrutiny of this definition, however, we begin to run into uncomfortable territories.

What seems to be an issue, then, in the definitional aspect of the correspondence theory of truth is its exclusive nature, namely, its apparent insinuation that the only true statements are those that correspond to the facts in the world. Indeed, this exclusive nature seems semantically implied by the conjunctive definition presented earlier, namely, true statements correspond to facts of the world and false ones do not. The second conjunct of this definition, to the effect that false statements do not correspond to the facts of the external world, may actually be incorrect. More specifically, suppose we define falsehood as follows: a statement is false if and only if it does not correspond to the external facts in the world. Accepting this claim may yield some difficulty if we fail to make important qualifications. Apparently, some true statements do not seem to correspond to facts in the world. For example, the law of noncontradiction, call it C, does not seem to correspond to any facts in the world. The facticity of this law seems contained in the law itself rather than in something external to C. In other words, upon examining the statement C that reads, "'p and not-p' is false," one knows *a priori* that C is true and that its contrary, not-C, is false without appealing to external facts to prove the claim. If this supposition is correct, we can cite at least one example outside the definitional correspondence theory of truth that seems true without appealing to facts external to the world.

Quite possibly, however, an objector to this critique of the correspondence theory of truth will make a fairly plausible comeback. The objector might note, for example, that the law of noncontradiction may, after all, be accurately descriptive of a specific instance of falsehood. It may be deemed as describing a non-obtaining state of affairs, a state whose being remains existentially impossible. Non-obtaining states of affairs may be regarded as non-facts. Accurate descriptions of non-obtaining states of affairs are, therefore, true and reliable, instructing the inquirer of what he or she should not expect to find in the external mind-independent world. Of course, the truth table method reveals that the law of non-contradiction is logically true and that its denial entails a contradiction. Described in this way, the law of non-contradiction may be seen to correspond to non-obtaining states of affairs in the world. Does this explanation rescue the correspondence theory of truth from the criticism that its definition does not cover the law of non-contradiction?

The law of non-contradiction, of course, is not the only claim we can appeal to in our attempt to show that the definitional aspect of the correspondence theory of truth, as presented herein, is too restrictive. Statements such as "no one is taller than himself" seem intuitive enough to help ground our feeling that the definitional aspect of the correspondence theory seems to exclude claims belonging to rival theories that appear to be true without appealing to external, mind-independent evidence or facts. Perhaps, then, rather than say that only true statements are those corresponding to the external world and that false ones do not, we could provide a weaker definition of the correspondence theory of truth such as the one earlier adumbrated: "All statements corresponding to the external world are true." This statement, however, is no longer a definition of truth. It seems to be a definition of the state of correspondence to the external world. More accurately, it seems to capture what "corresponding to the external world" implies.

With respect to Tarski's reformulation of the correspondence theory of truth, recall how he draws our attention to the liar's paradox. After giving an example of this paradox, Tarski shows how, apparently, acceptable premises of a given argument yield a contradiction following a series of inferential steps. In other words, the argument under consideration yields statement (8) of the following form: s is false if and only if s is true. Tarski takes this problem seriously enough to merit an attempt, on his part, to diffuse the contradiction. As noted, one method Tarski uses is to distinguish between what he calls "the object language" and "the meta-language," thereby suggesting that claim (8) be relegated to the level of object language.

Our decision, therefore, that the paradox is contradictory is made at the meta-language level.

Whereas Tarski's approach seems successful, we can also employ the method of self-referential incoherence in which a statement S self-stultifies by affirming and negating itself simultaneously. Take claim (8) as an example again. It reads, s is false if and only if s is true. Following the truth-table method, we discover at once that under no state of affairs will such a statement be true. In other words, the statement is logically false. Any standard logic text will show that logically false statements are self-contradictory, which, of course, is what we have been thinking about claim (8). They are self-contradictory because they remain essentially meaningless; thus, the liar's paradox is self-contradictory and essentially meaningless. It is self-referentially incoherent.

Perhaps the self-defeating nature of the liar's paradox will become clearer when we state it differently. Essentially, the utterer of the paradox seems to say "I speak the truth that I always do not speak the truth." Let me use the letter T to denote the "I speak the truth" clause and A to denote "I always do not speak the truth" clause. If T is true, then A is false. A, however, cannot be true because A has asserted its own falsity, so both T and A are false. Tarski's observation, therefore, that if s is true then s is false is really a self-defeating observation. Some philosophers employ this line of thinking to address the paradox, and I think their method is successful.[76]

Tarski also draws our attention to his concern that definitions of true statements do not, by themselves, prove the truths of those statements. The notion of proof is the procedure we need to ascertain the truths of sentences. This procedure revolutionized modern logic through the work of Gottlob Frege. The procedure employed the rules of logical inference to prove truths of a given sentence, the most famous of which, according to Tarski, is *modus ponens*. This observation by Tarski should strike anyone interested in the development of theories of truth as quite interesting.

In order to see this, I will use the letter F to denote the method of formal proof Tarski mentions—the method used by logicians to demonstrate the truth of certain axioms, or theorems, or derivations from axioms and theorems. The interesting thing to note here is that the use of F seems to employ the coherence theory of proof to prove the correspondence theory. Consider, for example, a re-expression of *modus ponens* as a conditional statement: if Fido is a dog implies that Fido is an animal, and Fido is a

---

76. See, for example, Geisler, *Christian Apologetics*, 141–45.

dog, then Fido is an animal. The set of atomic statements in this example could be labeled as follows: $A=\{$Fido is a dog implies Fido is an animal; Fido is a dog; Fido is an animal$\}$. Notice that the set has three members, even though it has only two atomic statements, namely "Fido is a dog" and "Fido is an animal." Since we know that *modus ponens* is, itself, a valid argument, re-expressing it as a conditional statement yields a theorem. A theorem is always logically true. Moreover, given these facts about *modus ponens*, the members of set A form a consistent set of statements. A set of statements is consistent if and only if the statements that form the members of that set are all possibly true.

Following different philosophers subscribing to the coherence theory of truth, it is the view that a sentence is true if and only if the sentence remains consistent with other sets of sentences in its universe of discourse, consistent in the sense that all members of that set can be true when conjoined. In order for a correspondence theorist to see whether the set of statements under consideration are true, he or she will have to employ the formal proof system, which seems to be a move coherence theorists find acceptable. Whether or not this state of affairs implies that the correspondence theory may, after all, collapse into the coherence theory of truth remains highly debatable. However, the correspondence theory of truth seems to need the coherence theory to establish the truth of its claim, assuming Tarski's observation about formal proof of axioms is correct.

A further concern we find with the attempt to define the correspondence theory of truth is Tarski's admission that a setback afflicts the formal method of ascertaining the truth of sentences specifically because the number of provable sentences is not identical to the number of true sentences. In other words, we cannot establish a one-to-one correspondence between sets of sentences and sets of numbers. This fact is evidenced by the observation that no expression with an empirical context would occur in the formulation of sentences definable in the language of arithmetic. Whereas this state of affairs has the advantage of avoiding the liar paradox, it demonstrates that provability cannot be substituted with the notion of truth.

The result of this finding leaves the idea of truth undecided under Tarski's semantic method. Tarski himself admits that the notion of truth remains an ideal limit, but it can never be reached even though we try to approximate it by gradually widening the set of provable sentences. Although Tarski's method is valiantly presented, it leaves several questions unanswered. For example, we are left wondering whether his very admission, that the notion of truth cannot be reached, is itself true or not. If that notion cannot be reached, then the statement that the notion of truth cannot be reached is false. However, if it can be reached, then the claim that it cannot be reached seems to conflict with Tarski's admission. The oddity itself falls prey to the very paradox Tarski is trying to avoid. Hence, whereas Tarski offers very helpful suggestions on how to tackle the paradox head-on, his admission seems to resign back into the paradox he is trying to solve. We can only use the suggestions he makes about distinguishing between the object language and the meta-language in avoiding the paradox. Beyond that, we remain helpless.

Let me now turn to Marino's account of the correspondence theory of truth to see whether, coupled with Tarski's, we will arrive at a more comprehensive understanding. Marino's description of the correspondence "with respect to 'how things are'" as opposed to correspondence "with respect to 'external mind-independent facts about the world'" seems helpful in accounting for true statements that appear to have no corresponding states of affairs with the external world. For example, one could say that in our world, the state of affairs is such that one cannot be dead and not dead simultaneously. Neither can we expect to see a state of affairs where triangles are not three-sided figures, or one in which someone is taller than himself or herself, or even one where bachelors are not single adult males. These kinds of states of affairs do not obtain in our world. As noted earlier, they are non-obtaining states of affairs. Statements that address these non-obtaining states of affairs correspond to them by offering an adequate description of what we would not expect to find if we observed our world. Admittedly, statements of these kinds do not claim to be comprehensively descriptive of our world. More importantly, the set of statements offering an adequate description of non-obtaining states of affairs in our world seems to be infinite. Hence, we cannot come up with a comprehensive list of these statements. However, I press the point that Marino helps us see how her distinction between "how things are" and "how things correspond to facts" helps to include statements that seemed invisible to initial definitions of the correspondence theory of truth.

Marino also draws attention to what she calls Property-hood with respect to truth. She seems to be referring to the idea that the expression "is-true" can be legitimately predicated of a subject as a property of that subject. Her use of this term in this way is an objection to the deflationist's account of truth—especially the account that prefers to drop the "is-true" predicate in their affirmations of certain propositions. Recall that a deflationist prefers to say, for example, that "snow is white" rather than to say "'snow is white' is true." According to Tarski, they do this to avoid, among other things, the liar's paradox.

How can we capture the Property-hood of truth? When we say "'snow is white' is true," what property are we ascribing to that statement? Part of the answer to that question, I think, is that we ascribe the idea that the statement in question is describing a certain aspect of perceived reality—an understanding of how things are from the speaker's perspective. If a certain claim is true, it seems to capture a certain aspect of reality. Hence, truth, we may say, predicates the notion of reality as a property of the subject.

Let me now draw attention to Lewis's charge that the correspondence theory does not seem to go beyond the redundancy theory.[77] According to Lewis, the correspondence theorist's formulation of truth seems to comport with the redundancy theorist's formulation such as the following: it is true that "cats purr" if and only if cats purr. Exactly what Lewis means by the redundancy theory remains largely unclear now that we have considered Tarski's view. If by redundancy he means "circularity," which is what some versions of redundancy could plausibly mean, then I think Tarski has addressed that concern sufficiently by restating the left side of the biconditional in a noncircular fashion.

Following Tarski, for example, we can restate the correspondence theory of truth adumbrated by Lewis in a noncircular way: "The string of letters beginning with the letter C, followed by the letter A, followed by the letter T, followed by the letter S, followed by another string of letters beginning with the letter P, followed by the letter U, followed by the letter R, followed by another letter R is true if and only if cats purr." With Tarski, we note that this definition says essentially the same thing as what Lewis calls claim (1),[78] even though it may not be as elegant as we would wish for it to be.

However, I would be surprised if Lewis is unaware of this approach by Tarski, and perhaps Lewis would complain that my reading of his critique of the correspondence theory erroneously accuses him of charging the theory with circularity. In other words, Lewis would possibly deny that by suggesting the correspondence theory does not go beyond the redundancy

---

77. Lewis, "Forget About," 277.
78. Lewis, "Forget About," 275.

theory, he means something different from my circularity charge. Assuming he means something different, what, then, does he mean?

The other option available would be the deflationist's account, one that drops the "is true" predicate from the sentence it is trying to modify. Claim (1), then, would read, "Cats purr if and only if cats purr." If this is what Lewis means, Tarski has taken pains to maintain the "is true" predicate on the left side of the biconditional in a way that remains uncommitted to the deflationist's account. Therefore, whether Lewis means "circularity" or "deflationism" by his redundancy theory, neither of these meanings remain similar to the correspondence theory of truth. Indeed, the correspondence theory seems to demonstrate a rather marked difference from the redundancy theory, no matter what Lewis might mean by that appellation.

Lewis also seems to suggest that the correspondence theory does not go beyond the pragmatic theory. He does not seem to justify this position at length except to note that an adherent of the coherence or pragmatic or epistemic theory of truth has no business denying that truth is correspondence to fact and that he should offer us his coherence or pragmatic or epistemic theory of what it is to be a fact. If, by pragmatism, we have in mind the theory of thinkers such as William James and Richard Rorty, their definitions of true statements seem markedly different from the correspondence theory of truth's definition. The basic motif of the pragmatic theory is its claim that true statements are those we find useful, that is, those that work. What we find in the correspondence theorist's definition, however, is far more removed in its tenets and postulates from the pragmatic theory, especially when we take Marino's formulation into consideration. For this reason, I cannot agree with Lewis that the correspondence theory does not go beyond the pragmatic theory.

At any rate, I did wonder earlier in this critique if Tarski's proof of the truth of statements using the formal system of proof collapsed into the coherence theory of truth. If that is the case, then Lewis may be right in suggesting that the correspondence theory would, perhaps, not go beyond the coherence theory of truth. Marino seems to give a promising way out in her recapitulation of the definition of facts as "the way things are." Whether her redefinition of facts here helps us to see the difference between the coherence theory and the correspondence theory remains debatable. Whereas it seems rather intuitive in its postulates, it might remain vulnerable to the charge that other intuitively true statements remain invisible to its definition of facts.

In short, though promising in its initial attempt to formulate an adequate theory of truth, the correspondence theory formulation falls short and fails to account for the nature of truth. Consider that with the correspondence theory, statements are true if and only if they correspond to the external world. This reading of truth remains heavily contingent upon statement-makers such as ourselves. As noted earlier, the correspondence theory of truth is a view more consistent with methodological naturalism. Just the same, a methodological naturalist would not explain, consistently, how truth would have been conceived before the arrival of humans into the universal scene. This is because, prior to our arrival into the universe, truth would not exist—at least not in the way the Judeo-Christian conception thinks it did exist. Perhaps we will have better luck with a different version of truth. I now turn to the coherence theory of truth.

7

The Coherence Theory of Truth

According to Alan R. White's entry in the *Encyclopedia of Philosophy*, the coherence theory of truth is characteristic of the great rationalist system-building metaphysicians Leibniz, Spinoza, Hegel, and Bradley, among others. This view holds that a statement is true if and only if it coheres with a system of other statements and false if it does not. The statement is a member of a system whose elements are related to each other by ties of logical implication in much the same way as elements in a system of pure mathematics are related. Proponents of the theory hold that each member of the system implies every other member. This observation by White seems especially applicable to the strong coherence theory of truth, which I will explicate. To test whether a statement is true is to test it for coherence with a system of other statements. The metaphysical supporters of the coherence theory of truth, also known as the strong coherence theory of truth, insist that a statement cannot properly be called true unless it fits into the one comprehensive account of the universe or reality. This account is, itself, a coherent system. Hence, no statement can be known to be true until it is known to cohere with every other statement of the system. To see how the coherence theory of truth works, consider how, in practice, we sometimes reject as false an ordinary person's assertions, for instance, that he saw a ghost, on the grounds that the idea of ghosts does not cohere with the other commonsense or scientific views that we hold to be true.[1]

White believes that a helpful way of understanding the meaning of truth under this theory is to consider how the logical test for truth, for

1. White, "Coherence Theory," 130.

example, in mathematics, is whether it coheres with some of the other propositions within that discipline and ultimately with the axioms of its system. In this test, for a proposition to cohere with other propositions is for it to be logically deducible from them. This coherence is what coherentists mean by calling a given proposition true. The meaning and truth of a mathematical proposition such as "two plus two equals four" is bound up with the meaning and the truth of all the other statements in the arithmetical system. Our knowledge of its meaning and its truth is bound up with our knowledge of their meaning and truth. According to metaphysical coherentists, this principle that nothing would be what it is if its relations to other things were different holds for every element whether in thought or reality.[2]

Coherence theorists admit that their arguments stem from *a priori* reasoning typical of mathematics and metaphysics. However, some coherentists have claimed that an examination of the *a posteriori* reasoning of the empirical sciences and ordinary life supports their theory, both as giving the meaning of truth and supplying a test of truth. They believe that in testing for truth, coherence is their only criterion, especially when we deal with statements about the past. No one, for example, can compare the statement that the battle of Hastings was fought in 1066 with anything else than other statements, such as those that occur in documents, history books, or works of art.[3]

What about a claim such as "a cat is sitting on the mat"? Suppose one were to ask you how you test the truth of this statement. Your reply might be as follows: "I can see the cat on the mat by merely looking at it. If what I saw corresponded to what was asserted, I would call the judgment true." By this answer, however, you assume the existence of a solid chunk of fact directly presented to your sense and beyond all question. What you take and use as fact, though, is really another judgment or set of judgments, and the coherence between the initial judgment and these is what provides the verification. Thus, your supposed perception of fact is really a judgment, since, without a stock of judgments, what is seen could never be identified as a cat and a mat respectively. Your test of the truth of the judgment that there is a cat on the mat or your comparison with what was there turns out to be a comparison of the original judgment with another judgment.[4]

---

2. White, "Coherence Theory," 130.
3. White, "Coherence Theory," 130.
4. White, "Coherence Theory," 130.

Hence, this example shows not only that coherence is the test or criterion of truth but also that it gives the meaning of "truth." It shows that the truth of the test judgment consists in its coherence with other judgments and not with something other than judgment.[5]

The Strong Coherence Theory of truth, as espoused by Harold Joachim, is metaphysical in its assumptions and is variously termed Metaphysical Coherentism or Realist Coherentism. This account will, hopefully, shed further light into what coherentism entails. I will then offer a brief survey of the weaker version of coherentism and, thereafter, provide an evaluation of both views.

HAROLD JOACHIM'S STRONG COHERENCE THEORY OF TRUTH

How does Harold Joachim define truth? For him, truth is, in its essence, systematic coherence or what he calls conceivability.[6] In other words, if something can be conceived, then it is true specifically because conceivability is the essential nature of truth. However, for Joachim, conceivability denotes the notion of thinking out clearly and logically. More specifically, to be *conceivable* means to be a *significant whole* or a whole possessed of meaning for thought. He puts forward the idea that a significant whole is such that all its constituent elements involve one another reciprocally. Stated differently, they determine one another's being as contributory features in a single concrete meaning. The elements cohering constitute a whole, which controls the reciprocal adjustment of its elements.[7]

In Joachim's view, conceivability means a systematic coherence. He describes it as the determining characteristic of a significant whole. This systematic coherence finds expression most adequately and explicitly in the system of reasoned knowledge, namely, science and philosophy.[8] If science can in any sense be seen as true, truth cannot be located in a sphere of being apart from mind.[9] Truth, for Joachim, falls on the side of the real.[10]

---

5. White, "Coherence Theory," 131–32.
6. Joachim, *Nature of Truth*, 68.
7. Joachim, *Nature of Truth*, 66.
8. Joachim, *Nature of Truth*, 67–68.
9. Joachim, *Nature of Truth*, 69.
10. Joachim, *Nature of Truth*, 68.

He believes the ideal of knowledge is a system not of truths but of truth. Coherence cannot be attached to propositions from the outside.[11]

For this reason, Joachim finds Descartes's indubitable truth so remote from the ideal so as to allow him to eliminate it from the name "truth." Cartesian truth is the smallest and most abstracted fragment of knowledge from the living whole, the very whole in which it would possess its significance. Joachim urges us to see the typical embodiments of the ideal in the organized whole of a science rather than in the isolated intuitions of the sort we find in Descartes's clear and distinct ideas.[12]

Moreover, Joachim believes that the systematic coherence in which we are looking for the nature of truth must not be confused with the consistency of formal logic. The reason for this thinking is that a strand of thought could be free from self-contradiction, could be valid, and could also be consistent in formal logic terms. However, it might fail to exhibit the systematic coherence characteristic of the nature of truth Joachim is trying to adumbrate.[13]

For this reason, to ensure clarity of understanding, Joachim formulates the coherence theory as follows: truth, in its essential nature, is systematic coherence whose character reflects that of a significant whole. A significant whole, in turn, is an organized, individual, self-fulfilling, and self-fulfilled experience. Additionally, the organization of this significant whole is the process of its self-fulfillment and the concrete manifestation of its individuality. The individuality of the whole, Joachim argues, is both the presupposition of the distinctive being of its moments or parts and the emerging resultant of their cooperation.[14]

This process of self-fulfillment, according to Joachim, is truth and what the theory means by *systematic coherence*. That process is what Joachim calls the very substance or essence of the moving elements. The coherence Joachim has in mind is a form that interpenetrates its materials through and through. These materials retain no inner privacy for themselves independently of the form. They hold their distinctive being, he argues, in and through their identical form rather than in defiance of it.[15]

---

11. Joachim, *Nature of Truth*, 72.
12. Joachim, *Nature of Truth*, 73.
13. Joachim, *Nature of Truth*, 76.
14. Joachim, *Nature of Truth*, 76.
15. Joachim, *Nature of Truth*, 77.

Further, Joachim believes that only one organized individual experience, which is both self-fulfilling and self-fulfilled, exists. He describes it as the absolute self-fulfillment, which is an absolutely self-contained significance, and that it is nothing short of absolute individuality. He holds the view that nothing short of the completely whole experience can satisfy this postulate, and human knowledge is certainly not a significant whole in this ideally complete sense. Therefore, truth, for Joachim, is an ideal—one that will never, as such or in its completeness, be actual as human experience.[16]

Moreover, Joachim believes certain categories exist that we use to express complete reality, and this fact holds even when such categories seem inadequate in enabling us to express reality. We use them, however, because they all come to express the whole in one way or another. Joachim identifies them as the categories of Life, Organism, and Self-Fulfillment. In our experiences they express wholes of a more complete and self-contained individuality than the categories under which we conceive a whole constituted by the limiting outline of its constituent environment. The reason for this fact, Joachim believes, is that the significant whole, which is truth, can, in the end, be most adequately described only in terms of categories of self-conscious thought. However, Joachim believes describing them in categories of Life, Organism, and Self-Fulfillment as against those lower grades of theory is certainly worthwhile.[17]

Also, for Joachim, only the ideal is solid, substantial, and fully actual. The finite experiences are rooted in the ideal. They share its actuality, drawing from it whatever being and conceivability they possess. For this reason, Joachim argues that condemning the ideal simply because the conditions, under which the finite experiences exhibit their fragmentary actuality, do not restrict its being as such is really a perverse attitude. Equally perverse, he says, is to deny that the ideal is conceivable simply because the conceivability of such incomplete expression is too confused and turbid to apply to it.[18]

For Joachim, the truth of true judgment involves the ideal especially when we consider the universal judgment of science and the universal judgment of fact. Consider an example of the universal judgment of science. It is a judgment that claims a necessary connection of content. For example, the proposition that $2 + 2 = 4$ is a claim that 4 is a necessary implication of the

16. Joachim, *Nature of Truth*, 78–79.
17. Joachim, *Nature of Truth*, 81–82.
18. Joachim, *Nature of Truth*, 82–83.

content that we express as *the addition of 2 and 2*.¹⁹ Joachim suggests that a universal judgment of science be conceived as a judgment naturally taking the form of a reciprocal hypothesis. For example, oxygen and hydrogen combined in determinate conditions necessarily form water.²⁰

Joachim believes these kinds of judgments furnish the strongest support for coherence theory. Every judgment of this kind is either true or false, and what is true is always true absolutely and completely. A so-called partial truth, in Joachim's view, is a judgment containing complete and absolute truth but when compared with another judgment, covers with its truth only a part of the subject matter of the latter judgment. For this reason, a partial truth is the same thing as a true but indeterminate judgment. Joachim believes that the determinate judgment is the whole truth about a matter where the indeterminate judgment affirms only part of the truth. Still, what the part affirms is absolutely, completely, and eternally true. Stated differently, it is the whole truth about part of the matter. Its truth, however, remains, for truth is timeless and cannot change. Joachim thinks this view seems evident and beyond dispute with respect to the universal judgment of science.²¹

The judgments of science are very abstract, Joachim notes, and this abstractness guarantees the precision of their affirmation and the purity of their truth. The truth of the original judgment, according to Joachim, persists as a solid unyielding fragment of the more perfect knowledge. He notes that this view seems unobjectionable and obvious specifically because what is once true remains always true. The view remains true at all times. For this reason, any science seems full of true judgments and their truths must be timeless, eternal, and, therefore, unalterable, just as all truths are. For example, the square root of three is nine, and nine has three as its square root. Joachim believes this claim is neither truer nor less true now than it was in the days of Adam.²²

When he turns his attention to judgments, Joachim considers them pieces of concrete thinking informed, conditioned, and, to some extent, constituted by what he calls the appercipient character of the mind. What he means by this expression remains unclear, but we could guess, from the context, that he is making reference to the mind's process of understanding

---

19. Joachim, *Nature of Truth*, 85.
20. Joachim, *Nature of Truth*, 86.
21. Joachim, *Nature of Truth*, 87.
22. Joachim, *Nature of Truth*, 88.

a judgment perceived in terms of previous experience. To see this possible interpretation of Joachim, he draws contrasts between a boy learning the multiplication table and an arithmetician who already knows the table. The boy understands that three is the square root of nine but only from memory. It is a truth he must not forget even though he does not fully understand it. The arithmetician, however, understands this fact as a shorthand symbol for the whole science of arithmetic. Hence, "as a piece of concrete thinking, it may signify all that could be read in it and expressed by the best arithmetical knowledge hitherto attained."[23]

In Joachim's view, the scientific mind commits us to the assumption of determinate and developing appercipient character. It charges the universal judgments of science wherein it finds its expression with determinate meaning. According to Joachim, the meaning of any judgment of science remains vitally dependent upon the system of knowledge that forms its context. This system of knowledge is the appercipient character of the scientific mind at the stage of its development.[24]

Joachim reiterates his earlier contention that the universal judgment of science would most naturally take the form of a reciprocal hypothetical, affirming a reciprocally necessary implication of two concepts. In other words, it states not merely that we always find A and B together but that given either of them, the other must obtain. The logical necessity, which this relationship must express, is to bind together two different contents formulated. The reason for this fact is that A is not to include any elements of B, nor B of A. However, A in its distinctness necessitates B, and vice versa. This occurrence remains impossible except insofar as A and B are rooted in a common ground as being the differences of a concrete identity. If A and B do not retain their reciprocally exclusive distinctness, Joachim believes the hypothetical judgment collapses into a tautology. Also, it loses all rational or logical necessity if A and B do not manifest one and the same individual significant content.[25]

Therefore, Joachim concludes that no universal judgment of science expresses in itself and by itself a determinate meaning. Every such judgment, he argues, is really the abbreviated statement of a meaning that would require a whole system of knowledge for its adequate expression. To take such a judgment in isolation is to take it in abstraction from the conditions

---

23. Joachim, *Nature of Truth*, 93.
24. Joachim, *Nature of Truth*, 94.
25. Joachim, *Nature of Truth*, 95.

under which alone its meaning can be determinate. He thinks completely isolating such a judgment is not possible strictly speaking, owing to the fact that some categorical basis seems involved in every hypothetical judgment. Moreover, some appercipient character of the mind must inform every piece of concrete thinking. This fact about the involvement of a categorical basis in every hypothetical judgment does not seem so obvious in the simple instances such as the square root of nine being three, because the assumptions have become so instinctive and familiar to us that we take them as a matter of course.[26]

In light of these considerations, Joachim warns us not to isolate single judgments especially because of the following observations. First, the categorical basis of a judgment such as $3^2 = 9$ is identical for all judging subjects. Second, these judging subjects, as a matter of fact, judge under the assumption of the same basis. Consider also that $3^2 = 9$ as a scientific judgment seems to be a piece of concrete thinking of the scientific mind and the appercipient character of that mind. Thus, Joachim maintains his view that the numerical system, in its fundamental features, is tacitly accepted as part of the framework of the world.[27]

By way of illustration, Joachim draws attention to how we suppose ourselves to understand the judgment $3^2 = 9$ even when we have no intelligent grasp of the arithmetical science behind it. The reason why this state of affairs obtains for us is because the terms are familiar and we possess at least some rudimentary acquaintance with the nature of number. However, we would not pretend to understand an isolated universal judgment of science, for example, in disciplines such as trigonometry, thermodynamics, or physiology unless we acquire the formulation of the judgment through what Joachim calls the methodical scientific investigation of the results on which it depends. The judgment would bear no meaning for a mind whose appercipient character had not been formed by special study or by the subject matter in question. This consideration allows Joachim to reiterate his contention: "If no universal judgment of science can be isolated from its scientific context without losing its determinate meaning, neither can it, in isolation, be 'absolutely true.'"[28]

For Joachim, therefore, treating science as a sum, aggregate, collection, or class of single independent truths, each of which remains what it is

26. Joachim, *Nature of Truth*, 96.
27. Joachim, *Nature of Truth*, 97–98.
28. Joachim, *Nature of Truth*, 98–99.

in its singleness and remains unchanged in the collection, seems to be an inadequate theory of knowledge.[29] He believes knowledge of the whole and knowledge of the parts involve one another, whether or not the parts form an intimate whole, such as what we find in the spatial system. Moreover, each involves the other at the same level. Immature knowledge of the parts entails immature knowledge of the whole, and full knowledge of the whole is full knowledge of each and all of the parts.[30]

In addition, when the single judgments get abstracted from their scientific context, their individual meaning is a caricature of their determinate meaning in the system of science. In that system alone, they possess their highest degree of truth wherein they possess their fullest significance. For this reason, even though the square root of nine is three unalterably, the significance of this judgment and, as a consequence, its truth, depends upon the numerical system in its totality and, ultimately, it depends upon the character of the universe within which the numerical system is a necessary subject of human thought.[31]

Hence, Joachim's conclusions about the Universal Judgment of Science entail the observation that every universal judgment in this category seems essentially a constituent of a system of judgment. The system as a whole affirms a relatively self-contained meaning, embodying a concrete and determinate significance. Moreover, Joachim argues that any constituent judgment of the system that remains in vital coherence with the other constituents affirms a determinate meaning, and that state of affairs obtains because the judgment in question is the emphatic and concentrated affirmation of a distinct but inseparable feature of the fuller significance. For this reason, determinate significance or meaning is the character of the context within which every single universal judgment of science has its logical being and function. This context, Joachim says, invests the several enunciations with determinate meanings as a concrete unity of significance.[32]

From his consideration of the Universal Judgment of Science, Joachim considers the Universal Judgment of Fact. He locates three types of universal judgment of facts and tries to show that their truth, so far as they are true, attaches to them through the involvement of a whole system of judgments. The three types of judgment are historical, descriptive and classificatory,

29. Joachim, *Nature of Truth*, 100.
30. Joachim, *Nature of Truth*, 102.
31. Joachim, *Nature of Truth*, 102–3.
32. Joachim, *Nature of Truth*, 103.

and judgment of perception. He admits that compared to judgment of science, judgment of facts even more obstinately seems to undercut the view he has been defending.[33]

However, Joachim argues that in spite of its apparent solidity and self-dependence, the judgment of fact comes in principle under what he says about the universal judgment of science. According to Joachim, what a judgment of fact affirms is subject to a complex mass of conditions that remain unexpressed but are certainly implied. If judgment of fact affirms definite meaning, it demands the articulate expression of this background in the form of an explicit system of judgment.

Joachim then considers an example of a judgment of fact, namely, Caesar crossed the Rubicon in 49 BC. The facticity of this claim, he argues, seems pregnant with significance. However, the actual event was not a nucleus of brute fact. Joachim reminds his readers that Caesar, at the head of his army and animated by conflicting motives of patriotism and ambition, did cross the Rubicon with a full consciousness of the effect of his action on the political crises of Rome. This fact, and many more, Joachim argues, is the meaning of historical judgment in its proper context, and it contains no bare crossing of a stream by a man in the abstract as a solid grain of fact separable from a complicated setting that particularizes it.[34] In the context of a biography, the judgment expresses a fact revealing Caesar's character. In the context of history, it reveals the decline of the Roman Republic. In either of these contexts, the judgments would have determinate meanings.[35]

With respect to descriptive judgments, Joachim notes that they do not really profess to be categorical statements of actual features of existing things. They do not stake their truth on the actual existence of their subjects, and, for that reason, they become hypothetical judgments affirming a connection of content. Consider, for example, the claim "the whale is a mammal." This claim is no assertion of a *de facto* coincidence of predicate and subject. The claim simply means, "If x is a whale, then x is a mammal." The classificatory judgment therefore passes at once into the universal judgment of science.[36]

The third judgment is that of perception. An example of this judgment is "this tree is green." According to Joachim, this judgment has its

---

33. Joachim, *Nature of Truth*, 104.
34. Joachim, *Nature of Truth*, 107.
35. Joachim, *Nature of Truth*, 108.
36. Joachim, *Nature of Truth*, 109.

definite meaning, and its truth depends upon a background implied in its formulation. It demands articulate expression as a system of judgments. In this respect, this judgment falls into line with other judgments of fact, exhibiting special affinity with the historical judgments.[37]

Hence, Joachim's overall goal is to show that so far as a judgment is true at all, its truth is really the character of a meaning that requires a system of judgments for its adequate expression. In his view, no judgment is ever entirely severed from a larger background of meaning, though the background may be relatively obscure except at that portion of itself, which is thrown into relief and formulated as this judgment. Moreover, according to Joachim, the truth of the judgment in question remains so insofar as it is the affirmation of a determinate meaning. The judgment affirms its most determinate meaning and is, therefore, true when the background is fully articulate as a system of judgments into which the judgment in question fits as a determining and determined member. The degree of its truth depends upon the degree of wholeness or, for that matter, self-containedness of the meaning expressed in such a system. In other words, it depends on the completeness and coherence of the system.[38]

Joachim thinks this result seems to confirm the ideal of truth as described in terms of the coherence notion of truth, specifically because the ideal of absolute truth, by reference to which we measure the relative degrees of truth in the various systems of judgment, is completely individual, self-sustained, and significantly whole. From this perspective, the truth emerges in its perfect completeness as an individual meaning with an internal logical connectedness and articulation. This seems to be the ideal that human knowledge involves and partly attains. However, Joachim believes it can never be adequately, fully, or finally embodied within the actual knowledge of finite subjects because actual human knowledge is never completely self-coherent given the fact that it is growing in time.[39] From Joachim, we move to L. Jonathan Cohen's defense of the coherence theory of truth.

---

37. Joachim, *Nature of Truth*, 109.
38. Joachim, *Nature of Truth*, 113.
39. Joachim, *Nature of Truth*, 113–14.

L. JONATHAN COHEN'S DEFENSE OF THE STRONG COHERENCE THEORY OF TRUTH

L. Jonathan Cohen believes he can demonstrate, quite rigorously, that if a collectively comprehensive, distributively compossible and co-entailing set C of propositions exists, then any proposition A is a member of C if and only if A is true. Hence, if C exists at all, Cohen concludes, it remains coextensive with the set that has all and only true propositions as its members.[40] Cohen contends that if a strongly cohering set of propositions C exists, then a proposition is true if and only if that proposition belongs to C. Cohen thinks that every necessary truth must be a member of the set C if the members of a comprehensive set of propositions have each to be possible. This fact holds, according to Cohen, because the successful negation of such a truth is impossible; therefore, every conditional linking one member of that truth with another must also be a member of C. This outcome is due to the fact that each such conditional is necessarily true.[41]

Cohen draws attention to a Hegelian claim Blanshard and Bradley make: ideally, coherent knowledge is also comprehensive knowledge. They argue that the ultimate truth about reality as a whole is a coherent system. However, they also note that provisional truths about parts of reality may well fail to constitute such a system. Still, this conception makes the strong coherence theory more defensible than opponents commonly suppose it to be. Also, Cohen thinks that, at most, only one comprehensive set of compossible and co-entailing propositions exists.[42]

Moreover, if we find ourselves easily tempted to suppose that we could have many sets of mutually cohering false propositions even if one set of true cohering propositions exist, this state of affairs depends on whether or not we are concerned with any set of propositions collectively comprehensive as well as distributively compossible and co-entailing. By collective comprehensiveness, Cohen refers to a set of propositions that contains an answer to every question.[43]

According to Cohen, whether or not someone is a Hegelian idealist, that individual will have to accept the strong coherence theory of truth if he or she assumes a strongly cohering set of propositions or judgments

---

40. Cohen, "Coherence Theory," 354.
41. Cohen, "Coherence Theory," 356.
42. Cohen, "Coherence Theory," 354.
43. Cohen, "Coherence Theory," 354.

exist, and this acceptance is possible whether or not the person thinks that he or she can gain knowledge about the nature of these propositions and judgments.[44] Hegelian idealists, Cohen possibly included, seem ready to defend this metaphysical assumption specifically because they believe that everything is interconnected with everything else. Stated differently, all true propositions entail one another. For this reason, the coherence theory of truth, when asserted unconditionally in its classically Hegelian form, seems to be a metaphysical theory. As Cohen notes, its validity depends on a factual assumption about the nature of reality as a whole.[45]

JAMES O. YOUNG'S DEFENSE OF THE WEAK COHERENCE THEORY OF TRUTH

Young tries to demonstrate that attempts to undercut the weak coherence theory have been unsuccessful.[46] His coherence view of truth, however, is different from the strong coherence theory because it remains neutral about idealism. Young locates areas of commonality between coherentists and their opponents. First, he believes they agree about which items are truth-bearers and about the relation between truth-bearers and truth conditions. He thinks judgments, sentences, statements, beliefs, and propositions are some of the candidates proposed as truth-bearers, though he limits his usage to propositions alone as bearers of truth-value. Second, they can also agree about the nature of the semantic relations between propositions and truth conditions. The speakers of a language, for example, adopt rules establishing relations between propositions and particular conditions. Hence, once the speakers adopt these rules, a proposition stands to its truth conditions in the relation of being true if and only if the conditions obtain.[47]

Young then locates areas of disagreement between coherentists and their opponents. He believes they part company when they begin to give accounts of truth conditions. Thus, correspondence theorists believe propositions have objective truth conditions. However, coherentists, presumably weak coherentists, maintain that the truth of any proposition consists in beliefs held by speakers of the proposition. A proposition in some speakers'

---

44. Cohen, "Coherence Theory," 356–57.
45. Cohen, "Coherence Theory," 357.
46. Young, "Defence," 89.
47. Young, "Defence," 90.

language is true if and only if the speakers' system of beliefs includes the beliefs warranting assertion of the propositions in question. Hence, weak coherentists reject the view that truth conditions are objective. They believe that truth conditions are internal to a system of beliefs. Their opponents, however, believe that truth conditions are external to systems of beliefs.[48]

How, then, do weak coherentists defend their position? According to Young, they begin with the observation that propositions do not just happen to stand in semantic relations to certain conditions. Semantic relations between propositions and certain conditions must be established by speakers by making a practice of asserting the proposition only when the conditions obtain. Moreover, the conditions under which speakers make a practice of asserting sentences are the conditions the speakers recognize as warranting assertion of the sentence. Speakers can scarcely make a practice of asserting sentences under objective conditions they cannot recognize as obtaining. They then appeal to the coherence theory of knowledge according to which speakers' other beliefs provide the speakers' only warrant for asserting a proposition. According to Young, this conception of warrant leads to the conclusion that the only thing speakers can recognize as warranting the assertion of a proposition is its coherence with their system of beliefs.[49]

Young, therefore, summarizes the argument for weak coherentism. First, the truth conditions of propositions are the conditions under which speakers regularly assert propositions. Second, speakers regularly assert propositions only under conditions that the speakers recognize as warranting the propositions. Third, the conditions under which propositions are warranted by a system of beliefs are the only conditions that speakers can recognize as warranting propositions. Therefore, the truth conditions of propositions are the conditions under which they are warranted by a system of beliefs.[50]

Young makes a few additional observations about this argument. For example, this weak version of the coherence theory of truth is a variety of antirealism, assuming antirealism is the view that if a proposition is true, it can be known to be true, and if it is false, it can be known to be false. Moreover, an antirealist account of truth involves the rejection of the principles of bivalence and transcendence. According to the former principle,

---

48. Young, "Defence," 91.
49. Young, "Defence," 91–92.
50. Young, "Defence," 92.

all propositions are either true or false, and according to the latter principle, propositions have their truth values independently of a speaker's capacity to determine these truth values.[51]

Young notes how early versions of coherentism presented by F. H. Bradley and Brand Blanshard remained committed to idealism. They were led to the conclusion that truth conditions consist in beliefs since they denied that anything mind-independent exists. Crucially also, Young notes that the argument he presents remains metaphysically neutral. He finds nothing in his argument committing him to denying the existence of objective conditions. Along with other coherentists committed to his view, he simply maintains that the truth conditions of propositions do not consist in objective conditions and that even if objective conditions exist, speakers cannot establish semantic relationships between propositions and these conditions.[52]

Moreover, to the objection raised by Ralph Walker that truth cannot consist in coherence with a system of propositions, given the fact that some coherent set of propositions are complete fictions, coherentists reply that they do not hold that truth consists in coherence with just any system of propositions. Rather, truth consists in coherence with a system of propositions held to be true or beliefs. According to Young, Walker notes that when coherentists specify the system of beliefs with which true propositions cohere, they embark on a vicious infinite regress. Young thinks, however, that truths are propositions that cohere with a system of beliefs rather than some arbitrarily selected set of propositions. Therefore, for a proposition p to be true, the coherentist thinks that this really means the proposition "p is believed" is true.[53] This state of affairs leaves coherentism vulnerable to some kind of an infinite regress because the question of what makes "p is believed" to be true then arises. According to Walker, the coherentist can only say that "'p is believed' is believed" is true. Hence, coherentists never explain what it is for a proposition to be true.[54]

Young thinks one could respond to Walker's challenge by adopting a hybrid account of truth. In other words, one could contend that the coherence theory provides the best account of the truth conditions of all propositions except for propositions about the kinds of systems that get

---

51. Young, "Defence," 92.
52. Young, "Defence," 92–93.
53. Young, "Defence," 93.
54. Young, "Defence," 94.

specified as systems. The correspondence theory could then provide the best account of the truth conditions of these propositions. Young still finds this response unsatisfactory because coherentists would have to explain how some propositions can have objective truth conditions while others cannot, especially when coherentists have taken pains to reject the notion of objective conditions for truth.[55]

How, then, should the coherentist respond to Walker's charge? Young suggests the following response. Coherentists will say that any proposition p is true if and only if p coheres with a specified system of beliefs. Coherentists can concede there is a fact about what system is accepted, but their position remains unthreatened by this concession. Even though this fact obtains, the truth conditions of propositions are those under which they cohere with a specified system and not any objective facts. Whereas this account of truth gives rise to regress, it is not a vicious regress, and the correspondence theory of truth faces a similar regress. If we say that p is true if and only if p coheres with a system of beliefs, we may be asked about the truth conditions of the claim "p coheres with a specified system of beliefs." The coherentist can only reply that this proposition is true just in case it coheres with a specified system of beliefs. Even though it is the beginning of a regress, it is not one the coherentist should worry about. Rather, it is one he or she should expect, given that the coherence theory states that it gives an account of the truth conditions of all propositions.[56]

Young admits that the answer remains incomplete here. Something still needs to be said concerning propositions about which systems of specified systems are true. According to Young, the short answer is simply to say that the coherence theory will give the same account of the truth of these sentences in the same way it gives of other sentences. Still, there will be propositions about which systems get specified that cohere with systems no one wants to say are specified systems. In Young's view, the key to solving this last difficulty is the recognition that all decisions about the truth or falsity of propositions about which systems are specified seem to be made from the perspective of some system or other. From the perspective of any system, call it S_1, no other system is a specified system. From the perspective of S_1, some system of propositions is simply a fiction held by no one.

---

55. Young, "Defence," 95.
56. Young, "Defence," 97–98.

The other alternative is that another system is believed by some speakers, but mistaken. Hence, in neither case is another system a specified system.[57]

EVALUATING STRONG COHERENTISM

Harold Joachim makes two initially important claims worth considering. First, I noted how he insists that truth cannot be located in a sphere of being apart from mind. Second, he suggests that truth falls on the side of the real. These three claims seem not only to cohere with idealism in general; they also resonate with the claims of Judeo-Christianity. In order to see this contention, we need to ask what relationship, if any, do we find between what we regard as true and what we regard as real. Seemingly, we would suppose that if anything is true then it must in some way be related to what is real. Stated differently, what is true must be real in some significant sense and what is real must be true. Contrapositively, however, what is false must be unreal and what is unreal must also be false.

Whereas this observation may seem intuitive, it may run into surprising problems. The problems seem to be a species of non-factuality issues that correspondence theorists routinely face: we can possibly locate certain statements we may well regard as true that also fail to be factual, hence failing to be real. Consider the following claim: all fairies are leprechauns. The set of things called fairies and the set of things called leprechauns are both empty sets because both entities are not known to exist. They are nonfactual entities. However, the claim "all fairies are leprechauns" is, presumably, true. If this observation is correct, then the strong coherentist would perhaps have a problem here. The strong coherentist could meet this objection quite easily by showing that the claim about fairies and leprechauns is really hypothetical rather than factual. In other words, the claim merely says that if fairies did exist, then they would belong to the class of things we would call leprechauns. The claim is neither a factual affirmation nor a presupposition of the existence of such entities. This response seems to meet the force of the non-factuality objection.

Still, what do we make of the claim that truth cannot be located in a sphere of being apart from mind? Whereas Hegelian idealists such as Joachim make this claim, one need not be a Hegelian idealist to agree. As we will see in the next section, Thomas Aquinas subscribes to a species of

---

57. Young, "Defence," 98.

this claim when he refers to God as the truth out of whom all other truths arise and find their basis.

Third, when Joachim contends that the ideal of knowledge is a system of truth rather than truths, he speaks a language resonating with Judeo-Christian claims. He seems to suggest, by this claim, that whereas truth may be an attribute of propositions, this attribute need not be regarded as the whole story. Truth is much more than mere propositions; it seems to have mentalistic factors as well. Quite importantly for our purpose, Joachim regards this truth as a significant whole, organized individual, self-fulfilling, and self-fulfilled experience. Curiously, he leaves this description of truth largely unexplained. The language of *self-fulfillment* and *experience*, coupled with his use of *mind* leaves us to wonder what he is trying to describe.

We find his explanation even more puzzling in light of his observation that this ideal of truth will never be actual as human experience, but it certainly is describable in terms of categories of self-conscious thought. Joachim denies its existence as a plurality of thought; rather, only one individual self-fulfilling and self-fulfilled experience exists. Joachim's language seems to be describing or affirming the existence of a nonhuman mind as the locus of truth—a self-conscious, non-human mind that possesses a whole system of knowledge.

Moreover, since such a self-fulfilling and self-fulfilled experience exists and is in possession of the whole system of knowledge, omniscience must be one of its major attributes. An omniscient entity, of course, is identical to the attribute of God as understood in the Judeo-Christian conception of deity. In this regard, Joachim's strong coherentism seems to point to God as the bedrock of all truth. Very few theists in orthodox Judeo-Christian tradition would disagree with this supposition. Whether or not such a conclusion appeals to the inquirer depends, of course, on his or her personal convictions about God. Orthodox Christian theists would find this view attractive. Non-theists would, quite likely, reject it.

Still, how does one know that the entire system of knowledge has its locus on truth? One may arrive at this knowledge *a priori* or *a posteriori*. If one arrives at this knowledge *a priori*, empiricists about knowledge will uphold their suspicions about the epistemological process warranting such a conclusion. The empiricists find such a process somewhat mysterious and possibly even occultic.[58] On the other hand, arriving at such a conclusion *a posteriori* seems well beyond one's reach because one will have to specify

---

58. Bonjour, *In Defense*, 16.

the empirical process allowing the acquisition of such knowledge—a process seemingly well beyond the reach of humans. Joachim himself admits that comprehensive cognitive access of all truths remains beyond the reach of humans even though omniscience is, in principle, possible. How, then, does anyone know that such knowledge exists even if it cannot be accessed? In other words, are we contradicting ourselves when we claim to know that p exists even if we do not know for sure that p?

We could form an answer to this objection as follows: one can know about the existence of p without having access to certain elements about p. Stated differently, partial knowledge of p seems sufficient to help us know of the existence of p, even if we remain incapable of determining every attributive element of p. Therefore, true coherentists need only have access to partial elements of knowledge in order to conclude, inductively, that a whole set of jointly exhaustive propositions descriptive of p exist in a way permitting the epistemologist to conclude that the entire system of what we call knowledge exists and is a system of what we call truth.

The upshot of this consideration seems to be that strong coherentism remains committed to belief in objective truth. It may be different from certain varieties of the correspondence theory of truth because some correspondence theorists seem committed to the existence of mind-independent objective truth. However, strong coherentists seem fundamentally committed to the existence of mind-dependent objective truth.

The question to ask, then, is whether strong coherentism is a promising theory of truth in the sense that it provides a reliable picture about the world. I argue that it does partially. What it does not seem to do, however, is identify what the actual locus of truth might be. In other words, it does not seem bold enough because it leaves the following question unanswered: is it a theistic approach or a nontheistic approach? Joachim's theistic commitments remain largely unstated. If truth does exist and if a Divine Mind is the locus of such truth, the inquiring mind would want to know about it even if such a desire may not seem a necessary outcome. Whereas strong coherentism furnishes us with important pointers as far as the nature of truth is concerned, it does not give us the whole story.

Jonathan Cohen has tried to provide a logical demonstration of the plausibility of the strong coherence theory of truth. Since I have already provided a summary of his argument, I need not repeat his postulations here except to point out a certain line in one of his logical steps. His goal is to show that any true statement in the entire set of necessarily true statements can be derivable from that set. The demonstration, though quite valiant, fails to prove his point specifically because one of his deductions from the set turns out to be a contingent truth rather than a necessary truth. I refer to a specific step he arrives at in his paper, which he symbolizes as follows: *cB* → ~ *c (A & B)*. I imagine he uses the arrow as a conditional understood, of course, in the sense of symbolic logic. Also, I do not have to state the entire proof of his work here in order to show where this step seems to fall short. All I need to do is to contend that the statement does not seem to be a necessary truth. Cohen uses the small letter *c* to represent an object-language operator intended to signify the following expression: "The strongly coherent set C includes the proposition that . . ." Whereas this statement is a well-formed formula in the logical sense, it is certainly not a necessary truth.

Another flaw afflicting Cohen's logical deductions can be located in the step following the claim, which he determines by the application of specific rules of natural deduction as follows: *(cA & cB)* → *cA & c ~(A & ~B)*. A closer look at this step in the deduction reveals an obvious mistake: the statement is not a well-formed formula because we have no way of determining what the main operator is. For this reason, the proof Cohen presents for the plausibility of the coherence theory of truth cannot be logically determined. Secondly, no matter what one decides the main operator should be, whether it is the arrow or the ampersand,, we still do not arrive at a necessary truth from Cohen's deductions. Either way, the demonstration Cohen presents may not necessarily succeed in proving his theory because of the typographical errors afflicting his proofs. Thus, whereas the strong coherent theory of truth *may* be plausible in itself, Cohen has not demonstrated that it really *is* plausible.

AN EVALUATION OF WEAK COHERENT THEORY OF TRUTH

Consider Young's explications that weak coherentism does not exclude the correspondence theory as a way of arriving at truth. The recognition that certain conditions must obtain to warrant assertions of a sentence seems to be a recognition of certain facts about the world described by those conditions. Stated differently, weak coherentism seems to depend on certain factors external to them to obtain in order for them to specify conditions that will guarantee the truth of an assertion.

Second, if weak coherentism rejects the view that truth conditions are objective, then obviously truth conditions are subjective. Indeed, we find this implication assumed in Young's argument when he states that the conditions under which propositions are warranted by a system of beliefs are the only conditions that speakers can recognize as warranting propositions. If truth conditions are subjective, then weak coherentism seems to be subjective about truth. More pointedly, weak coherentism, apparently, abandons any sort of serious commitment to objective truth as we find in strong coherentism. This absence of commitment to objectivity remains at odds with its inclusion of the correspondence theory about truth. The oddity arises from the fact that the correspondence theory appears to remain fundamentally objective. It is objective to the extent that the truth of many propositions, from the correspondence theorists' perspective, seems independently verifiable by the inquiring epistemologist. If subjectivism about truth characterizes weak coherentism, one would expect them to be uneasy about correspondence theories of truth.

Third, Young rejects what he calls the principle of bivalence: all propositions are either true or false. To reject such a claim is to deny it as follows: "It is false that all propositions are either true or false." Such a claim would, in turn, logically imply the following: "Some propositions are not either true or false." In other words, some propositions are not true and not false,[59] and this claim entails that some propositions are neutral about truth. Whatever else this conclusion might imply, the implications will include two things.

First, the implications will include the observation that some propositions seem logically undetermined. In other words, their truths cannot be known. However, to say that the truths of some statements or propositions cannot be known seems to be at odds with Young's claims that if a proposition is true, it can be known to be true, and if it is false, it can be known to be false. The oddity arises from the consideration that truth and falsity are essential attributes of propositions. Any proposition under consideration may be true or may be false. If it is true, then going by Young's statement we should be able to know it. If it is false, again, going by Young statements, we should be able to know that it is false. But under the same breath, Young seems to insist that some propositions are not true and not false. Clearly, we have an oddity.

Second, the conclusion can mean the proposition is meaningless. This second alternative does not fare better, for it provides us with the possibility

---

59. I apply Quantifier Negation and DeMorgan's rules in locating these implications.

that some statements are true and false at the same time. To make such a claim, of course, is contradictory. Logically speaking, such a statement is a necessary falsehood. Young's rejection of the principle of transcendence betrays the oddity we find with his rejection of the principle of bivalence. Since I have already identified that oddity, I do not have need to repeat it here.

Having given a brief survey of the coherence theory of truth, I now wish to focus on a different view of the nature of truth—one that seemed to gain currency in the medieval period but seems largely ignored in contemporary philosophical thought, owing specifically to its religious underpinnings. I turn to this theory of truth because what it presents seems fundamentally foundational and, for that reason, merits some attention. I refer here to the relationship between logos and truth as found in the Christian Scriptures, namely, the Bible.

8

The Bible and Truth

Having looked at the coherence account of truth, let us now focus on what Smit would call the Christocentric account of truth, though she applies the term Christocentrism to epistemology in general rather than to truth in particular. In order to understand this version of truth, let me turn, as I did in the introduction, to its main source of information, the Bible. I begin with a well-known statement found in the Gospel of John—well-known for its exclusivity and for its controversial nature in philosophical and theological circles. In John 14:6, Jesus claims to be the way, the truth, and the life. He also describes himself as truth in additional texts in the Gospel of John. The Old Testament has specific references to God as truth, as I will point out later in this section. What meaning do we find conveyed by these expressions, and what relationships do they have with other expressions from the Gospel of John depicting Jesus Christ as the Word of God? Beginning with the Old Testament, and also drawing from *The Theological Dictionary of the New Testament*, I will try to sketch possible answers to these questions. In the Old Testament, we find that the Hebraic term for truth is *emeth*. The Old Testament uses this term in an absolute sense to denote a reality regarded as firm and, therefore, solid, valid, and binding. The conclusion from these considerations is that *emeth* signifies what is true.[1]

The Greek equivalent of *emeth* is *aletheia*. Etymologically, the term has the meaning of non-concealment. Therefore, it denotes a state to the extent that one perceives a particular entity or that something gets indicated or expressed and that in such seeing, indication, or expression, the

---

1. Kittel, *Dictionary*, I. 232.

entity is disclosed or discloses itself as it really is. The implication here is that the revealed entity might be concealed, truncated, or suppressed. The term, therefore, denotes the full real state of affairs. In a sense, it is the unveiling of a certain reality.[2] In the practice of history, as well as in historical and philosophical inquiry, the task of *logos* is, essentially, to reveal and indicate. The task of *aletheia* can also denote an aspect of the *logos*, and this task is proper to *logos* as revelation to the extent that it causes that which exists to be seen.[3]

The point of John 1:1 is that the *logos* is the pre-incarnate Christ and that the transition from pre-incarnation to history is the true theme.[4] This theme is also present throughout the gospel as seen from sayings such as those we find in John 1:30, 6:20, and 8:38. In meaning, statements of the sort in John 1:1 simply express the fact that this *logos*, or Word, always goes forth as the divine Word and that it cannot be detached from God. In other words, it is always the Word of God.[5]

Moreover, the formulation goes further in the direction of apparent personification. The Word is personal, and its foundation is the fact that the thinking of the New Testament authors does not begin with speculation even if they apply their thought process to the creation event. Rather, even the process of creation began with the person of Christ. The preincarnation of the *logos* is, in fact, the preincarnation of Christ.

In addition, we discover that in philosophy the usage of *aletheia* seems understood as true being in distinction from the worldly phenomena appearing in the first instance as being. Plato understands this true being as the world of ideas immune from changing and perishing. According to Plato, the true being remains concealed from the senses. However, we comprehend it in thinking. From his writings, *aletheia* takes the sense of *true* and *genuine* reality. For this reason, the only thing genuinely true is that which always is. However, only the divine is that which always is.[6]

From Plato's understanding, therefore, we begin to see how truth and divinity are linked. Moreover, if Plato still uses *aletheia* formally to denote genuineness or something truly existing, in Hellenism it seems simply to imply the *eternal* or *divine* but in the sense of cosmological dualism. Still,

2. Kittel, *Dictionary*, I. 238.
3. Kittel, *Dictionary*, I. 239.
4. Kittel, *Dictionary*, II. 129–30.
5. Kittel, *Dictionary*, II. 132.
6. Kittel, *Dictionary*, II. 239–40.

it retains the sense of genuineness specifically because the divine being is that in which humans must come to share in order to be saved. One consequence of this salvation is that humans attain to their own genuine and proper being. In other words, that is when they will be truly, fully, and genuinely human because they will be in possession of perfect knowledge. We find this expression considerably underscored in Plato's apology.[7]

The early Christian usage of the term *aletheia*, though, varies depending on the contexts in which Scripture uses the term. For example, Eph 4:1 uses the term to signify something with certainty and force. John 3:21 takes the weaker sense of uprightness. The word also takes the meaning of "something on which one can rely," as evidenced by Rom 3:3–7. Here, God's truth is nothing other than his faithfulness. In 2 Cor 7:14, it signifies "sincerity" or "honesty." In Rom 1:18 and following, it begins to take the shape of truth as "the real state of affairs disclosed." Here, we understand truth either as the divine claim or as uprightness. Verse 19, however, seems to argue that God's reality is revealed.[8]

Aletheia seems also to have the sense of *truth of statement*. It can be used to denote "true teaching of faith." In this sense, righteous individuals get described as the children of truth.[9] More importantly, the term means *genuineness, divine reality*, or *revelation*. The usage of the term in this way developed out of the dualism of Hellenism. The usage reflects that of the apostle John's, where *aletheia* denotes *divine reality* with reference to several facts. First, it is a fact different from reality in which humans first find themselves and by which they are controlled. Second, it is a fact that discloses itself and is, for that reason, revelation.[10]

Whereas the Gospel of John's account of truth remains consistent with the Hellenistic view, we find a unique distinction of the gospel's aspect of truth from the fact that its use of *aletheia* and *pseudos* is not a cosmological use. Rather, it presents genuine possibilities of human existence rather than substances.[11] When Jesus speaks the truth, the presentation of Christ depicts the formal meaning of *speaking the truth*. However, it also seems to mean *bringing the revelation in words*. We find the same twofold sense when John speaks of John the Baptist as testifying to the truth. We find

7. Kittel, *Dictionary*, II. 240.
8. Kittel, *Dictionary*, II. 243.
9. Kittel, *Dictionary*, II. 244.
10. Kittel, *Dictionary*, II. 245.
11. Kittel, *Dictionary*, II. 245.

a similar expression in John 18:37. In this section, the question Pontius Pilate asks Jesus gives emphasis to the word *aletheia,* and the continuation of that *aletheia* seems to be the self-revealing divine reality. Its comprehension appears to be grounded in the determination of the existence of divine reality.[12]

We also read in John 3:32 and 2 John 1 how *aletheia* is the object of knowledge as revelation. What these passages denote by the use of these words is the knowledge of revelation. The Word of revelation is not a complex of statements or ideas. It is neither cosmological nor soteriological speculation. Rather, it is an address fulfilled in concrete encounter. More importantly, *aletheia* is demonstrated by the fact that it cannot be separated from the person of Jesus and the events fulfilled in his history. Jesus brings the *aletheia* not simply as an impartation mediated by his Word but as he sanctifies himself for them. In this way he can say, "I am the way, the truth and the life" (John 14:6). For this reason, revelation is not the means to an end. It is, itself, both the way and the goal—the goal, here, being understood as life. *Aletheia* is taken seriously as a divine occurrence that God becomes disclosed in revelation. He is the reality given in the revelation.[13]

John also uses *pneuma* and *aletheia* in 4:23 to denote the sphere of divine essence and occurrences as distinct from human ones. For this reason, the meaning is not that true worship takes place in spirituality and pure knowledge on the basis of a concept of God purged of anthropomorphic conceptions. Rather, it takes place as determined by God's own essence, namely, by the *pneuma.* Adding *aletheia* indicates that such worship can take place only as determined through the revelation accomplished in Jesus. Consequently, the revealer who is also the only way of access to God determines it.[14]

The Holy Spirit, presented by John as the Paraclete, is interpreted in John 14:17 and John 15:26, among other texts, as the Spirit of truth. Unquestionably, John intended us to understand the traditional concept of the Holy Spirit (*pneuma hagion*) that God had granted to the community. The Spirit of truth is primarily the Spirit of God, for the sphere of God is denoted no less by *hagios* than by *aletheia* as John 17:17–19 seems to demonstrate. However, when John 16:13 says that the Spirit will guide you into all truth, this claim shows that for John, the divine truth is always that

---

12. Kittel, *Dictionary,* II. 246.
13. Kittel, *Dictionary,* II. 246.
14. Kittel, *Dictionary,* II. 246–47.

which works in revelation such that the function of the Holy Spirit, who also works as the Spirit of Truth, is described as the revelation that continues to work in the community. In 1 John 5:6, however, the witnessing spirit is simply equated with truth.[15]

Drawing from Exod 34:6 and Isa 65:16, New Testament scholar Craig Keener points out how truth characterizes God's nature. In Exod 34:6, God lists "faithfulness" as one of his main attributes in his revelation to Moses, and this faithfulness is translated as *emeth*. In Isa 65:16 we read the following: "Whoever invokes a blessing in the land will do so by the God of truth; he who takes an oath in the land will swear by the God of truth." Keener notes how truth became a Jewish title for God. However, the primary significance of the statement in John 14:1 is that Jesus is the embodiment of truth—God's covenant faithfulness. This faithfulness was embodied in God's Word in the Old Testament.[16] Consider, for example, Ps 119:142 and 151: "Your righteousness is everlasting and your law is true.... Yet you are near, O Lord, and all your commands are true."

According to Keener, many philosophers used the Greek term *logos* translated *word* to mean *reason*, denoting its role in structuring the universe. Philo combined this image with the Jewish conception of the *word*. Keener believes that Greek conceptions had some influence on how John's hearers understood this phrase. His hearers (or readers) were not philosophically trained. Still, the most relevant background is the one all of them shared. This fact holds, at least, from what they heard in the synagogues or churches each week. God's word was Scripture and the personification of this word makes sense. Consider also, Keener suggests, that the Old Testament had personified Wisdom in Prov 8 and ancient Judaism eventually personified Wisdom, the Word, and the Law, sometimes using them synonymously.[17]

By calling Jesus "the Word," John describes him as the "embodiment of God's revelation in the Scripture" (John 1:1, 14) and thus encourages his Jewish Christian hearers, marginalized from some of their synagogues, that only those who accept Jesus truly honor the law fully. Jewish people considered Wisdom, or the Word, divine yet distinct from God the Father. Hence, it was the closest available term John had to describe Jesus.[18]

---

15. Kittel, *Dictionary*, II. 247.
16. Keener, *Bible Backgrounds*, 248.
17. Keener, *Bible Backgrounds*, 249.
18. Keener, *Bible Backgrounds*, 249.

Keener makes two important claims in his description of Jesus. With respect to truth, he describes Jesus as the embodiment of truth. With respect to *logos*, he also describes Jesus as the embodiment of God's revelation. The relationship between these two descriptions ought to be clear: the embodiment of truth is also identical to the embodiment of God's revelation. Stated differently, *truth* as a person is also identical to *the word*. Keener, perhaps, did not intend to arrive at this conclusion; however, his descriptions of Christ do warrant this conclusion. The relationship between the embodiment of God's revelation and the embodiment of truth seems to be one of identity. More importantly, and somewhat going beyond current theories of truth, the biblical meaning of truth portrays truth as a person rather than as a property of propositions. This fact dominates theocentric descriptions of truth as I will show briefly in a later section in this chapter. Before doing so, however, let me now turn to a survey of how a variety of some church fathers viewed logos and truth, and how they understood this relationship.

THE CHURCH FATHERS ON LOGOS AND TRUTH

I begin with Theophilus of Antioch. According to James Donaldson and Alexander Roberts, Theophilus was an apologist in the tradition of Justin Martyr and Bishop Irenaeus.[19] The writings of Theophilus depict an understanding of the Word as an embodiment of the divine. According to him, because God cannot be contained, the Word, by which he created all things and which assumed the person of God, went into the garden and conversed with Adam. When Scripture teaches us that Adam heard the voice of God, Theophilus urges us to conclude that this voice is nothing other than the Word of God, namely, Jesus Christ.[20]

Moreover, Theophilus warns against viewing Jesus Christ in the same way the poets and writers of myths view sons of gods begotten biologically from women. Rather, we view the Son as the Word that is eternal, residing within the heart of God. He argues how God had the Word as counselor before anything came into existence. More pointedly, the Word was and presumably is God's own mind and thought. Hence, when God wished to create all he had decided to create, he begot his Word without emptying himself of that Word. For Theophilus, reason is this word, and having

19. Donaldson, *Ante-Nicene Fathers*, 87.
20. Theophilus, *Autolycus*, XXII.

begotten reason, God always converses with reason. Thus, John 1:1 teaches us that "in the beginning was the Word and the Word was God."[21]

Hence, when Keener postulates how medieval thinkers interpreted *logos* as reason, and how Christ is the embodiment of one as well as the other, he is absolutely correct. We find this theme reflected in the writings of Theophilus. We also find it reflected in the writings of Athenagoras. Strangely, Donaldson points out that in early ecclesiastical history, the name of Athenagoras is scarcely mentioned. Only two references to him and his writings have been discovered, one occurring in the work of Methodius, entitled *On the Resurrection of the Body*, as preserved by Epiphanus and Photius. The other notice of him appears in the writings of Philip of Side who flourished in the early part of the fifth century in Pamphylia.[22]

According to Donaldson, Athenagoras was an Athenian philosopher who had embraced Christianity. His work, *Apology*, which he called Embassy, was presented to Emperors Aurelius and Commodus around AD 177. He converted to Christianity while reading Scriptures in order to controvert them. Donaldson finds him by far one of the most elegant and able of the early Christian apologists.[23]

Athenagoras's writings echo a theme similar to the one we find in Theophilus. He argues consistently with Scripture that the Son of God is the Logos of the Father both in idea and operation specifically because this Logos made all things in the pattern consistent with God the Father. The Son himself is in the Father and the Father is in the Son. Consequently, in oneness and the Spirit's power, the understanding and reason (or Logos) of the Father is the Son of God.[24] Consistently with the writers we have considered so far, Athenagoras ties the etymology of Logos to reason.

Also, Clement of Alexandria, a church father more famous than Athenagoras, notes how this Christ, who is also "the Word," is the cause of our being specifically because he was in God. Moreover, he was the cause of our well-being. This very Word, Clement of Alexandria says, has now appeared as a human being.[25] As with other writers, the theme of the embodiment of the word recurs here.

---

21. Theophilus, *Autolycus*, XXII.
22. Donaldson, *Ante-Nicene Fathers*, 127.
23. Donaldson, *Ante-Nicene Fathers*, 127.
24. Athenagoras, *Plea*, 223.
25. Clement of Alexandria, *Exhortation*, 173.

Similar motifs appear in the writings of Hippolytus. According to him, God brought forth the Logos by an exercise of reflection. Logos was not the word in the sense of being articulated by voice. Rather, it was a ratiocination of the universe conceived and residing in the divine mind. According to Hippolytus, God the Father constituted existence. The Logos born from him was the cause of all produced things. More accurately, the Logos was in God the Father bearing the will of his progenitor. He was not unacquainted with the mind of the Father. He has a voice in himself in such a way that when God ordered the world to come into existence, the Logos completed each object of creation one by one. Hippolytus concludes that the Logos alone of this God is from God himself; hence, this Logos is also God because he is the very substance of God.[26]

In addition, Novatian's *Treatise Concerning the Trinity* notes how Christ would not have said he came from God if he was only a human being. God created humans; thus, humans did not proceed from God in the same way Christ did. Because Christ proceeded from God as the Word of God, he is also reason with God. This Word, whereby all things were made, is God; hence, God proceeded from God in that the Word that proceeded is God.[27]

We find a more extended treatment of the idea of the Logos as God in Athanasius. He argues how, through the Word, or Logos, creation comes to existence. This Word is the living will of God the Father. It is an essential energy and a real Word in whom all things exist and remain excellently governed.[28] Even though Christ remains identical with the Word, Athanasius reminds us that Christ is not composed of syllables as we find in human words. Rather, Christ is the unchanging image of his own Father. Humans are composed of parts and made out of nothing. God, however, professes true existence and is not composite. For this reason, his Word also has true existence and is not composite. His Word is the only begotten God, who proceeds in his goodness from the Father as a good fountain, ordering all things and holding them together.[29] Whereas the Word of God is also God, the Godhead is both indivisible and inseparable. Athanasius also contends that the Father of the Word is himself not Word, nor is the offspring of the Father a creature. Rather, the offspring is the own-begotten essence

26. Hippolytus, *Heresies*, X.XXIX.
27. Novatian, *Treatise*, 1094.
28. Athanasius, *Discourse*, III.41.1, 2.
29. Athanasius, *Discourse*, IV.1.

of the Father. The Word that proceeded is not the Father, either, nor is the Word one word out of many words. The Word alone, Athanasius argues, is the true and genuine Son by nature. This Son is in him and is eternally and indivisibly within him; therefore, the Lord is both Wisdom and Truth.[30]

In a similar fashion, Gregory of Nyssa argues that a person who admits that God is not without Logos must also accept that such a being certainly possesses Logos. He then observes that humans use analogous terms to describe themselves. If they say that they understand how the Logos applies to God in a fashion analogous to how it applies to us, their reasoning will lead them to a loftier idea. Necessarily, then, the utterance of a given entity will correspond to that entity. Gregory asks us to consider how a certain kind of force and life and wisdom observed in humans exists. From the similarity of the terms, no one would suppose, according to Gregory, that the life or power or wisdom, in God's case, would be of such a kind as that of humans.[31]

According to Gregory of Nyssa, the meanings of such terms get lowered with the standard of our nature. Our nature is liable to corruption and weakness, he argues correctly. However, with God's transcendent nature, everything we say about that nature becomes elevated with that very nature. Hence, whenever we mention Logos as the Word of God, it remains intransient, in contrast to human words, which vanish away into nonexistence when uttered. Our nature, which remains liable to mortality, seems endued with mortal speech as well. By contrast, the imperishable and ever-existing nature of God possesses a similarly immortal, nonperishable, and eternal speech. Suppose, then, that logic requires an eternal subsistence of God's Word, the Logos. Necessarily we must also admit that the subsistence of that Word consists in a living state. Supposing that the Logos has a soulless subsistence is impious.[32]

Hence, Gregory concludes, the Logos subsists as something with intellect but incorporeal. If it subsists, then it lives. The idea that the Word of God does not subsist has been shown to be blasphemous. The Word has consequently been considered as being in a living condition. The nature of the Logos has been reasonably believed to be simple. According to Gregory, no one would contemplate the existence of the living Logos as dependent on a mere participation of life. Such a supposing would necessarily include

---

30. Athanasius, *On the Opinion*, 186.
31. Gregory of Nyssa, *Catechism*, 475.
32. Gregory of Nyssa, *Catechism*, 475.

the idea of compositeness. The simplicity, however, has been admitted. For Gregory, the Logos has an independent life and is not a mere participation in life. If, then, the Logos lives, it certainly has the faculty of will. Not even one of the living creatures is without such a faculty.[33] A devout mind will also conclude that such a will has the capacity to act. Impotence is quite removed from our conception of deity.[34]

Moreover, Gregory encourages us to suppose also that this will, in its power to do all things, will have no tendency to do anything evil; rather, whatever is good, this will wishes. To be sure, it can perform the act of wishing, and being able to perform it, it will not fail to perform it. It will bring all its proposals for good to effectual accomplishment.[35] Gregory makes an interesting postulate here, namely, that God's ability implies God's intentionality. Stated differently, in God's scheme of activity, *can* implies *ought*. If God can do x, he will do x.

For Gregory, the world is good. All its contents are wisely and skillfully ordered. Therefore, all of them are the works of the Word. The Word is from the mind and no more entirely the same as the mind altogether other than the mind. Similarly, the Word of God, by its self-subsistence, is distinct from him from whom it has its subsistence. Still, it exhibits in itself qualities recognized in God. Hence, it is identical in nature with God who is also recognizable by the same distinctive marks.[36]

Gregory reiterates the postulates of Scripture when he states that the Word of God made the heavens and all their powers. He did this by the breath of his mouth. Only the power of God, arising from speech or breathing, could be powerful enough to establish the heavens and its powers therein. If God's Word is like our speech and his breath like our breath, then from these sorts of things there must certainly come a likeness of power. Then God's word will have just as much force as our word and no more. Our words and our breaths are ineffective and unsubstantial, so those who would compare Deity with our word render his Divine Word and Spirit altogether ineffective and unsubstantial.[37]

Gregory of Nyssa also finds the claim that thought and skill rule the world abundantly plain. He thinks God's Word is not an actual utterance

33. Gregory of Nyssa, *Catechism*, 475.
34. Gregory of Nyssa, *Catechism*, 476.
35. Gregory of Nyssa, *Catechism*, 476.
36. Gregory of Nyssa, *Catechism*, 476.
37. Gregory of Nyssa, *Catechism*, 476.

of speech or possession of some kind of science or art. God's Word is the power essentially and substantially existing and willing all good and having strength to execute all its will. Moreover, according to Gregory, this power, appetitive and creative of good, is the cause of a world that is good. Suppose, then, that if the subsistence of the whole world has been made to depend on the power of the Word, we must necessarily reject the thought that another cause exists that organized the parts of this world.[38]

From Gregory of Nyssa, I turn to Jerome. Not much about the Word and the truth seems to feature in his writings. However, what we find is just as significant as what we have already explored. According to Jerome, Logos in Greek has many meanings. It signifies Word and reasoning and reckoning. It is the cause of individual things by which the existing ones subsist. According to Jerome, we predicate all these things to Christ.[39]

One of the thinkers linking Logos with Truth is Gregory Nazianzen. Consistently with John 1:1, he notes that Christ is called the Word specifically because he is related to the Father as Word is related to Mind. Gregory Nazianzen thinks that this relation might be compared to the relation between the definition of a thing and the thing defined, and this claim follows because the definition is also called Logos. The reason Nazianzen makes this claim is because a person with the mental perception of the Son has also perceived the Father. The Son, Gregory notes, is a concise demonstration of the nature of God the Father.[40]

Also, according to Nazianzen, Logos is called wisdom, as the knowledge of things divine and human, because we find impossible the supposition that he who made all things is ignorant of the reasons he made them. He is also called power as the sustainer of all created things. He is the furnisher to them of the power to keep themselves together, and truth, as being in nature one and not many, is the pure seal of the Father and his most unerring impress.[41]

From Nazianzen, we find a clearer description of truth in the writings of Thomas Aquinas. According to Aquinas, truth is a certain perfection of understanding, or of intellectual operation. The understanding of God, however, is his being specifically because this understanding is the divine being—a being that does not get perfected through any form of superadded

---

38. Gregory of Nyssa, *Catechism*, 476.
39. Jerome, *Letter*, LIII.4.
40. Nazianzen, *Theological Orations*, 4.XX.
41. Nazianzen, *Theological Orations*, 4.XX.

perfection. It is already perfect and gets its perfection from itself. For this reason, Aquinas concludes that the divine substance is truth itself.[42] Moreover, drawing from Aristotle's argument in the *Nichomachean Ethics*,[43] Aquinas maintains that truth is a certain goodness of the intellect in the sense that God is his own goodness. For that reason, he is his own truth.[44] This allows Aquinas to hold that truth exists in God not from a source external to God but from God's essential nature as God. God, therefore, is his truth.[45] That is why, Aquinas concludes, Jesus said in John 14:6, "I am the way, and the truth and the life."[46]

This demonstration, Aquinas says, shows that pure truth exists in God. By pure truth, he seems to refer to truth that cannot be mingled with falsity.[47] He draws this conclusion from the consideration that truth is incompatible with falsity. God is not only true. He is truth itself, and falsity cannot be found in him.[48] Aquinas believes that all knowledge of the divine intellect is the kind that knows what a thing is. This observation allows him to see the impossibility of finding error, deception, or falsity in the divine knowledge.[49]

According to Aquinas, the intellect does not err in the case of first principals, even though it errs sometimes in the case of the conclusions at which it arrives by logical reasoning from first principles. The divine intellect, however, is not ratiocinative or discursive. In other words, the divine intellect does not ramble or meander thought-wise. This observation allows Aquinas to believe that no deception can be found in the divine intellect.[50]

Another argument Aquinas advances for his position on truth is analogous in nature. For example, he holds that the higher a knowing power is, the more universal is its proper object. However, the power of the divine intellect is at the zenith of elevation in knowing. Hence, all knowing objects are related to the divine intellect as properly and essentially knowable, and

---

42. Aquinas, *Summa Contra Gentiles*, I.60.2.
43. Aristotle, *Nichomachean Ethics*, VI, 2, 1139a 27.
44. Aquinas, *Contra Gentiles*, I.60.3.
45. Aquinas, *Contra Gentiles*, I.60.4.
46. Aquinas, *Contra Gentiles*, I.60.5.
47. Aquinas, *Contra Gentiles*, I.61.1.
48. Aquinas, *Contra Gentiles*, I.61.2.
49. Aquinas, *Contra Gentiles*, I.61.3.
50. Aquinas, *Contra Gentiles*, I.61.4.

the divine intellect cannot be in error in the case of any knowable object.[51] Moreover, things external to the human intellect, in a certain sense, cause the knowledge of the human intellect. In this way, knowable things measure human knowledge. The divine intellect, however, is the cause of things, and for that very reason, its knowledge is the measure of things in the same way art is the measure or the standard of artifacts. The artifacts are perfect to the extent that they agree with the art. Similarly, the divine intellect is related to things as things are related to the human intellect. No falsity can be found in things because each thing has being. To that extent, each thing has truth. Therefore, we find on inequality between the divine intellect and things and there cannot be found any falsity in the divine intellect.[52]

Aquinas's description of truth also takes an ethical dimension. Once again, drawing from Aristotle,[53] Aquinas contends that the true is the good of the intellect, and the false, by contrast, is the evil of the intellect. To demonstrate his contention, he observes how we naturally seek to know the truth and flee from being deceived by what is false.[54] However, no evil can be found in God; thus, no falsity can be found in him. That process of reasoning enabled the apostle to say in Rom 3:4, "But God is true." It also allowed a prophet to say in Num 23:19, "God is not a man, that he should lie."[55]

These observations give Aquinas the warrant to conclude that the divine truth is the first and highest truth.[56] In agreement with Aristotle's claim in *Metaphysics*,[57] he contends that things get disposed in truth as they are disposed in being. The reason for this state of affairs, Aquinas argues, is that the true and being follow one another. This observation stems from Aquinas's consideration that the true exists when what exists is said to be and that which does not exist is said not to be. The divine being, however, is first and most perfect. Therefore, the truth of the divine being is the first and highest kind of truth.[58]

---

51. Aquinas, *Contra Gentiles*, I.61.5.
52. Aquinas, *Contra Gentiles*, I.61.7.
53. See Aristotle, *Nichomachean Ethics*, VI, 2 1139a 27.
54. Aquinas, *Contra Gentiles*, I.61.8.
55. Aquinas, *Contra Gentiles*, I.61.9.
56. Aquinas, *Contra Gentiles*, I.62.1.
57. See Aristotle, *Metaphysics*, Ia, 1 993b 30; IV, 7, 1011b 25.
58. Aquinas, *Contra Gentiles*, I.62.2.

Moreover, Aquinas adds, whatever belongs to a thing essentially belongs to that thing most perfectly. Truth, however, belongs to God essentially. Therefore, God's truth remains the highest and first truth. It belongs to God most perfectly, Aquinas would say. In another instance of agreement with Aristotle,[59] unity is the cause of equality. In the divine intellect, however, the intellect and whatever that intellect understands remain absolutely one. Therefore, the truth of the divine intellect is the first and highest truth.[60]

The apparent upshot of what Aquinas is trying to convey in his discourse on truth may be seen in the following consideration: the divine truth is the measure of all truth specifically because the truth of our intellect is measured by the thing outside the soul. After all, we find our intellect true because our intellect agrees with the thing it knows. On the other hand, the divine intellect measures the truth of a thing, and this divine intellect is the cause of all things. God is the first intellect; God's intellect must, therefore, be the measure of the truth of any intellect. Aristotle did make this argument,[61] according to Aquinas, by contending whatever is first in the genus of anything really is the measure of each thing. Therefore, the divine truth is the first, highest, and most perfect truth.[62]

GREG WELTY'S THEISTIC THEORY OF TRUTH

We find one of the most recent formulations of the theistic theory of truth in the work of Greg Welty entitled "Truth as Divine Ideas: A Theistic Theory of the Property 'Truth.'" In this article, Welty responds to David Armstrong's criticism of traditional theories of universals by defending a realist conception of truth from a theocentric perspective.[63] The final consequence of his defense becomes compatible with the claim of Jesus Christ when he said he was the truth in John 14:6. This consequence emerges, Welty observes, when we bear in mind that Christian theists remain firmly committed to defining truth in some sense with respect to a person. Thus, Welty believes the defense of his theocentric version of truth supports the claims of Christ specifically because if his version is the right theory of truth in particular,

---

59. See Aristotle, *Metaphysics*, V, 15, 1021a 10.
60. Aquinas, *Contra Gentiles*, I.62.3.
61. See Aristotle, *Metaphysics*, X, 1, 1052b 25.
62. Aquinas, *Contra Gentiles*, I.62.5.
63. Welty, "Truth," 56.

then the existence of truth is fundamentally bound up with the existence of a person whose ideas constitute the very existence of truth.[64]

In what follows, I will offer an outline of Welty's argument, which I think presents a view of truth I find compatible with what other thinkers, explored in this section, affirm. Welty begins by noting that any adequate theistic theory of truth must say something about the ontological status of properties and propositions. It would have to deal with the fact that properties and propositions remain irreducibly different kinds of things. Hence, Welty argues, each will require a different theistic account, bearing in mind, for example, the following considerations: propositions have truth value while properties do not; propositions have intentionality while properties do not; propositions are declarative but properties are not.[65]

Welty, therefore, begins by describing the nature of a theistic theory of universals—a theory he calls Theistic Conceptual Realism, or TCR, for short. He locates three theses to facilitate this description. First, Welty observes that TCR is a realism about universals, and he defines universals, in this context, as ideas in the mind though he seems unsure of how to characterize these ideas. These universals, ideas, or entities have what Welty calls "extra-mental" existence but "extra-mental" relative to finite minds. In his view, properties exist independently of any human cognitive activity, and the entire range of properties would exist even if no corresponding concrete substance ever comes into existence.[66]

The second thesis Welty advances is the contention that TCR is a form of conceptualism about universals. A universal is something that explains attribute agreement among particulars, or identity of nature among particulars, or the nature of different tokens as tokens of the same type. To this extent, then, "universal" is a functional concept. Hence, TCR is a form of conceptualism about universals because it proposes that mental items of a certain sort play the metaphysical role that satisfies the functional concept of a universal.[67]

Third, and more importantly for the purpose of this section, TCR is a theistic conceptual realism about universals. What implication does this supposition have? According to Welty, the ideas to be identified as universals are not merely mental things in just any mind. Specifically, they

64. Welty, "Truth," 68.
65. Welty, "Truth," 56.
66. Welty, "Truth," 57.
67. Welty, "Truth," 58.

are divine ideas. Welty finds the conviction that God has ideas eminently reasonable by drawing attention to two fundamental considerations.[68]

First, suppose God is a person. We must then understand God to have justified true beliefs, to have powers and intentions. Moreover, if God is both the creator of the universe and an intelligent one in this regard, his creative act consists of divine power to actualize divine intentions. Hence, with the exception of God alone, the existence of all concrete substances remains contingent upon God's creative act, and this act of creation is intelligent insofar as it realizes a divine purpose. Welty correctly recognizes how a majority of theists in the Christian tradition favor a model of creation that understands God as an architect of this universe who intentionally chooses to design a world according to a specific blueprint in his mind. They avoid the alternative Neoplatonic model that sees creation as some form of divine emanation. Hence, for Welty, intelligent creation is one that presupposes the existence of divine ideas. Here, it presupposes correspondence between God's idea of the world he wishes to create and the world that is created.[69]

Also important, intelligent creation presupposes an asymmetrical dependence of any created world upon the existence of divine ideas, according to Welty. In other words, Welty thinks, rightly I believe, that the existence of any created world entails the existence of divine ideas, but the converse does not follow. In other words, the existence of the divine ideas does not entail the existence of a world created according to their pattern specifically because God could have chosen not to create any world and would still have the ideas of the worlds he could have created.[70]

The second consideration Welty postulates is the rationality of believing that God possesses divine ideas specifically because of his omniscience. Suppose part of that omniscience is exhaustive divine self-knowledge. God would know which worlds he would create as a consequence because exhaustive divine self-knowledge entails God's knowledge of the full range of his power. Suppose this knowledge includes justified true belief as an essential component, which, in turn, presupposes the possession of concepts. Then divine omniscience, according to Welty, would entail the possession of a multitude of concepts or ideas; hence, God's omniscience and the fact of his intelligent creation entail the existence of divine ideas. Welty, therefore, lays out what he takes as the characteristic claim of TCR as a theory

---

68. Welty, "Truth," 58.
69. Welty, "Truth," 58.
70. Welty, "Truth," 58.

of universals. According to this claim, these divine concepts function as properties insofar as they are entities that can be exemplified and actually exist. They are entities that explain all cases of attribute-agreement in any universe God has created, and they exist independently of any created universe.[71]

Welty then tries to show how TCR can fit the three models of concept nominalism, predicate nominalism, and transcendental realism without being vulnerable to the objections David Armstrong raises against them specifically because of their theocentric origin. I will not try to show how Welty demonstrates their imperviousness to an Armstrongian refutation because doing so would not add much to the overall argument I am trying to develop in this work. What I intend to do is to provide an outline of how Welty maps the structure of TCR on the three models cited here. Let me begin with his mapping of TCR on concept nominalism.

Armstrong defines concept nominalism as follows: "*a* has the property *F* if and only if *a* falls under the concept '*F*.'" Welty then shows how to apply this description to TCR. One would simply need to replace the phrase "the concept '*F*'" appearing on the right-hand side of the material biconditional with a phrase reflecting a theocentric understanding such as "the divine concept '*F*'" or "God's concept of '*F*.'" The biconditional would then be reworded as follows: "*a* has the property *F* if and only if *a* falls under the divine concept '*F*'" or "*a* has the property *F* if and only if *a* falls under God's concept of an '*F*.'" This formulation would capture a version of TCR that remains consistent with concept nominalism. According to Welty, this formulation would be a version of nominalism insofar as the divine concepts are concrete entities. Moreover, an advocate of TCR could subscribe to a traditional nominalist view by contending that concrete substances are the only existing things. This nominalism concedes that universals really exist insofar as it also accepts that the thoughts of one concrete substance in particular satisfy the function concept of universals.[72]

Welty still thinks this interpretation of TCR would be some sort of realism about universals, provided it thinks of divine concepts existing independently of any human cognitive activity. The concepts would exist irrespective of whether or not human thinkers existed at all to have them in their minds. To be sure, they would exist irrespective of whether or not

---

71. Welty, "Truth," 58.
72. Welty, "Truth," 59–60.

concrete substances existed. God would be the only concrete substance exempt from this rule because he would be the entity hosting the concepts.[73]

Welty also believes TCR would not only fit the pattern or model of concept nominalism. It would also fit the pattern of predicate nominalism. Armstrong defines predicate nominalism as follows: "*a* has the property *F* if and only if *a* falls under the predicate '*F*.'" In order to see how TCR fits into this pattern, Welty suggests we replace "the predicate '*F*'" with "the divine predicate '*F*.'" According to Armstrong, "the divine predicate '*F*'" is "the predicate God would use to characterize to himself what we would refer to as '*F*.'" The predicates of a divine language by which God possesses and expresses to himself his knowledge serve as those relevant to a predicate nominalism theory of universals. In this way, we could see why TCR is a version of predicate nominalism insofar as the divine predicates are concrete entities. However, it would be a version of realism insofar as the divine predicates exist independently of human thinkers and all concrete substances except God.[74]

With respect to transcendental realism, Armstrong sketches it as follows: "*a* has the property *F* if and only if *a* has a suitable relation to that transcendent universal or form of '*F*.'" As he did with the previous two versions hitherto considered, Welty shows how TCR could fit the descriptive pattern of transcendental realism. According to Welty, doing so would fit the pattern insofar as the divine concepts or predicates are themselves transcendent and functionally equivalent to "the transcendental universal or form of *F*." Welty notes how concept nominalism differs from predicate nominalism chiefly in whether interpretations of TCR consider divine thoughts as language transcendent or not, in some sense. Whether language transcendent or not, the divine thoughts remain divine and transcendent with respect to any concrete substances exemplifying them. As with the previous two versions, however, God is the only exception.[75]

What implication does this chapter's survey have for truth and human access to truth? If truth is fundamentally rooted in God's character, in what ways would we say humans know anything at all? Smit provides a possible clue to answering this question, which she draws primarily from Bonaventure. Her answer, as I will show later, seems consistent with what René Descartes offers in his *Meditations*. According to Smit, the person

---

73. Welty, "Truth," 60.
74. Welty, "Truth," 60.
75. Welty, "Truth," 60.

of Christ is relevant to any conversations concerning our act of grasping or knowing the truth. Appealing to Bonaventure, Smit thinks identifying Christ with the truth suggests that all our life experiences with the truth must in some way relate back to Christ. The experiences, stated differently, must participate in Christ.[76]

For Smit, Christ is relevant to our cognition of reality and to our grasp of truth, along with our epistemic functioning. For this reason, any epistemological theories falling short of taking Christ into account in their elucidations will be wrong and incomplete. In light of Christ's claim that he is the truth, Smit believes Christian philosophers have three options. The first option is, possibly, to ignore Christ's claims by taking the view of scriptural authority less and less seriously or by demythologizing those claims, perhaps in the Bultmannian tradition, in some way. The second option is, possibly, to view philosophy as a discipline that fails to address epistemological questions. The third option is to be more concerned with the question at hand and less concerned with disciplinary boundaries placed upon the epistemologist. Smit believes Bonaventure takes the third view, which she also endorses, and includes Alvin Plantinga in the cohort as well.[77]

Hence, in the process of trying to arrive at truth, Smit appeals to Bonaventure's suggestion that one should begin from Christ himself specifically because Christ is the mediator between God and humans. He holds everything together, which, in Smit's view, should be seen as the central position in all things. For this reason, one must necessarily begin with Christ as the starting point in order to arrive at Christian wisdom. All the treasures of wisdom and knowledge, Smit argues, are hidden in Christ, specifically because he is the central point of all understanding. Understanding a created thing is impossible except in trying to understand it by the agent who created it. Therefore, Christ, the Word, must necessarily go before the epistemologist in order to gain a correct understanding of his creation. God is the author of everything that exists, including ourselves. Therefore, without reference to him, understanding ourselves or anything in existence is impossible.[78]

Smit delves deeper into the aforesaid by appealing to the theological claim that God is the source of every existing thing. However, she notes that Christ, the word of God, conveys and specifies to his creation the nature

---

76. Smit, "In Your Light," 170.
77. Smit, "In Your Light," 170–71.
78. Smit, "In Your Light," 171.

of everything God has created. Christ makes concrete all the ideas present in God the Father and speaks everything into existence. However, in order for us to have correct, reliable, and true knowledge of something S, we must penetrate the illusion surrounding S and see S's essential nature. If this exercise must succeed, Smit argues, our intellect must, in some way, possess illuminating contact with the likeness of S as expressed in Christ. This exercise applies for all certain knowledge and remains true for all humans, not just for Christians. It is true for all humans who find anything true irrespective of whether they realize they have such contact.[79]

Smit believes God's knowledge of anything S remains more expressive of S than S is expressive of itself. For example, suppose God knows a tree. The true "treeness" of that tree remains fully expressed in God, and the treeness cannot be without God's knowledge. This fact applies to every created thing. "The truth of" every created thing remains fully expressed and fully known in Christ, the logos. Our senses receive the perceptible world S, allowing us to receive internally those objects of experience. Our minds convert the perceptions of S to an image of S. This process of imagination is a matter of discovery and recognition. It is not creativity. Moreover, the presence of Christ illuminating the mind makes this process of discovery and recognition possible. In this way, humans arrive at true knowledge, rather than illusion, of the external world they perceive. This way of knowing is God's design for humans—to understand and grasp the truth of the external world around them, thereby reflecting Christ's image, which contains the essential forms of every existing thing as the exemplar. In our knowing in this way, we become Christlike because we are able to reflect and understand the objects of our perception in a manner similar to how Christ understands them.[80]

Smit believes this way of understanding true knowledge, especially in theological matters, helps to solve two epistemological problems in theology. First, it solves the problems of how finite humans can possess reliable knowledge of an infinite God. Christ bridges the gap between God's incorporeal essence and our corporeal nature because Christ's physical human form contains God's fullness. Second, it solves the problem of how our mental faculties as humans interact with the physical world. Christ channels this knowledge even for individuals who seem ignorant of his presence and his work. This fact obtains because Christ is *the truth*. Therefore, we

---

79. Smit, "In Your Light," 172.
80. Smit, "In Your Light," 173–74.

know anything at all through the incarnation of God in Christ. The power of Christ equips sinful human beings such as ourselves with the capacity to gain reliable information about the external sensory world, enabling us to see traces of God therein.[81]

Exactly what kind of knowledge of the external world do we gain as a result of this contact that we, as humans, have with God? Our knowledge is dependent on God as being, truth, and goodness. With respect to our knowledge of God as being, Smit draws our attention to Bonaventure's supposition that our intellect cannot know that a certain being is defective and incomplete without knowledge of a perfect being, free from all defect. God, of course, is the only one who fits this categorization of perfection. Such knowledge of a perfect being is innate in us based on the power of memory, which has the power to process events from the past, present, and future simultaneously though, of course, not with the kind of simultaneity that God possesses. Reminiscent of Plato's account of recollection, Smit draws attention to Bonaventure's contention that the power of memory is evident in our direct apprehension, *a priori*, of mathematical principles and the foundational principles of science wherein we know God, ourselves, and the world around us.[82]

With respect to know our knowledge of God as Truth, Smit points us to Bonaventure's claim that our understanding is joined to eternal truth itself. Suppose, then, that if this light does not teach us, we will fail to grasp any truth with certitude. Moreover, owing to the fact that truth is immutable, all true things are lasting. Our understanding, however, is limited. Thus, in order to understand an eternal essence, we must necessarily see it within the person of Christ. Christ is the immutable, undisturbed and unconfined truth, containing within himself the essence of every existing thing. Our connection to Christ makes the power of understanding to function possible, including individuals unaware of Christ's presence.[83]

With respect to God as goodness, Smit argues, the mind makes value judgments and judgments of ethical behavior. Such judgments, Smit argues, are possible only, and because humans possess an intrinsic love of goodness. Humans desire the good; they also desire happiness. Our innate desire for the good is evidenced by our desire for happiness, even though

---

81. Smit, "In Your Light," 175.
82. Smit, "In Your Light," 177.
83. Smit, "In Your Light," 177–78.

those desires may seem displaced.[84] This dependence on our contact with God as goodness suggests the possibility of practical knowledge, going beyond the limits of theoretical knowledge.

So from Smit's suppositions, the experience of truth in humans is possible by participating in Christ, consciously or unconsciously. Smit and, for that matter, Bonaventure uphold the view that Christ is truth and in him all truths find their foundation. How, exactly, would Smit respond to a nontheistic objection that finds this supposition false? Smit would perhaps respond by demonstrating that the objector simply ignores what might be too obvious to be seen. Smit finds it easy to fail to pay attention to our dependence on God for truth in the way just specified. According to Smit, what we find among nontheists is not that their intellect fails to see being or truth or goodness. More accurately, the intellect sees being in all these ways but remains unaware of seeing being. In other words, God easily becomes a part of reality taken for granted in a way that makes the epistemologist be inattentive to his or her reality. Smit points to Bonaventure's contention that our mind's eye fails to notice being because we are intent on particular and universal beings. This unawareness is analogous to how our physical eye fails to see the light by which it sees other things, or if, in fact, it does see the light, it fails to recognize or notice it because it is intent on seeing other things illuminated by that light.[85]

All these authors make an important observation missing in other explications of truth I have been exploring throughout this work. As already noted, the observation describes truth as a person rather than confining it to propositions. If Scripture presents God as truth, this view needs to be taken seriously by those committed to the fact that truth matters. Just as important is the commitment to the view that objective truth does exist and ought to be understood as far as is reasonably possible.

Current theories of truth routinely present it as a property of propositions specified in the form "a statement is true if and only if x." For example, according to the correspondence theory of truth, a statement S is true if and only if S corresponds to states of affairs obtaining in the external world, or, qua Tarski, *snow is white* is true if and only if snow is white. Also, according to the coherence theory of truth, a statement S is true if and only if S coheres with a set of statements in question. For all these examples, the first part of the biconditional betrays the assumption or the conviction that truth is a

---

84. Smit, "In Your Light," 178.
85. Smit, "In Your Light," 179.

property of statements or, more accurately, of propositions. Characterizing truth in this way seems convenient for purposes of explication. The logical outcome of such characterizations, however, may appear epistemologically odd for a specific brand of metaphysics that finds any epistemological move beyond the natural world problematic.

Consider, for example, that statements do not occur independently of rational and intelligent statement-makers. Their existence seems contingent upon the existence of rational creatures such as ourselves. Without the existence of rational, intelligent statement-makers, statements would not exist. This fact further suggests that if staters did not exist, statements would not exist either, and if statements would not exist, truth would not exist. Following the theory of natural selection, finite sentient creatures such as ourselves came into existence billions of years after the physical universe existed. This would imply, therefore, that truth was nonexistent for billions of years before finite intelligent creatures came into being. Statements came into being only when finite staters came into existence.

Truth, however, seems to have infinite qualities. The set of all true statements is infinite. This fact is not hard to see. Showing that truth has infinite attributes or qualities is quite possible. Examining the entire collection of an infinite set of true statements to confirm the infinite nature of truth would, of course, be impossible. We only need to demonstrate, from one example, that a set of true statements exists and, by some simplified form of mathematical induction, locate the infinite nature of such a statement. To do this, let me begin with a well-known logically true statement, namely, the law of noncontradiction. It is the understanding that a statement cannot be both true and false at the same time with regard to the same thing. Intuitively, the law is true. A denial of this law only serves to prove its truth because by denying its application to reality, one uses that very law to make the move. At no time is this law ever false. The truth-table method also demonstrates the law is true on every horizontal line of the truth table. The law of noncontradiction, therefore, is logically true. A negation of that law entails a contradiction.

In order to demonstrate, then, the infinite nature of truth using this law, let me assign the letter L to the law of noncontradiction as follows: $L = \sim(p\ \&\ \sim p)$. If L is true, then the claim (call it L^1) that "L is true" is itself true. If L^1 is true, then the claim (call it L^2) that "L^1 is true" is also true. If L^2 is true, then the claim (call it L^3) that "L^2 is true" is just as true as L^1 and L^2. And if L^3 is true, then the claim (call it L^4) that "L^3 is true" is also true, and so on *ad infinitum*. The whole infinite set of true statements characterized in this way, $L^i = \{L^1, L^2, L^3, L^4, \ldots\}$, is infinite. More correctly, the set of subsequent truth-value interpretations of statements derived from an initially logically true statement forms an infinite conjunction of true statements, the whole set, itself, being true as a conjunction of those statements.

We can make similar derivative remarks about every logically true statement, including necessary truths. Presumably, the set of such statements is infinite. If truth has infinite qualities, then truth has always existed. The reason for this supposition follows from the fact that staters of propositions, of which truth is a predicate, will have to be in existence for an infinite period of time to make an infinite number of truth-claims of the sort characterized by L^i. Moreover, if truth has always existed, then propositions or statements have always existed because truth is contingent upon statements. The claim, therefore, that a period existed in which truth did not exist, is false.

If truth has always existed, then at no time did the universe exist without truth, and if truth is a property of propositions, then an infinite number of propositions exist that would entail the infinite existence of truth. This would imply that either an infinite number of statement-makers exists or an infinite statement-maker exists to account for the infinite number of truths already in existence. If truth is contingent upon statements, and statements are contingent upon statement-makers, then either an infinite number of finite statement-makers have always existed or at least one infinite statement-maker has always existed to make the infinite conjunction of true statements. From science, or even from Scripture, the claim that an infinite number of statement-makers have always existed is false. The only other option we have is to conclude that at least one infinite statement-maker has always existed to make the infinite conjunction of true statements, specifically because an infinite conjunction of true statements seems too long to be made by finite statement-makers who only appeared on the scene of the universe much later.

As already noted, both science and the Judeo-Christian Scriptures postulate that statement-makers such as ourselves have not been in existence from the beginning, though, of course, the duration for both seems vastly different, depending on one's interpretation of the first chapter of the book of Genesis. Just the same, both underscore the finite nature of humans by agreeing that humans are latecomers to the universe compared to the rest of creation. Truth, however, being infinite, has been in existence prior to our existence. But if truth is a property of propositions *P*, then *P* came into existence through the action of makers of *P*, or what I have hitherto called statement-makers. If so, the observation implies that a statement-maker distinct in nature from ourselves has been in existence to make the sort of statements belonging to the infinite set of true statements. This conclusion comes from the observation that statements or propositions require statement-makers.

Notice how this conclusion coheres with John 1:1 and John 1:14. John 1:1 claims that the word has been in existence from the beginning. John 1:14 claims that this Word, Jesus, is full of grace and truth. It therefore identifies Jesus as both the word and the truth. In this way, the biblical nature of truth affirms that truth is a property of a proposition, identified as the word in Scripture, but revealed to the world as the incarnation of a unique person called Jesus Christ. This reality enables one to see that Truth is an objective, immutable benchmark with divine authority to enforce itself on everything in the universe it sustains.

The conviction from all these considerations entails the idea that divine truth and divine knowledge remain identical in being, and that the triune God is in possession of all knowledge and, for that very reason, all truth. We find this conviction among the church fathers and chiefly championed by Thomas Aquinas. We also find the same conviction in Welty's and Smit's explications; therefore, when Jesus tells his disciples he is the truth, he unequivocally affirms that truth is his attribute. More importantly, this claim implies, in Aristotelian language, that truth is a predicate, a character, or, more accurately, *the nature* of Christ. Truth is the nature of Christ in a way identical to how omniscience is also the nature of Christ. Truth and omniscience remain synonymous in this context specifically because Christ's omniscience implies he possesses all knowledge. If we follow Leibniz's law of identity, truth and omniscience presented in this way are one and the same thing.

Most orthodox Christian scholars seem to concur that the Judeo-Christian triune God is in possession of infinite knowledge. In other words, no information remains beyond God's cognitive reach. If that were not the case, this state of affairs would void omniscience. God, in this case, would be a very knowledgeable being but would lack all the knowledge an infinite being should have in order to be God. This outworking, in turn, would imply that God would not be in possession of all truth because some truths would remain beyond God's reach. Thus, Christ's claim to be the truth seems to imply, on the one hand, that no truth or knowledge lies outside his cognitive reach and, on the other, that God is in possession of knowledge simultaneously in all of eternity.

The implication of this contention, as Aquinas noted, is that the knowledge God has is maximally reliable information about reality—information that contains no error or falsity. By this very information, we can individuate false ones from true ones. In his treatment of this subject, Wolfhart Pannenberg quotes Sirach's explanation that God knows all things and the exact time everything occurs. According to Pannenberg, things hidden from us remain open to God, and this fact applies both to the future and to the things hidden from us. Quoting Ps 139, Pannenberg observes how those fleeing from God's presence have nothing to hide even though God's child has no real reason to flee from him. When we speak of God's knowledge, therefore, what we mean is that everything in all creation is present before him and nothing is hidden from his cognition. His knowledge, however, is different than human knowledge despite its analogous nature to human knowledge. Human experience of knowledge provides only a feeble hint of what divine knowledge really entails.[86]

In reference to God's knowledge, Millard Erickson describes the understanding of God as immeasurable in the sense that his knowledge is vast. According to Erickson, humans remain fully exposed before God because God sees and knows everything. God knows every truth, even those hitherto undiscovered by human beings. This reality, according to Erickson, owes itself to the fact that God built his truth into the objects of his creation. For this reason, God knows all genuine possibilities, including those appearing limitless in number. What Erickson refers to here is what I will call God's factual knowledge.[87]

From this treatment of factual knowledge, Erickson turns to God's practical knowledge, also called wisdom. According to Erickson, the actions of God are based on facts and on correct values all of which remain in his possession. Hence, God knows what is good because God knows all things. Since God has access to all information, he makes his judgments wisely without needing to revise possible estimations of a certain cause of action stemming from additional information; thus, we can trust God's knowledge in this regard.[88] Moreover, three aspects of God's nature always

---

86. Pannenberg, *Systematic Theology*, I. 379–80.
87. Erickson, *Christian Theology*, 301.
88. Erickson, *Christian Theology*, 301–2.

converge to produce correct action on God's part: God is wise, and for this reason he knows what he needs to do. Second, he is good and, therefore, chooses the right course of action. Third, God is powerful and possesses the ability to accomplish what he wills to do.[89] Erickson points out that God's knowledge is not merely factual as we find with the correspondence theory of truth; it includes skillful knowledge, an aspect Lyotard found to be missing in other theories of truth such as the correspondence and the coherence theories.

Both Pannenberg and Erickson believe, as many theologians do, that God is in possession of all knowledge. More accurately, God has immediate cognitive access to all facts and has the ability, or skill, to make judgments and act on those facts when and where necessary. The implication here, then is that God is omniscient. Stated differently, God is all-knowing. More correctly for our purposes, God is all-truth. All truths belong to him properly as his nature, irrespective of whether we are making references to truths of logical reasoning or truths based on fact or practical knowledge.

This sense of truth, I claim, seems to be what Christ implied when he identified himself with truth as his nature in the same way we identify God with his infinite attributes such as omniscience, omnipresence, and omnipotence. For example, when we talk of *omniscience* as the subject of a sentence, our audience would understand us to be making reference to the triune God in some way. We can make analogous remarks with omnipresence and omnipotence. Less familiar but certainly no less accurate, we would be making analogous remarks with truth as we do with omniscience when we talk of truth as the subject of our sentence. In this way, we would be making reference to God in much the same way omniscience, omnipresence, and omnipotence make reference to God. Hence, when Jesus says he is the truth, we should understand him to say he is God, for only God qualifies to be described in this way. Indeed, only God is big enough to fit such a description.

---

89. Erickson, *Christian Theology*, 303.

Bibliography

Abel, Reuben. *Man Is the Measure: A Cordial Invitation to the Central Problems of Philosophy.* New York: Free Press, 1976.

Acton, H. B. "The Correspondence Theory of Truth." *Proceedings of the Aristotelian Society* 35 (1934) 177–94. http://www.jstor.org/stable/4544256.

Alston, William. *Realism and Antirealism.* Edited by William Alston. Ithaca, NY: Cornell University Press, 2002.

———. *A Realist Conception of Truth.* Ithaca: Cornell University Press, 1997.

Aquinas, Thomas. *Summa Contra Gentiles Book One: God.* Translated by Anton C. Pegis. Notre Dame, IN: University of Notre Dame Press, 1975.

Aristotle. *Metaphysics.* In *The Basic Works of Aristotle*, edited by Richard McKeon, 689–934. New York: Modern Library, 2001.

———. *Nichomachean Ethics.* In *The Basic Works of Aristotle*, edited by Richard McKeon, 935–1125. New York: Modern Library, 2001.

Athanasius, "On the Opinion of Dionysius." In *A Select Library of Nicene and Post-Nicene Fathers of the Christian Church: Translated into English with Prolegomena and Explanatory Notes*, 173–188. Vol. IV. Edited by Schaff, Philip and Henry Wace. Grand Rapids: Eerdmans, 1953.

Athenagoras. "A Plea for the Christians." In *The Ante-Nicene Fathers: Translations of the Fathers Down to A.D. 325*, 153–217. Vol. 2. Edited by A. Roberts, J. Donaldson, and A. Cleveland Coxe. New York: Charles Scribner's Sons, 1926.

Baronett, Stan. *Logic.* New York: Oxford University Press, 2013.

Beckwith, Francis, J., and Gregory Koukl. *Relativism: Feet Firmly Planted in Midair.* Grand Rapids: Baker Academic, 2000.

Bergmann, Merrie, et al. *The Logic Book.* 4th ed. New York: McGraw Hill, 2004.

Bloom, Alan. *The Closing of the American Mind.* New York: Simon & Schuster, 1988.

BonJour, Laurence. *In Defense of Pure Reason: A Rationalist Account of A Priori Justification.* Cambridge Studies in Philosophy. Cambridge: Cambridge University Press, 1997.

Clement. "Exhortation to the Heathen." In *The Ante-Nicene Fathers: Translations of the Fathers Down to A.D. 325*, 200–236. Vol. 2. Edited by A. Roberts, J. Donaldson, and A. Cleveland Coxe. New York: Charles Scribner's Sons, 1926.

Cohen, L. Jonathan. "The Coherence Theory of Truth." *Philosophical Studies: An International Journal for Philosophy in the Analytic Tradition* 34.4 (1978) 351–60. http://www.jstor.org/stable/4319261.

Crump, David. "Truth." In *Dictionary of Jesus and the Gospels*, edited by Joel B. Green, Scott McKnight, and I. Howard Marshall, 861. Downers Grove, IL: InterVarsity, 1992.
Derrida, Jacques. "Différance." In *From Modernism to Postmodernism: An Anthology*, 2nd ed., edited by Lawrence Cahoone, 225–40. Malden, MA: Blackwell, 2003.
———. *Of Grammatology*. Translated by Gayatri Chakravorty Spivak. Baltimore: Johns Hopkins University Press, 1997.
Donaldson, James, and Alexander Roberts, eds. *The Ante-Nicene Fathers: Translations of the Fathers Down to A.D. 325*. Vol. 2. New York: Charles Scribner's Sons, 1926.
Erickson, Millard. *Christian Theology*. Grand Rapids: Baker Academic, 1998.
Evans, C. Stephen. "Critical Dialogues in Philosophy of Religion." In *Philosophy of Religion: Selected Readings*, 5th ed., edited by Michael Peterson et al., 120–26. New York: Oxford University Press, 2014.
Ezorsky, Gertrude. "The Pragmatic Theory of Truth." In *The Encyclopedia of Philosophy*, edited by Paul Edwards. 6:427. New York: Macmillan, 1967.
Foucault, Michel. "Truth and Power." In *From Modernism to Postmodernism: An Anthology*, 2nd ed., edited by Lawrence Cahoone, 252–53. Malden, MA: Blackwell, 2003.
Geisler, Norman. *Christian Apologetics*. Grand Rapids: Baker, 2007.
George Barna Group. "Americans Are More Likely to Base Truth on Feelings." https://www.barna.com/research/americans-are-most-likely-to-base-truth-on-feelings/.
Gibson, Peter. *Philosophy: Everything You Need to Know to Master The Subject—In One Book!* London: Arcturus, 2024.
Gregory of Nyssa. "The Great Catechism." In *A Select Library of Nicene and Post-Nicene Fathers of the Christian Church: Translated into English with Prolegomena and Explanatory Notes*, 471–513. Vol. V. Edited by Schaff, Philip, and Henry Wace. Grand Rapids: Eerdmans, 1953.
Guinness, Os. "Time for Truth." In *A Place for Truth: Leading Thinkers Explore Life's Hardest Questions*, edited by Dallas Willard, 39–54. Downers Grove, IL: InterVarsity, 2010.
Hippolytus. "The Refutation of All Heresies." In *The Ante-Nicene Fathers: Translations of the Fathers Down to A.D. 325*, 12–472. Vol. V. Edited by A. Roberts, J. Donaldson, and A. Cleveland Coxe. New York: Charles Scribner's Sons, 1926.
Horowitz, Carol R., and J. Carey Jackson. "Female 'Circumcision': African Women Confront American Medicine." https://pmc.ncbi.nlm.nih.gov/articles/PMC1497147/.
James, William. "The Pragmatic Notion of Truth." In *The Twentieth Century*, edited by Louis Pojman, 128–34. Classics of Philosophy 3. New York: Oxford University Press, 2001.
———. "What Pragmatism Means." In *The Twentieth Century*, edited by Louis Pojman, 120–28. Classics of Philosophy 3. New York: Oxford University Press, 2001.
Jerome. "Letters." In *A Select Library of Nicene and Post-Nicene Fathers of the Christian Church: Translated into English with Prolegomena and Explanatory Notes*, 1–295. Vol. VI. Edited by Schaff, Philip, and Henry Wace. Grand Rapids: Eerdmans, 1953.
Joachim, Harold H. *The Nature of Truth*. Oxford: Clarendon, 1906.
Kant, Immanuel, *A Critique of Practical Reason*. 3rd ed. Translated by Mary Gregor. Cambridge. Cambridge University Press, 2015.
Kaufman, Gordon D. *Relativism, Knowledge and Faith*. Chicago: University of Chicago Press, 1960.

BIBLIOGRAPHY

Keener, Craig. *The IVP Bible Backgrounds Commentary: New Testament*. Madison: InterVarsity, 2014.

Keller, Timothy. "Reasons for God." In *A Place for Truth: Leading Thinkers Explore Life's Hardest Questions*, edited by Dallas Willard, 55–71. Downers Grove: InterVarsity, 2010.

Kierkegaard, Søren. *Concluding Unscientific Postscript*. 5th ed. Edited and translated by Howard V. Hong and Edna H. Hong. In *Philosophy of Religion: Selected Readings*, edited by Michael Peterson, et al., 116–19. New York: Oxford University Press, 2014.

Kittel, Gerhard. *Theological Dictionary of The New Testament*. Vols. 1 & 2. Grand Rapids: Eerdmans, 1977.

Lewis, David. "Forget About the 'Correspondence Theory of Truth.'" *Analysis* 61.4 (2001) 275–80. http://www.jstor.org/stable/3329005.

Luper, Stephen. "Epistemic Relativism." *Philosophical Issues* 14 (2004) 271–95.

Lyotard, Jean-François. *The Postmodern Condition: A Report on Knowledge*. Translated by Geoff Bennington and Brian Massumi. Manchester: Manchester University Press, 1984.

Marino, Patricia. "What Should a Correspondence Theory Be and Do?" *Philosophical Studies* 127 (2006) 415–57.

Marshall, Bruce D. *Trinity and Truth*. Cambridge: Cambridge University Press, 2000.

Moore, G. E. *Principia Ethica*. New York: Prometheus, 1988.

Mosteller, Timothy. *Relativism: A Guide for the Perplexed*. New York: Continuum, 2008.

Murano, Grace. "10 Most Chilling Stories of Modern Day Cannibalism." Oddee, Jun. 20, 2013. http://www.oddee.com/item_98622.aspx.

Nazianzen, Gregory. "Theological Orations: The Fourth Theological Oration." In *A Select Library of Nicene and Post-Nicene Fathers of the Christian Church: Translated into English with Prolegomena and Explanatory Notes*, 203–437. Vol. VI. Edited by Schaff, Philip, and Henry Wace. Grand Rapids: Eerdmans, 1953.

Neuhaus, Richard J. "Is There Life After Truth." In *A Place for Truth: Leading Thinkers Explore Life's Hardest Questions*, edited by Dallas Willard, 23–38. Downers Grove, IL: InterVarsity, 2010.

Novatian. "Treatise Concerning the Trinity," In *The Ante-Nicene Fathers: Translations of the Fathers Down to A.D. 325*, 1071–1140. Vol. 5. Edited by A. Roberts, J. Donaldson, and A. Cleveland Coxe. New York: Charles Scribner's Sons, 1926.

Pannenberg, Wolfhart. *Systematic Theology*. Vol. 1. Grand Rapids: Eerdmans, 1988.

Pascal, Blaise. *Pensées*. Translated by A. J. Krailsheimer. New York: Penguin Books, 1966.

Peirce, Charles S. "How to Make Our Ideas Clear." *Popular Science Monthly* 12 (Jan. 1878) 286–302. https://courses.media.mit.edu/2004spring/mas966/Peirce%201878%20Make%20Ideas%20Clear.pdf.

Peterson, Michael. *Reason and Religious Belief: An Introduction to the Philosophy of Religion*. New York: Oxford University Press, 2013.

———., et al. *Philosophy of Religion: Selected Readings*. 5th ed. New York: Oxford University Press, 2014.

Plato. *The Republic*. Translated by Tom Griffith. Cambridge: Cambridge University Press, 2000.

———. *Theaetetus*. Edited by Bernard Williams. Indianapolis: Hackett, 1992.

Popkin. Richard H. "Fideism." In *The Encyclopedia of Philosophy*, edited by Paul Edwards, 3:201-2. New York: Macmillan, 1967.

BIBLIOGRAPHY

Prior, A. N. "Correspondence Theory of Truth." In *The Encyclopedia of Philosophy*, edited by P. Edwards, 2:223–31. New York: Macmillan, 1967.

Putnam, Hilary. "Pragmatic Realism." *Metaphysics: An Anthology*, edited by Jaegwon Kim and Ernest Sosa, 591–606. Malden, MA: Blackwell, 1999.

Rorty, Richard. "Dismantling Truth: Solidarity Versus Objectivity." In *Classics of Philosophy*, edited by Louis Pojman, 541–48. Vol. 3 of *The Twentieth Century*. New York: Oxford University Press, 2001.

Russell, Bertrand. *The Problems of Philosophy*. New York: Oxford University Press, 1997.

Sire, James. *The Universe Next Door: A Basic Worldview Catalog*. 4th ed. Downers Grove, IL: InterVarsity, 1997.

Smit, Laura A. "In Your Light, We See Light." In *Realism and Antirealism*, edited by William P. Alston, 167–80. Ithaca: Cornell University Press, 2002.

Smith, James K. A. *Who's Afraid of Postmodernism? Taking Derrida, Lyotard and Foucault to Church*. Grand Rapids: Baker Academic, 2006.

———. *Who's Afraid of Relativism? Community, Contingency and Creaturehood*. Grand Rapids: Baker Academic, 2014.

Tarski, Alfred. "Truth and Proof." *Scientific American* 220.6 (1969) 63–77. http://www.jstor.org/stable/24926385.

Tertullian. "Against Hermogenes." In *Latin Christianity: Its Founder, Tertullian*, 823–74. Vol. 3 of *Ante-Nicene Fathers*. Edited by A. Roberts, J. Donaldson, and A. Cleveland Coxe. Grand Rapids: Eerdmans, 1957.

———. "Five Books Against Marcion." In *Latin Christianity: Its Founder, Tertullian*, 432–822. Vol. 3 of *Ante-Nicene Fathers*. Edited by A. Roberts, J. Donaldson, and A. Cleveland Coxe. Grand Rapids: Eerdmans, 1957.

———. "The Prescription Against Heretics." In *Latin Christianity: Its Founder, Tertullian*, 383–431. Vol. 3 of *Ante-Nicene Fathers*. Edited by A. Roberts, J. Donaldson, and A. Cleveland Coxe. Grand Rapids: Eerdmans, 1957.

Thayer, H. S. "Pragmatism." In *Encyclopedia of Philosophy*, complete and unabridged reprint edition, edited by Paul Edwards, 5–6:430–35. New York: Collier Macmillan, 1972.

Theophilus. "Theophilus to Autolycus," In *The Ante-Nicene Fathers: Translations of the Fathers Down to A.D. 325*, 135–196. Vol. 2. Edited by A. Roberts, J. Donaldson, and A. Cleveland Coxe. New York: Charles Scribner's Sons, 1926.

Vision, Gerald. "Lest We Forget 'The Correspondence Theory of Truth.'" *Analysis* 63.2 (2003) 136–42. http://www.jstor.org/stable/3329220.

Wainwright, "Omnipotence, Omniscience and Omnipresence." In *The Cambridge Companion to Christian Philosophical Theology*, edited by Charles Taliaferro and Chad Meister, 46–65. New York: Cambridge University Press, 2010.

Welty, Greg. "Truth as Divine Ideas: A Theistic Theory of the Property of Truth." *Southwestern Journal of Theology* 47 (2004) 57–70.

Westacot, Emrys. "Relativism." In *Internet Encyclopedia of Philosophy*, edited by James Feiser and Bradley Dowden. http://www.iep.utm.edu/relativi/.

White, Alan R. "Coherence Theory of Truth." In *The Encyclopedia of Philosophy*, edited by Paul Edwards, 2–130. New York: Macmillan, 1967.

Willard, Dallas, ed. "Introduction." In *A Place for Truth: Leading Thinkers Explore Life's Hardest Questions*, 15–21. Downers Grove: InterVarsity, 2010.

Wittgenstein, Ludwig. *Tractatus Logico-Philosophicus*. Translated by C. K. Ogden. New York: Routledge, 1999.

BIBLIOGRAPHY

Young, James O. "A Defence of the Coherence Theory of Truth." *Journal of Philosophical Research* 26 (2001) 89–101.

Index

Abel, Reuben, 19, 42
ability to be right, 87, 99
absence of truth, 4, 17, 39, 87
absolute truth, 37, 143
absolutism, 19, 34–35, 46, 55
absolutist epistemologies, 65, 75–76
absolutists, 25–26, 34–35
abstract truth, difference in, 48, 54
Acton, H. B., 105
aletheia, 155–59
alethic ontological argument, 8, 11
Alston, William, 72–75
anti-foundationalism, 3
antinomy of the liar, 108–14
antirealism, 146–47
Apology (Athenagoras), 161
a posteriori reasoning, 134, 150–51
appercipient character of the mind, 138–40
a priori reasoning, 97, 99, 134, 150, 175
Aquinas, Thomas, 149–50, 165–68, 179–80
Aristotle, 4, 48, 104, 106, 166–68
arithmetic, 86, 98, 113–14, 118, 128, 139–40
Armstrong, David, 121–23, 168, 171–72
artifacts, 167
assertability, 70–71
asserting sentences, 146
Athanasius, 162–63
Athenagoras, 161
atomic sentence, 111
axioms/axiomatic method, 81, 86, 112–13, 127–28, 134

Barna Research, 16–17
Beckwith, Francis, 16, 18–20
behavior, 57, 175–76. *See also* epistemic behaviorism
beliefs, 6, 43–47
Bergson, Henri, 41
Berkeley, George, 48
Bible, 155–60
biconditionals, 8, 107, 121–22, 130–31, 171, 176–77
bivalence principle, 146, 153–54
Blanshard, Brand, 144, 147
Bloom, Allan, 16
Bonaventure, 6–7, 172–76
Bradley, F. H., 133, 144, 147

capitalism, 90–91
causality, 68
Christocentric epistemology, 6–7, 155
circularity, 107, 130–31
clarity, 42–43, 47–48
classical conception of truth, 106–9
Cleavage, 115, 116–17, 119
Clement of Alexandria, 161
The Closing of the American Mind (Bloom), 16
cognitive access/reach, 11, 36, 151, 179–80, 181
cognitive status, 59
Cohen, L. Jonathan, 144–45, 151–52
coherence theory of truth, 133–54
    and correspondence theory, 131
    formal proof system, 127–28
    and propositions, 144–48, 150–51, 176–77

INDEX

(coherence theory of truth continued)
  strong coherence theory of truth, Cohen's, 144–45
  strong coherence theory of truth, evaluating, 149–52
  strong coherence theory of truth, Joachim's, 135–43
  weak coherence theory of truth, evaluation, 152–54
  weak coherence theory of truth, Young's, 145–49
coherent knowledge, 144
color, 65–69
common language, 109–10
commonsense, 59, 65, 68–69, 71, 133
compositeness, 75, 162–64
comprehensive knowledge, 144
conceivability, 135–37
concept nominalism, 171–72
conceptualism about universals, 169
conceptual relativism, 65, 69, 71, 75
concreteness, 51
concrete substances, 169–72
concrete thinking, 138–40
conduct, 47–48
consciousness, 27, 30–31, 43, 44, 91, 142
consensus, 34, 74, 79, 83, 85, 86, 97–99
constitutive meaning, 91, 93, 101–2
Content Implication, 118–20
Correspondence Platitude, 115–16
correspondence theory of truth, 104–32
  critique of the, 124–32
  definitional aspect of, 124–26
  hybrid account of truth, 148
  intuitiveness, 124–26
  Lewis's objection to, 121–24
  Lyotard's objection to, 78
  Marino's Correspondence Platitude, 115–16
  Modest Correspondence Theory of Truth (MCT), 105, 114–15, 120
  and propositions, 176–77
  Rorty's pragmatism, 58
  strong coherence theory of truth, 151
  and Tarski, 5, 105, 106–14, 126–31, 176
  weak coherence theory of truth, 153
creation, 170, 173–74, 180
Crump, David, 7
cultural relativism, 70, 98, 100
cultures, 19, 28, 32, 38, 60, 64–65, 83
cybernetics, 93

death of the book, 93
declaration, 88
defense of relativism, 34–35
definiens, 107
deflationism, 129–31
denotative utterances, 79–80, 85, 88, 95–97
Derrida, Jacques, 91–95, 101–3
Descartes, Rene, 43, 45, 66, 68, 136, 172–73
descriptive judgments, 142
Descriptiveness, 119–20
desires, 175–76
Dewey, John, 49–50
dichotomies, 70–71
dispositions, 33, 46–47, 48, 66–68
distinctness, 43
divine concepts, 171–72
divine ideas, 170
divine intellect, 166–68
divine reality, 157–58
divine truth, 158–59, 167–68, 179
Donaldson, James, 160–61
double legitimation, 80
doubt, 43

emeth, 155–56, 159
empiricism, 30, 48, 78, 83
Encyclopedia of Philosophy, 104
Epiphanus, 161
epistemic behaviorism, 58–59
epistemic merit, 19, 22–23, 25–26
epistemic relativism, 22–23, 32, 39
epistemological naturalism, 8
epistemological relativism
  definition of, 22–23
  evaluation of, 32–34
  inadequate as a theory, 39
  James's pragmatism, 55

Mosteller's defense of, 23–32
epistemology, 119, 155
equivalences of form, 108, 111–12
Erickson, Millard, 180–81
ethical claims, 118
ethical skeptics, 117–18, 120
extension, 70
external relativism, 27–28, 31
external world, 106, 126, 129, 132, 174–77
Ezorsky, Gertrude, 47

facts in the world, 125
factual knowledge, 180–81
factual rightness, 99
faithfulness, 157, 159
falsehood, 124–26
finite experiences, 137
first-person relativist, 33–34
force, 44–45
formal logic, 136
Foucault, Michel, 89–91, 99–101
Frege, Gottlob, 112, 127

Galileo, 94
Geisler, Norman, 41–42
genuineness, 156–57
getting it right relationship, 2
Gibson, Peter, 2
God
    Aquinas's understanding of, 165–68
    Bible and truth, 155–63
    God's knowledge, 170, 174–75, 180–81
    and omniscience, 150
    Welty's theistic theory of truth, 170–81
Gödel, Kurt, 86, 98
God's Word, 155–59, 160–65
Gospel of John, 4–7, 155–59, 179
grand narrative, 78, 79, 81
Gregory Nazianzen, 165
Gregory of Nyssa, 163–65
Guinness, Os, 3–4

habit, 43, 45–46
Hahn, Hans, 41
hardness, 44, 60–61

Hegelian idealists, 144–45, 149
Hellenism, 156–57
hermeneutics of meaning, 78, 79
Hippolytus, 162
Holy Spirit, 5, 158–59
"How to Make Our Ideas Clear" (Peirce), 42
humanities, 59–60
humanity, 59, 85
human origins, 76
human sensation, 87
Hume, David, 48
Husserl, Edmund, 40–41, 66
hypothetical judgments, 139–42

idealism, 145–49
identical subjective viewpoints, 32
ideology, 90–91
Independence-Congruence, 119
individual personality, 27
infinitely long true statements, 9–10
infinite nature of truth, 177–78
information retrieval, 92
intellect, 166–68, 174
intellectuals, 22, 90–91
intelligent creation, 170
intelligible, 94
intentionality, 8, 169
inter-and intra-cultural variation, 36
internal epistemological relativism, 38
internal realism, 69, 71–72
internal relativism, 27–28, 31
interpretation of the world, 94–95
intersubjectivity, 31–32
intrinsic properties, 65, 67–68, 71
investigation, 44–47

James, William, 41, 47–57, 58–59, 66–67, 131
Jaspers, Karl, 94
Jerome, 165
Jesus Christ, 1–7, 155–60, 168–81
Joachim, Harold, 135–43, 149–51
Judeo-Christian tradition
    and absolutism, 19
    infinite truth in the person of an omniscient God, 39
    model of creation, 170

INDEX

(Judeo-Christian tradition continued)
   pragmatism as a theory of truth, 57
   statement-makers, 178–79
   strong coherentism, 149
   truth exists, 3–4
judgment(s)
   coherence theory of truth, 134–35
   descriptive judgments, 142
   Hegelian idealists, 144–45
   hypothetical judgments, 139–42
   judging a true statement false, 36–37
   of perception, 142–43
   theistic theory of truth, 175–76
   universal judgment of fact, 141–43
   universal judgment of science, 137–42
   value judgments, 30, 46, 175–76
justice, 80, 85
justification, 22, 33, 61–64, 84, 88, 112, 119

Kant, Immanuel, 97
Kaufman, Gordon D., 16, 22, 26–31, 36–39
Keener, Craig, 159–60, 161
Keller, Timothy, 3–4
knowing, 38–39
knowledge
   Christian wisdom, 173
   coherent knowledge, 144
   comprehensive knowledge, 144
   factual knowledge, 180–81
   of God, 170, 174–75, 180–81
   Hegelian idealists, 144–45
   ideal of, 136, 150
   knowledge claims, 24
   and learning, 83–85
   mercantilization, 86
   narrative knowledge, 80, 82, 84–85, 97
   and opinion, 60–62, 64
   Peirce's pragmatism, 43
   as postmodern, 78
   practical knowledge, 176, 180
   pre-scientific form of, 81, 96
   Rorty's pragmatism, 59
   scientific, rejection of, 79–83

   scientific knowledge, 79–83, 84, 96–97
   skillful knowledge, 181
   strong coherence theory of truth, 135–43, 150–51
   theoretical knowledge, 176
   true knowledge, 174–75
Koukl, Gregory, 16, 18–20
Kuhn, Thomas, 22, 60

language, 83–85, 88–89, 92–95, 98, 108–14
language games, 59, 79–82, 84, 87, 88, 97, 99
law of noncontradiction, 96, 106, 125–26, 177–78
laws of logic, 24
learning, 83–85
legitimation, 80–83, 84–85, 87, 96–98
Leibniz, Gottfried, 43, 45, 133, 179
Le Roy, Edouard, 41
Lewis, David, 105, 121–24, 130–31
liar's paradox, 108–9, 126–30
linguistic objects, 106, 110
local neutrality, 24–25
Locke, John, 48
logic, 24, 37, 43, 86, 106–10
logos/Logos, 7, 91–92, 156, 159–60, 160–65, 174
Luper, Stephen, 17–19, 21, 22–23, 25–26, 31, 32, 34–36, 39
Lyotard, Jean François
   postmodernism, evaluation of, 95–99
   postmodernism, overall view of, 77–89
   skillful knowledge, 181

Manheim, Karl, 27, 37
Man Is the Measure (Abel), 19
Marino, Patricia, 105, 114–20, 129–31
Marshall, Bruce D., 4–6
materialism, 68
Meditations (Descartes), 172–73
mental experiences, 93–94
meta-language, 86, 111, 113, 126–29
metanarratives, 77–78, 79, 82, 84–85, 95–99

INDEX

metaphysical coherentism, 133–35
metaphysics, 47–49, 53, 91–94, 134, 177
Metaphysics (Aristotle), 104, 167
Methodius, 161
methodological naturalism, 10, 39, 132
"might is right" ideology, 100
mind-independent, 10, 115, 119, 120, 125–26, 129, 147, 151
modern, 79
modernism, 78
Modest Correspondence Theory of Truth (MCT), 105, 114–15, 120
modus ponens, 113, 127–28
Moore, G. E., 46
moral objectivism, 96
moral power, 101
moral rightness, 96–99
moral truths, 16–17, 38, 98
Moses, 159
Mosteller, Timothy, 18–19, 22, 23–31, 32–34, 39
Muller-Freienfels, Richard, 41

narration, 83–84
narrative knowledge, 80, 82, 84–85, 97
naturalistic fallacy, 46–47
natural sciences, 60
nature, 163–66
necessary truths, 31, 144, 152, 178
Neoplatonic model, 170
Neuhaus, Richard John, 2–4
neutral framework, 33
neutrality conjunct, 22
neutral standards, 24
New Testament, 4–5, 155–56
Nichomachean Ethics (Aristotle), 166–67
nihilistic approach, 109
no-deadlock principle, 34
non-absolutist conception of truth, 27, 46
non-factuality, 118, 149
nonmoral power, 101
non-obtaining states of affairs, 126, 129
non-repeating truth-conditions, 116, 120
non-sentential expression, 108, 112–13

nontheists, 176
norms, 28–31, 38, 49
no-ties principle, 35
Novatian, 162
numbers, 9–12, 20, 113–14, 128
numerical system, 140–41

objections against relativism, 27, 75
objective principle, 37
objective truths, 3, 18, 20, 50, 60–61, 77–78, 91–95, 100, 102, 145–48, 151, 176
objectivism, 20, 59–60, 68, 96
objectivist assumptions, 68
objectivity, 47, 59–62, 70–71
object language, 111, 113, 126, 129
Of Grammatology (Derrida), 91, 101
Old Testament, 155, 159
omnipotence, 181
omnipresence, 181
omniscience, 9–11, 39, 150–51, 170–71, 179, 181
On the Resurrection of the Body (Methodius), 161
ontological realist, 73, 74–75
ontology, 118–19
opinion, 44–47, 50, 60–62, 64
organized individual, 137, 150
Ostwald, Wilhelm, 40–41
ought-ness, 96–97

Pamphylia, 161
Pannenberg, Wolfhart, 180–81
Papini, Giovanni, 41
Peirce, Charles S., 41, 42–47, 54–55
perfection, 165–68
performative utterances, 80, 88
performativity, 87, 99
petitioning the addressee, 86
Philip of Side, 161
Philo, 159
philosophy, 40–41, 47–48, 59, 67–69. *See also* pragmatism as a theory of truth
phonetic writing, 92–95
Photius, 161
physics, 68–69
Plantinga, Alvin, 173

INDEX

Plato, 10, 18, 80, 100, 156–57, 175
pluralistic relativism, 22–23, 25–26, 31–32, 35–36
pneuma, 158
politics of truth, 89–91
postmodernism, 40, 77–89, 95–99, 102
power, 86–87, 89–91, 100–101
powerset objection, 11–12
practical knowledge, 176, 180. *See also* pragmatism as a theory of truth; wisdom
pragmatic realism, 65–76
Pragmatism (James), 47
pragmatism as a theory of truth, 40–57
    and correspondence theory, 131
    definition of, 41–42
    and James, 47–57
    Lyotard's postmodernism, 99
    and Peirce, 42–47
    and Putnam, 65–76
    and Rorty, 58–65
predestinate opinion, 45–46
predicate nominalism, 171–72
pre-scientific form of knowledge, 81, 96
prescriptive utterances, 97
Prior, A. N., 104
production of proof, 87
projection, 68–71
proof, 112–14, 127–28
properties, 169–71
Property-hood, 115, 117–18, 119, 129–30
propositions, 7–12, 169–71, 176–79
    bivalence principle, 153
    correspondence theory of truth, 105
    and deflationism, 130
    mathematical, 134
    origins in sentient beings, 2
    and pragmatism, 42, 44
    redundancy theory, 123–24
    and relativism, 32
    strong coherence theory of truth, 144–45, 150–51
    systematic coherence, 136
    weak coherence theory of truth, 145–48
Protagoras, 18–19

Protagorean relativism, 18–19
provability, 114, 128
Putnam, Hilary, 41, 65–76

rationality, 58–62
rationally justifiable, 33
realism about universals, 169–72
realist coherentism, 135
reality
    Cohen's strong coherence theory of truth, 145
    correspondence theory of truth, 104–5
    divine reality, 155–58, 176–80
    language games, 87
    Life, Organism, and Self-Fulfillment, 137
    Peirce's pragmatism, 44–47
    Property-hood of truth, 130
    Putnam's pragmatism, 72–73, 76
reason. See *logos*/Logos
redundancy biconditionals, 121–22
redundancy theory, 11–12, 121–24, 130–31
relativism, 16–39
    brief evaluation of in general, 31–32
    conceptual, 65, 69, 71, 75
    defense of, 34–35
    definition of, 18–22
    epistemic relativism, 22–23, 32, 39
    epistemological relativism, 22–31, 32–34
    external relativism, 27–28, 31
    internal relativism, 27–28, 31
    objections against, 27, 75
    pluralistic relativism, 22–23, 25–26, 31–32, 35–36
    and postmodernism, 98, 102
    Protagorean relativism, 18–19
    relativistic truth, 18–19
    Rorty's pragmatism, 61
    subjective relativism, 22–23, 25–26
    subjectivist relativism, 21, 23, 25–26, 34–35
Relativism, Knowledge and Faith (Kaufman), 16
relativistic standard, 63–64
Republic (Plato), 100

INDEX

revelation, 156–60
Roberts, Alexander, 160
Rorty, Richard, 22, 41, 58–65, 131
Russell, Bertrand, 104

Schiller, Friedrich, 49–50
science(s), 49–51, 59–62, 71, 78–83, 90–91, 92, 96–98, 135–43, 178–79
Scientific American (magazine), 109
scientific community, 47, 80, 85, 96
scientific knowledge, 79–83, 84, 96–97
scientists, 80, 82, 96–97
self-contained meaning, 137, 141, 143
self-contradiction, 26, 43, 96, 127, 136–37
self-fulfillment, 136–37, 150
semantic relationships, 145–47
semantics, 106
sense datum, 66–67
sensible, 94
sentences, 6, 106–14
Siegel, Harvey, 22, 24–25, 32–34
significant whole, 135–37, 150
signifier and the signified, 93–95
Simmel, Georg, 40–41
Sirach, 180
Sire, James, 78
Smit, Laura A., 3, 6–7, 155, 172–76, 179
Smith, James K. A., 17, 19, 40, 78, 94–95, 102
social bonds, 79, 84, 88–89
society, 58–59, 61–64, 89–90, 97–98, 99–100
Socrates, 100–101
solidity, 65–69
solipsism, 33
specified system of beliefs, 148–49
standards, 7, 22–23, 24, 26, 29, 32, 35, 38, 54, 84, 86
statement-makers, 8–10, 132, 177–79
statements, 8–10, 133, 176–79
strong coherence theory of truth, 135–43, 144–45, 149–52
subjective non-absolutist realism, 65
subjective relativism, 22–23, 25–26
subjectivism, 20, 31, 59–60, 153

subjectivist relativism, 21, 23, 25–26, 34–35
subjectivity, 66, 70–71
subsistence, 163–65
surface syntax, 119
sympathetic interpretation, 28–29, 38
syntactical rules, 107–8, 110–12
systematic coherence, 135–36
system of beliefs, 146–48, 153
system of propositions, 147–49

Tarski, Alfred, 5–6, 105, 106–14, 126–31, 176
technological equipment, 87, 99
telling a lie, 55–56
testing for truth, 133–35
Thayer, H. S., 40–41
Theaetetus (Plato), 18
Theistic Conceptual Realism (TCR), 169–72
theistic theory of truth, 168–81
The Theological Dictionary of the New Testament (Kittel), 155
Theophilus of Antioch, 160–61
theorems, 127–28
theoretical knowledge, 176
thinking, 30–31, 39, 43–44, 127, 135, 156. *See also* concrete thinking
Tractarian facts, 121–23
transcendental realism, 171–72
Treatise Concerning the Trinity (Novatian), 162
Trinity and Truth (Marshall), 4–6
triune God, 179–81
true knowledge, 174–75
true or false, 70, 106–7, 110, 112, 118
true sentences, 6, 9, 105, 113, 114–15, 117–18, 120, 127–28
true statements
  and Content Implication, 119
  and correspondence theory, 115, 124–26, 129, 131
  definition of, 107
  and Descriptiveness, 119–20
  infinitely long, 9–10
  judging a true statement false, 36–37
  and Property-hood, 115, 117

(true statements continued)
   strong coherence theory of truth, 151–52
   theistic theory of truth, 177–79
truth, 1–12
   Bible and, 155–60
   church fathers on, 160–68
   and correspondence to reality, 60–61, 64
   and Derrida, 102–3
   and Foucault, 89–91, 99–101
   human origins, 76
   infinite nature of, 177–78
   Lyotard's postmodernism, 96–99
   objective truths, 3, 18, 20, 50, 60–61, 77–78, 91–95, 100, 102, 145–48, 151, 176
   politics of, 89–91
   Putnam's pragmatism, 71–72
   relativistic truth, 18–19
   scientific view of, 79–83
   sphere of being apart from mind, 149–51
   Tarski's semantic theory of, 106–14
   Welty's theistic theory of truth, 168–81
   See also coherence theory of truth; pragmatism as a theory of truth
"Truth as Divine Ideas" (Welty), 168–81
truth-bearers, 145
truth conditions, 116–17, 120, 145–48, 153
truth-makers, 121–24
truth-table method, 127, 177
truth values, 36, 79, 93, 147, 169

uncritical dogmatisms, 27, 36–37
understanding, 173–75
undesirable results, 55–56
universal judgment of fact, 141–43
universal judgment of science, 137–42
universal objective principle, 37
universals, theories of, 168–72
universal values, 90, 100
unjust power, 100
untrustworthiness, 26
utterances, 79–80, 82, 85, 88, 95–97

Vaihinger, Hans, 41
Vailati, Giovanni, 41
validation, 52
value judgments, 30, 46, 175–76
values, 18, 19, 27, 28, 29, 38, 51, 63, 180. *See also* truth values; universal values
verification, 52–53
Vision, Gerald, 105, 123–24
vulnerability, 97–98

Wainwright, William, 11
Walker, Ralph, 147–48
weak coherence theory of truth, 145–49, 152–54
weight, 44
well-formed formulas, 86, 152
well-justified beliefs, 61–62, 64
Welty, Greg, 168–81
Westacott, Emrys, 18, 19, 21
White, Alan R., 133
Willard, Dallas, 2–3
wisdom, 165, 173
Wittgenstein, Ludwig, 104–5
world and language, 94–95
writing, 91–95

Young, James O., 145–49, 152–54

www.ingramcontent.com/pod-product-compliance
Lightning Source LLC
Chambersburg PA
CBHW062037220426
43662CB00010B/1544